AF079893

Intertextuality in modern Arabic literature since 1967

MANCHESTER
1824

Manchester University Press

Intertextuality in modern Arabic literature since 1967

edited by Luc Deheuvels,
Barbara Michalak-Pikulska
and Paul Starkey

Manchester University Press
Manchester and New York

Published by Manchester University Press
Oxford Road, Manchester M13 9NR, UK
and Room 400, 175 Fifth Avenue, New York, NY 10010, USA
www.manchesteruniversitypress.co.uk

Distributed exclusively in the USA by
Palgrave, 175 Fifth Avenue, New York NY 10010, USA

Distributed exclusively in Canada by
UBC Press, University of British Columbia, 2029 West Mall,
Vancouver, BC, Canada V6T 1Z2

British Library Cataloguing-in-Publication Data
A catalogue record for this book is available from the British Library

Library of Congress Cataloging-in-Publication Data
A catalog record for this book is available from the Library of Congress

ISBN 13: 978 0 7190 8189 7

First published 2006 by Durham Modern Languages Series
This edition first published 2009 by Manchester University Press

Printed by Lightning Source

Contents

Preface and Acknowledgements, *Paul Starkey* vii

Intertextuality in Modern Arabic Literature since 1967, *Roger Allen* 1

The Narrative of the Ship: al-Mu'aqqit, Maḥfūẓ, and Jabrā, *Richard van Leeuwen* 13

D'arbres et de lunes : parcours intertextuel dans la littérature arabe contemporaine, *Luc-Willy Deheuvels* 33

Intertextuality Gone Awry? The Mysterious (Dis)appearance of 'Tradition' in the Arabic Novel, *Wen-chin Ouyang* 45

Appropriating, or Secretly Undermining, the Secular Literary Heritage? Distant echoes of *Mawsim al-Hijra* in a Muslim writer's novel: Leila Aboulela, *The Translator*, *Stephan Guth* 65

Intertexte et mémoire dans l'écriture romanesque de Rabīᶜ Jābir : Essai sur le roman *Ralph Rizqallah fī 'l-mir'āt*, *Sobhi Boustani* 83

Transformations of the *Thousand and One Nights*: Zakariyyā Tāmir's 'Shahriyār wa-Shahrazād' and Muḥammad Jibrīl's *Zahrat al-Ṣabāḥ*, *Ulrike Stehli-Werbeck* 103

Intertextual and Intratextual Processes in *al-Malik huwa al-malik* by Saᶜd Allāh Wannūs, *Rosella Dorigo* 117

From Intertext to Mixed Media: the case of Edwār al-Kharrāṭ, *Robin C. Ostle* 133

Intertextuality and the Arabic Literary Tradition in Edwār al-Kharrāṭ's *Stones of Bobello*, *Paul Starkey* 149

The Past in the Present: aspects of intertextuality in modern literature in the Gulf, *Gail Ramsay* 161

The Mosaic of Quotations and the Labyrinth of Interpretations: the problem of intertextuality in the modern literature of the Gulf, *Barbara Michalak-Pikulska* 187

Select Bibliography 201

Index 219

Preface and Acknowledgements

Paul Starkey
Durham University

The chapters of the present volume represent edited versions of papers originally presented at the Conference on Intertextuality in Modern Arabic Literature since 1967 held at the Jagiellonian University, Kraków in May 2003 under the auspices of EMTAR (European Meeting of Teachers of Arabic Literature).[1]

The subject of intertextuality has aroused a good deal of interest in recent years, both on a theoretical and a practical level, and the investigation of the phenomenon in the context of modern Arabic literature, with its twin roots in the Middle Eastern and Western literary traditions, is a particularly fruitful one. Since the 'watershed' year of 1967, which witnessed the disastrous Arab defeat in the so-called 'Six-Day' War with Israel, many Arab authors have, for a variety of reasons, deliberately chosen to incorporate intertextual elements in their works. The present volume, which opens with a general account of the subject by Roger Allen, explores this phenomenon from a variety of angles, and includes discussion of a number of lesser known authors as well as some more familiar ones. It is hoped that the papers included in the volume will not only make a useful contribution to the field but also perhaps inspire others to pursue further research into the subject.

***

The editors are grateful to EURAMAL for a financial contribution towards the costs of preparing this volume; to Janet Starkey, who typeset the work and prepared the index; and for assistance at various stages of the production process to David Baguley, Catherine Dousteyssier-Khoze and staff at Prontaprint, Durham.

1 Subsequently renamed EURAMAL (European Association for Modern Arabic Literature).

Intertextuality and Retrospect: Arabic fiction's relationship with its past

Roger Allen
University of Pennsylvania

Introduction

I am sure that, as we have all contemplated the potential significances of the general topic of this volume, it will not have escaped anyone's attention that the topic itself contains a delicious and creative paradox. It resides principally in the English word 'since'. The title demands that we focus our attention on the writings of Arab *littérateurs* that have been published after a particular date — 1967. In other words, we are presented with a particular time-period from which to cull the textual contributions to modern Arabic literature that will be the focus of our critical analyses, a time period that is designated by its 'afterness' ('since 1967'). However, I am sure that the readings that we may all have undertaken into the concept of 'intertextuality' have made it clear that one of its primary features is cultural contextualisation and thus inevitably retrospect. Julia Kristeva notes that 'every text is from the outset under the jurisdiction of other discourses which impose a universe on it'.[1] In commenting on Kristeva's writings and those of other theorisers in this domain, Jonathan Culler notes that intertextuality 'calls our attention to the importance of prior texts', but that it moves beyond the more traditional games of allusion to become an investigation into a text's 'participation in the discursive space of a culture'.[2]

Our topic's linkage of 'intertextuality' and '1967', then, presents us all with an interesting posture somewhat reminiscent of the Roman house-god, Janus, traditionally portrayed as looking simultaneously in two directions. We find ourselves using a crucial historical moment, a

1 Julia Kristeva, *La Révolution du langage poétique* (Paris: Seuil, 1974), 388–9, quoted in Jonathan Culler, *The Pursuit of Signs: semiotics, literature, deconstruction* (Ithaca, New York: Cornell University Press, 1981), 105.
2 Culler (1981), 103.

'watershed' perhaps — the year 1967 — as a starting-off point for a process of assessing the ways whereby the creativity of Arab *littérateurs* during the last thirty years or so is the consequence of the kind of 'imposition' to which Kristeva refers in her discussion of the concept of intertextuality.

Intertextuality, then, aims to identify and then explore the creative tensions between present and past that are an intrinsic part of the reading of any text. In such a context the designation of that past and the principles involved in its definition become of primary importance. I would suggest that it is precisely for that reason that, in the context of a discussion of intertextuality in Arabic literature, the date of 1967 moves beyond the merely exclusive delineation of a time-period to become what I suggested above, one of those historical watersheds that not only divide one historical period from another but also call radically into question the very principles by which literary-historical periods, and thereby the definitions of the relationships between present and past, are established in the first place.

Post-1967

The chapter in Albert Hourani's renowned *A History of the Arab Peoples* that is devoted to the post-1967 period is entitled 'A Disturbance of Spirits', an apt commentary on the generally unpromising cultural environment within which the texts that we are to consider have been created, published and read.[3] Such severe and practical realities as the fragility of the right to freedom of expression, together with the direct linkage of publication possibilities to the interests of the cultural establishment in many, if not most, Arab countries, impose heavy restrictions on creative writing and thus inevitably compromise the picture of 'cultural context' within which an investigation of intertextuality can take place. The June War of 1967 itself produced some notable fictional commentaries on this general situation: one thinks, for example, of Ḥalīm Barakāt's novel, *ᶜAwdat al-ṭā'ir ilā al-baḥr*, and the series of shocking short stories that Najīb Maḥfūẓ penned in the

3 Albert Hourani, *A History of the Arab Peoples* (New York: Warner Books, 1991), 434–58.

immediate aftermath of *al-naksa* ('the setback').[4] Over the longer term, the post-1967 period was marked by a profound re-examination of the very bases of Arab culture, leading to the publication of a whole series of extremely important contributions to the re-examination and even redefinition of Arab culture and approaches to its heritage. The authors of these works were distinguished Arab scholars: Ḥasan Ḥanafī, Muḥammad ᶜAbid al-Jābirī, ᶜAbdallāh al-ᶜArwī, and al-Ṭayyib Tizzinī (to name just some of the major contributors).[5] While the ramifications of these writings have obviously been widely debated within the cultural communities of the Arab world, I would like to suggest that a very particular concern within the context of post-1967 Arabic literature, and thus the application of intertextual notions to it, is the need to revisit and even to redefine the historical framework of the cultural context and its concept of heritage, both recent and more distant. More topically, one might pose the following questions: what are those 'prior texts' that impose themselves on our readings of post-1967 Arabic literature, and how exactly did they achieve their status?

I would like to illustrate this problematic by reference to an author and circumstance with whom and which we are all familiar: the career of Najīb Maḥfūẓ. In any literary historical perspective from the year 1967 (and I have been in this field for long enough to be able to recall such a scenario) the novels of Maḥfūẓ would have been placed, indeed were placed, into an intertextual framework that was grounded heavily, or perhaps exclusively, in the development of the various European traditions of fiction. In such a literary-historical context a work like al-

4 Ḥalīm Barakāt, *ᶜAwdat al-ṭā'ir ilā al-baḥr* (Beirut: Dār al-Nahār, 1969), English translation: *Days of Dust*, tr. Trevor LeGassick (Wilmette, Ill.: Medina Press International, 1974); Najīb Maḥfūẓ, *Taḥta al-miẓalla* (Cairo: Maktabat Miṣr, 1968), English translation of several stories in *God's World*, tr. Akef Abadir and Roger Allen (Minneapolis: Bibliotheca Islamica, 1973).

5 Ḥasan Ḥanafī, *Qaḍāyā muᶜāṣira*, 2 vols (Cairo: Dār al-Fikr al-ᶜArabī, 1977; Beirut: Dār al-Tanwīr, 1981, 1983); Muḥammad ᶜAbid al-Jābirī, *Naḥnu wa-al-Turāth* (Beirut: Dār al-Ṭalīᶜa, 1980); ᶜAbdallāh al-ᶜArwī (Laroui), *al-ᶜArab wa-al-Fikr al-Ta'rīkhī* (Beirut: Dār al-Ḥaqīqa, 1973); Ṭayyib Tizzinī, *Mashrūᶜ Ru'yā jadīda lil-Fikr al-ᶜArabī min al-ᶜAṣr al-Jāhilī Ḥattā al-Marḥala al-Muᶜāṣira* (Beirut: Dār Ibn Khaldūn, 1978), I : *Min al-turāth ilā al-thawra*. These works and others are analysed by Issa J. Boullata, *Trends and Issues in Contemporary Arab Thought* (Albany, New York: State University of New York Press, 1990).

Muwayliḥī's *Ḥadīth ᶜĪsā ibn Hishām* is seen as a kind of bridge between a so-called classical tradition and the emergence of modern fiction in Arabic, a process that brings to the fore, as we all know, the familiar names of Haykal, al-Ḥakīm, al-Māzinī, and so on (with their analogues at different times in other Arab-world regions). Within such a cultural framework this process of novelistic development is seen as culminating in the novels of Maḥfūẓ. However, I would like to suggest that the kind of historical scenario that I have just essayed represents a highly problematic intertextual situation that I am inclined to term 'translational', not in the particular sense of translation as a textual process but in its literal sense of 'carrying something across' two or more cultural traditions. The situation has, I believe, been clearly illustrated by the Nobel Award of 1988 and its aftermath. Exactly twenty-one years after 1967, Maḥfūẓ was awarded the international recognition that accompanies the West's most prestigious literary award, and yet he found himself regularly termed 'the Balzac [or Zola, or Dickens, etc.] of Cairo'. There was a severe chronological disjuncture here, but I would suggest that more is involved than merely that.

I wish to make it clear at this point that I am not talking here (although I have elsewhere) about whether the Nobel Award certified the ability of an Arab author to write the kind of European family saga that was so popular in the nineteenth and early twentieth century in Europe. What I am more concerned with in the context of our combination of intertextuality and post-1967 is that the Nobel Award in 1988 conspicuously ignored and ignores those later works of Maḥfūẓ that, along with those of his younger colleagues, represent those trends in fiction that not only encourage the invocation of different intertextual approaches but also call radically into question the balance in the selection of 'prior texts' that is characteristic of many pre-1967 studies of modern Arabic fiction, including, I admit, some of my own. It is to some of these post-1967 trends that I now turn.

Ḥabībī and al-Ghīṭānī

I would like to suggest that, in the wake of the 1967 'setback' (*naksa*) and the profound period of self-examination that followed, two important works of Arabic fiction appeared that not only brilliantly reflected the *Zeitgeist* of the 1970s but, equally, if not more, important, required of their readers that the works in question be culturally contextualised in ways radically different from those that I have just discussed with reference to the pre-1967 works of Maḥfūẓ. In other words, their intertextual frame of reference was one that reflected a totally different attitude towards and utilisation of the relationship of present to past. I refer, as is probably already clear, to Émile Ḥabībī's *al-Waqā'i*ᶜ *al-gharība fī ikhtifā' Sa*ᶜ*īd Abī al-Naḥs al-Mutashā'il* (1972, 1974) and Jamāl al-Ghīṭānī's *al-Zaynī Barakāt* (1975). Both these texts have now become some kind of 'classics' in modern Arabic fiction, and rightly so. As such, they have been widely studied and from many points of view. It is not my intention here to add to the list of studies devoted to these two works (not least, because I have already contributed some of my own in my book, *The Arabic Novel*,[6] but rather to suggest that the timing of their publication in a post-1967 Arab world is no accident of chronology but is representative of an emerging new and different approach to the heritage of the past and, in the context of intertextual approaches, a renewed interest in the relationship between history and narrative in the pre-modern era. One might suggest that the possibility of a new retrospective continuum was being investigated by these two authors.

In the case of Ḥabībī's narrative, we can begin with the very title itself: its preposterous length, the bane of librarians, and its predilection for word-play inevitably call to the reader's mind the elaborate and *saj*ᶜ-laden titles given to Arabic works in all fields, a phenomenon that may be seen as reaching a high (or low) point during the pre-modern era. The juxta-position *of al-Waqā'i*ᶜ *al-gharība* ... to such contemporaneous (that is, post-1967) fictional contributions as Maḥfūẓ's *al-Marāyā* (1972) and *Ḥikāyāt ḥāratinā* (1974)[7] or, to cite another Palestinian author, Jabrā Ibrāhīm Jabrā's *al-Safīna* (1969)[8] only serves to emphasise the nature of

6 (2nd ed., Syracuse University Press, 1995). Among recent contributions, see Peter Heath, 'Creativity in the novels of Émil Habiby, with special reference to Saᶜid the Pessoptimist', in *Tradition, Modernity, and Post-Modernity in Arabic Literature: essays in honor of Professor Issa J. Boullata* (Leiden: E.J. Brill, 2000), 158–72; Maher Jarrar, 'A Narration of "deterritorialization": Imil Habibi's *The Pessoptimist*', *Middle Eastern Literatures* 5 (1) (January 2002), 15–28; and Rula Jurdi Abisaab, 'The Pessoptimist: breaching the state's *da*ᶜ*wa* in a fated narrative of secrets', *Edebiyat* 13 (1) (May 2002), 1–10.

7 Najīb Maḥfūẓ, *Ḥikāyāt ḥāratinā* (1974; Cairo: Dār Miṣr lil-Ṭibāᶜa, 1975).

8 Jabrā Ibrāhīm Jabrā, *al-Safīna* (Beirut: Dār al-Adāb, 1970); *The Ship*, English tr. Adnan Haydar and Roger Allen (1985; Colorado Springs: Three Continents

Ḥabībī's gesture. Incidentally, I mention those two works of Maḥfūẓ in particular at this point because, in spite of my observations above about the reception of Maḥfūẓ's works, both *al-Marāyā* and *Ḥikāyāt ḥāratinā* illustrate clearly that he was as aware of the tensions in the relationship of modern Arabic fiction to its indigenous past as were his younger contemporaries. Neither of these two works by Maḥfūẓ was initially designated as being a 'novel'; indeed, the preface to the original publication of the former specifically noted that the series of vignettes was something new, but not a novel, while the latter work was initially termed '*qiṣaṣ qaṣīra*', then '*shakhṣiyyāt wa-mawāqif*' (and I wonder if the Sufi connotations of the latter term were intentional), and finally '*riwāya*'.[9] I am, of course, not concerned here about the pedantries of generic designation — never a terribly fruitful area of investigation — but rather about the ways whereby these works of Maḥfūẓ suggest both new directions in fictional experiment (the linkage to the biographical tradition, for example, and the clear interest in Sufism already evident in previous works and reaching some kind of climax in *Aṣdā' al-sīra al-dhātiyya* (1994)) and an apparent process whereby the reading community is endeavouring to reformulate its generic assumptions and expectations in the light of new cultural trends and the changed circumstances of the post-1967 era. But I now return to Ḥabībī's narrative. Beyond the title itself we can point to the role of the narrator, the discrete function of each episode, the games with language and allusion, and many other features so redolent of the earlier traditions of Arabic narrative — and especially that of the *maqāma.*

In the case of al-Ghīṭānī's novel, the linkage of present and past involves not merely an act of interpretation but also a direct encounter with historical texts and pastiches of them — a process that some critics have dubbed 'transtextuality'.[10] *Al-Zaynī Barakāt* contains not only

Press, 1995).

9 For *al-Marāyā*, see the preface to the original episodes published in the magazine, *al-Idhāᶜa wa-al-Television* (beginning on 1 May 1971); for *Ḥikāyāt ḥāratinā*, see the changing designations in the listing of Maḥfūẓ's *œuvre* in subsequent fictional works.

10 Among many studies of al-Ghiṭānī's novel that seem particular relevant to the current topic, I would mention Samia Mehrez, *Egyptian Writers between History and Fiction* (Cairo: American University in Cairo Press, 1994), especially pages 96–118.

citations from Ibn Iyās's history of Egypt describing events in the sixteenth century, but also brilliant replications of historical accounts, public proclamations, and 'translations' of accounts by a Venetian traveller, all from the pen of al-Ghīṭānī himself. In yet another aside, I might record that al-Ghīṭānī was the guest of EMTAR at its first meeting in Nijmegen, the Netherlands, in 1992.[11] When I spotted him busy writing in the garden, I went over and asked what his next project was going to be. He informed me that what he was writing was actually not part of a fictional text — at least as yet, but rather a preliminary in that he was setting himself to replicate the style of a previous author and genre. With al-Ghīṭānī then there is a move beyond earlier evocations of history in novel form, whether for purposes of community-building through general education or merely for entertainment, to the replication of a particular historical period — that surrounding the Ottoman capture of Cairo in 1516 — but for a very contemporary purpose, a trenchant analysis of Egyptian society in the wake of the June War of 1967. The record of the secret police system operated by Zakariyyā ibn Raḍī and the rise to fame and power of al-Zaynī Barakāt, as recorded by Ibn Iyās and his twentieth-century replicator, remind the reader of Santayana's famous quotation that 'those who cannot remember the past are condemned to repeat it'. Furthermore, al-Ghīṭānī's resort in his evocation of the past to trans-textuality, the incorporation of other texts within his own fiction, places his novel into the very context that I alluded to above. The genres of Arabic *adab* have such citations and pastiches of them as a primary characteristic, and no more so than in the *maqāma*, as any number of studies of the generic imitations contained within al-Hamadhānī's *œuvre* have shown.

In the remainder of this study, I would like to examine the works of a few of those writers who may be considered as al-Ghīṭānī's successors, but not before suggesting that, if indeed *al-Zaynī Barakāt* merits such significant status in the post-1967 period of Arabic fiction, do its intertextual strategies not lead us back, as indeed do those of Ḥabībī's fictional masterpiece, to strong precedents in earlier works such as al-Shidyāq's *al-Sāq ᶜalā al-Sāq* (1855) and al-Muwayliḥī's *Ḥadīth ᶜĪsā ibn Hishām* (1898, 1907), where pastiches of other genres and styles not only

11 EMTAR = European Meeting of Teachers of Arabic Literature (since 2005 renamed EURAMAL = European Association for Modern Arabic Literature).

look back to earlier periods but also presage a re-examination of the past in the post-1967 era?

The Uses of History

In my brief discussion above of the cultural context in the post-1967 era, I mentioned the fragility of the right to freedom of expression that is a daily reality for many, if not most, writers of Arabic fiction. Those realities clearly have a major impact upon what creative writers choose to write about and what not to write about. However, at the same time I think we are all abundantly aware of the fact that that very situation serves to establish not only a linkage between literary creativity and political interpretations of it that is much closer than tends to be the case in most Western literary traditions, but that it also fosters a readership that is almost inevitably attuned to the process of 'reading between the lines', which is what the term 'intertextuality' presumably implies on the most literal level. In a period from 1967 to the present day (2003) when we have seen Hourani's 'disturbance of spirits' illustrated on international, regional and local fronts, 'reading between the lines' and a recontextualisation of fiction's focus on the need for and process of societal change has been the primary means for the expression of the politically controversial and often inexpressible. That the revival and exploitation of history, its genres and textual strategies — what Harold Bloom refers to as 'the family archive', should be a principal resort in such a political context is hardly surprising.[12]

While the works of many authors could be cited as examples of more recent contributions to this trend in fiction, I will concentrate in what follows on certain Maghribi authors, a reflection, I admit, of my own recent interest in the Arabic fictional output in that region. The most obvious candidate for analysis is probably Ben Sālim Ḥimmīsh. During the 1990s, Ḥimmīsh revealed his continuing interest in the philosophy of history, and Ibn Khaldūn in particular, in two distinct ways: first, in the form of the novel, *al-ᶜAllāma* (1997), and, almost at the same time, in monograph form, *al-Khaldūniyya fī Ḍaw' Falsafat al-Ta'rīkh* (1998), a study of the great historian's historical method. In *al-ᶜAllāma*, which won

12 So described by Jonathan Culler (1981), 108.

the 2002 Naguib Mahfouz Prize in Cairo, the world-renowned historian Ibn Khaldūn, now resident in Cairo, is portrayed as discussing with his amanuensis, Ḥamū al-Hīhī, his approach to historical writing in the light of his own lifelong experience with the capricious nature of power and the rampant abuses of both political and religious authority. The process involves, almost automatically, the citation of extracts from both *al-Muqaddima* and *al-Taᶜrīf*, along with samples of Ibn Khaldūn's own poetry, his favourite samples of Andalusian verse, and criticism of the methodology of his much–travelled contemporary, Ibn Baṭṭuṭa, in *Tuḥfat al-nuẓẓār*. Here, one might suggest, the linkage of fiction and history becomes almost vertiginous, as a novel is penned by a contemporary Moroccan philosopher of history about a historian utilising his own earlier studies of history to muse about the role of history and its relationship to contemporary power structures. To be sure, the novel itself has its cerebral qualities, but, as with Ḥimmīsh's other prize-winning novel, *Majnūn al-Ḥukm* (1990), the invocation of a particular historical period and personage (in this latter case, the Fatimid caliph, al-Ḥākim) and the use of historical texts and pastiches of them to analyse the abuse of religious and political authority are not lacking in contemporary relevance.

The text of Ibn Khaldūn's famous study of history and its theorisation is also cited in another Maghribi novel, Rashīd Abū Jadra's (Boudjedra) *Maᶜrakat al-zuqāq* (1986), which also exists in a French version, *La Prise de Gibraltar* (1987). However, in the context of intertextuality, the strategies of the author and the processes of reading seem to be completely different from those of Ḥimmīsh's novels. For, whereas Ḥimmīsh's works, by their citation of actual historical sources and their incorporation into the narrative of pastiches of various genres and styles of text, clearly seek to utilise an Arabic textual past for contemporary purposes, Abū Jadra's work places Ibn Khaldūn's descriptions of the conquest of al-Andalus into a much more complicated intertextual and indeed intercultural environment. As is well known, the Algerian novelist and poet began his career by writing in French (with *La Répudiation* (1969) as his most famous novel of that period). In 1981 he announced that henceforth he would be writing his fiction in Arabic; *Maᶜrakat al-zuqāq* thus belongs to this latter period. However, many scholars have wondered out loud quite what the implications of this process of language-transfer actually are; one possibility among many suggests that the Arabic version of a work originally conceived either in French or a mixture of French and Arabic is now the first to be published.[13] Whatever the case may be, Abū Jadra's works provide a wonderful example of that post-colonial '*métissage*' that is so characteristic of much fictional writing in the Maghrib. The reader of *Ma^{c}rakat al-zuqāq* is introduced to the obsessive musings of Ṭāriq, a doctor in contemporary Algeria whose memories of childhood are emblematic of the entire course of the Algerian Revolution and of attempts to place it within a historical framework. Ṭāriq's very name provides a direct linkage to part of that framework; his father, totally obsessed with history in general and the linkage of the Maghrib to al-Andalus in particular, has named his son after Ṭāriq ibn Ziyād. A visual intertext — if such a concept is permitted — is provided by elaborate and lengthy descriptions of a miniature (attributed in the French version only to al-Wāsiṭī) showing the Muslim forces in the year AD 710 massed in preparation for the crossing of the straits to Gibraltar, which gives its names to both Ṭāriqs, the historical and the contemporary. When Ṭāriq's school-teacher casts doubts on the veracity of the historical account, and especially of Ṭāriq ibn Ziyād's ringing address to his troops, the contemporary Ṭāriq's father and indeed his school-friends who are heavily involved in the Algerian revolutionary movement declare that the teacher is a traitor. History and historical texts are thus portrayed as having a crucial contemporary function in nation-building.

Neither the Arabic nor French version of this highly complex novel is a complete version of the other; each has substantial additions and omissions not found in the other language-version. However, Ibn Khaldūn's account does appear in both texts (in varying quantities), thus providing a linkage to the Arab-Islamic past. Ṭāriq finds himself compelled by his school-teacher and, above all, by his father to read and memorise parts of *al-Muqaddima*, but at the same time his school curriculum also requires him to translate passages from the account by the Roman general, senator and historian, Sallustus (d. 34 BC), of his war against the Numidian ruler, Jugurtha — yet another link to Maghribi history. Given Abū Jadra's fondness for elaboration, it comes as no

13 I have discussed this issue in detail in 'Translation translated: Rashīd Abū Jadrah's *Ma^{c}rakat al-zuqāq*', *Oriente moderno* 16 (77), n.s. nos. 2–3 (1997): 165–76.

surprise to find the Latin text included in the novel, along with the process where Ṭāriq's father requires that he prepare vocabulary lists — also incorporated into the text.

This attempt at describing *Ma^{c}rakat al-zuqāq* comes about as the result of a process of reading that might itself almost be called a '*ma^{c}raka*', one of intercultural and intertextual proportions. Throughout the text there is a truly obsessive concern with particular scenarios that are repeated over and over again: al-Wāsiṭī's miniature, the Ibn Khaldūn passage, and the contemporary Ṭāriq's traumatic and brutal treatment by the shaykh at the Qur'ān school (*kuttāb*), these are just a few among many. Narrators are switched on a regular basis, and with little or no indication as to their identity except via the process of reading (and indeed re-reading). While there is some punctuation, sentences will often blend into each other; single noun sentences are common, often accompanied by associations which are appended in parentheses followed by a question mark. Thus, while Ibn Khaldūn and al-Wāsiṭī may lead the reader in one direction, these discourse features and the pervasive mood of narrative plurality and uncertainty reveal a close affinity with another cultural tradition and intertext, namely the French '*nouveau roman*'. It is here, of course, that the existence of a French version of the novel (with its different title) and the fact that it is described as having been translated 'with the author's collaboration' becomes particularly interesting. In this context it is also interesting to note, as my colleague Richard Serrano has, that *La Prise de Gibraltar* (and my use of the French title here is deliberate) owes a great deal to the model provided by Claude Simon in his novel, *Pharsalie*. Whatever the case may be regarding Abū Jadra's language of original creativity, there can be little doubt that this novel and others create a vivid and complex picture of the social and cultural environment of his much troubled homeland which has ever since its long and violent revolution been emblematic of the post-colonial condition. It is perhaps ironic in such a context that, whatever the original language of the fictional work in question, the intertextual linkages to the French tradition still seem the more prevalent and applicable.

Conclusion

This brief examination of the applicability of the methods of intertextuality to the fictional output of Arab *littérateurs* in the post-1967 period has shown, I believe, the richness and variety of the tradition as it pursues its course along paths that are quite different from each other — differences that reflect creative explorations of language, genre, and regional attitudes of the writers of the present in their confrontation with the general and particular past. Indeed, such is that variety and so specific are some of the local factors, both contemporary and historical, that, having suggested elsewhere that attempts to subsume so much productivity under the single rubric of 'Arab' or 'Arabic' become so general as to be less than useful, I would now posit that, in the particular context of intertextual analyses, we now need to pose the question as to precisely which 'discursive space' and in which 'culture' we are proposing to base our discussions. However, whatever bases we choose for anchoring our chosen texts in a 'culture', I would suggest that the especially useful function of modern Arabic literature, indeed of the Arabic literary heritage in general, is its intercultural aspect. In a return to my opening comments, I might suggest that the founding figures of the intertextual approach seem to have grounded their theories in a generally unicultural or at least Eurocentric context (but one might suggest that, in Western comparative literature studies, there is little new about that situation). With that in mind, the sheer richness of the patterns of trans-regional and trans-cultural influence that have always been and remain a primary feature of Arabic literature seems to provide a source of potentially fruitful studies of and adjustments to the concept of intertextuality. To such efforts this volume is clearly a significant contribution.

However, I cannot close without returning once again to a problem that seems to me to impact directly on the efficacy of our researches in this domain. It relates to the concepts of heritage and literary canon and how the works identified within such terms of reference are categorised and historicised. As we continue to wrestle with the organisation of a history of modern Arabic literature in which a continuingly problematic concept of *'nahḍa'* is preceded by several centuries, the literary products and aesthetic criteria of which we have studied so little, we must surely suggest that the application of intertextual approaches requires — almost as a prerequisite — a more detailed questioning of the basic validity of Arabic's 'family archive'

The Narrative of the Ship: al-Mu'aqqit, Maḥfūẓ, and Jabrā

Richard van Leeuwen
University of Amsterdam

In his survey of Arabic literary history, Roger Allen observes that the topographical focus in Arabic literature has always been on the land, as opposed to the sea. Over the centuries, spatial motifs in Arabic literature, whether used as metaphors or referential evocations, are overwhelmingly associated with the land. It is conceptions of land which provide the parameters for narratives of identity; it is the land which provides the basic conditions for social life; it is the land which is the focus of political concerns. In some ways, this observation is remarkable, since at various times during their history the Arabs upheld an important tradition of seafaring. From the early ages of Islam, merchants travelled eastward, building a trade network which covered a large part of South-East Asia and included the eastern coast of Africa. In the Mediterranean the Arab presence was less prominent, but the Red Sea and the Persian Gulf were intensively explored by Arab dhows, fishermen, smugglers and traders. Arabic nautical handbooks were the basis of European knowledge of navigation, and Arabic maps inspired the emergence of the European tradition of cartography.[1]

In spite of these remarkable achievements, Arabs, or perhaps we should say Arab *literati*, retained an uneasy relationship to the sea. Of course, Arabic literature produced such a quintessential seafarer as Sindbād the Sailor, who cannot resist the lure of the sea and stubbornly plunges from one adventure into another. Indeed, Sindbād has become the symbol of man challenging the waves and addicted to sailing and maritime trade. On closer inspection, however, the stories of Sindbād cannot

1 Roger Allen, *The Arabic Literary Heritage; the development of its genres and criticism* (Cambridge: Cambridge University Press, 1998), 14; see also G.F. Hourani, *Arab Seafaring* (Princeton: Princeton University Press, 1995); Xavier de Planhol, *L'Islam et la mer: la mosquée et le matelot; VIIe–XXe siècle* (Paris: Perrin, 2000).

be considered to unambiguously sing the praise of the ocean. In fact, they are more concerned with the horrors of the sea than with its virtues. Since the stories, plots and sub-plots consist of shipwreck, ferocious monsters, storms, mysterious cliffs, dangerous islands, and unexpected dangers, they reflect the fear of the sea rather than love of seafaring. They characterise the seas as a domain of Fate, of ultimate contingency, of fatal natural catastrophes. This image of the sea is confirmed by such authors as Ibn Jubayr and Ibn Baṭṭūṭa, who both elaborate on the dangers of travelling on ships and give lively descriptions of shipwrecks.

If seafaring, as a literary *topos*, is so scarce and has such a negative connotation, the instances in which it is used in a prominent way are the more remarkable. In these cases we can be sure that it is used in a deliberate way to create sharp contrasts and to profit from a wide range of implicit and explicit connotations. We can be sure that the text is related to a rich 'metatext' in which these associations have been cultivated and explored, and with which both the author and the reader are familiar, as common, 'inherited' knowledge. The sea will not be a marginal setting or a mere backdrop; it will be an essential part of the metaphoric structure and of the thematic purport.

In this essay I examine three texts in which ships play a major role and which, in my view, fully exploit the potential of the ship as a metaphoric concept. The works are *Ahl al-safīna* by the Moroccan scholar Muḥammad al-Mu'aqqit, published in 1934;[2] the well-known novel *Tharthara fawq al-Nīl* by Najīb Maḥfūẓ (1966);[3] and the equally famous novel *al-Safīna* by Jabrā Ibrāhīm Jabrā (1969).[4] The discussion will focus on the ways in which the ship is used in these texts as a central metaphor

2 I have not been able to consult the original Arabic text, so here I have used the French translation: Mohammed ibn Abdallah al-Mu'aqqit al-Murrâkushi, *Les Gens du navire, ou le XIVᵉ siècle. Réforme et politique dans le Maroc des années 1930*, ed. and tr. Alain Roussillon and Abdallah Saaf (Casablanca: Afrique Orient, 1998); quotations are taken from this edition. I am grateful to Gonzalo Fernández Parrilla, who informed me about the existence of the text. See also his 'La novela en Marruecos; un nuevo género literario en el proceso de formación de una literatura árabe nacional: el papel de la crítica', Tesis Doctoral, Universidad Autónoma de Madrid (Madrid, 2000) , 1.

3 (Cairo: Maktabat Miṣr, 1966). Quotations are taken from Naguib Mahfouz, *Adrift on the Nile* (New York: Doubleday, 1994), English tr. Frances Liardet.

4 Jabra I. Jabra, *The Ship*, English tr. Adnan Haydar and Roger Allen (Colorado Springs: Three Continents Press, 1995); quotations are taken from this edition.

structuring the meaning of the narrative and on the common features and strategies exploiting the connotations of the ship, from which we could perhaps extract a metatextual notion: the constituents of a narrative of the ship. In this context it is only possible to formulate a hypothesis, the 'model' of the ship as a narrative *topos*, which should be compared to other texts. On this limited level, the term 'intertextuality' will be interpreted in its most general definition, as a structural link between texts which obliges the reader to refer to one text to interpret another and which bind texts to a 'metatext' or a network of different texts.[5]

Ahl al-safīna

In 1932 Muḥammad ibn ᶜAbd Allāh al-Mu'aqqit al-Murrākushī, an Islamic scholar and thinker,[6] published his *al-Riḥla al-Murrākushiyya*, an account of an imaginary journey to Marrakesh in which the conditions of contemporary Moroccan society are discussed and criticised. The book was an ambitious effort to defend the values of traditional Muslim society and to expose various forms of innovation, corruption and religious laxity. Apparently, the book was not received without criticism, which induced the author to write a continuation of the text in the form of an allegorical story, entitled *Ahl al-safīna*, or 'The people of the ship'. After some pious introductory formulae, the author relates how injustice has been done to him after the publication of his treatise and how, instead of heeding his admonitions, his enemies subjected him to ridicule and insults. He therefore left his home town and set out to join the Aṣḥāb Jamᶜiyya al-Ṣawāᶜiq al-Samāwiyya (Association of the Heavenly Tempests), a kind of wandering brotherhood founded to discover the

5 Graham Allen, *Intertextuality* (London / New York: Routledge, 2000).

6 Some information about al-Mu'aqqit's life and work can be found in Adolphe Faure, 'Un réformateur marocain: Muḥammad b. Muḥammad b ᶜAbd Allāh al-Muwaqqit al-Marrākusī,' *Hespéris* 39 (1952); al-Mu'aqqit was born about 1894 and was appointed *muwaqqit* of the Beni Youssef Mosque in Marrakesh. He was influenced by reformist thinkers such as Muḥammad ᶜAbduh and Rashīd Riḍā, and was acquainted with the work of Ibrāhīm and al-Muwayliḥī. He wrote several works criticising the morals of his contemporaries and especially corruption, modernisation and European influences. He died in 1949.

marvels of the world and to eliminate the manifold threats to the Muslim *umma*.

While the members of the group, on the seaside, are discussing the problems facing the Muslims, they see a ship approaching which is so large and strong that it is compared to a city: 'We contemplated the extension of this sea and "ships raised above the sea as mountains",[7] as cities whose basis is built by science and whose foundation is provided by the waters.'[8] And 'It was as if the seas were traversed by "Iram the many-columned city, a city such as nobody could ever create its likeness, in whatever country".'[9] This ship, in its magnificence, is seen as a symbol of power, which throughout history has served as a means to achieve hegemony and superiority:

> What a marvel are these ships which go and come for commerce and profit, for war and peace. How numerous are the nations, now and in the past, which have traversed these seas in all directions, and the dominance which they achieved is the result of the care taken in their preparation. In this way, they were able to vanquish nations that were inferior to them, through science, and they could impose their yoke in the interior and the exterior, as Titans. But the cycle of the stars does not turn in vain and time will bring about that which escaped the visions of the wisest sage.[10]

The group is allowed on board, but they have to pay a large amount of money and are treated with hostility. On board, they explore the inside of the ship, which is the size of a whole country and which contains everything that can satisfy human desires and that pleases the eye. The technical devices in particular arouse their admiration and concern:

> In truth, all these marvels of technical precision, all the elegance of these extraordinary inventions, besides ancestral technical secrets, could plunge the spirit into confusion and could stupefy the eye. All the signs of pleasure came from commercial establishments and everything bathed in electric light.[11]

7 Sura 55:24.
8 Al-Mu'aqqit, 22.
9 Ibid.; Sura 89:6–8.
10 Al-Mu'aqqit, 22–23.
11 Ibid., 25.

The captain of the ship is a European who distinguishes himself by his haughtiness and impoliteness. He allows the group to stay on board, on condition that they do not mix in 'politics'. They decide to keep a low profile, since they know that Europeans are prone to condemn a 'nation' for a mistake of one of its members.

The population of the ship consists of people of various nations, Muslims and non-Muslims. The Europeans are praised for their inventiveness, their rational vision and practical sense of organisation, but their leadership is unstable, because everyone wants to be an independent chief. The Muslims have not adopted the virtues of the Europeans, but only their vices. They live in disorder, as an 'exhausted nation', and suffer from heresy, corruption, the debasement of women, and bad habits, such as smoking tobacco, using drugs, drinking alcohol, eating pork, and practicing fornication and homosexuality. In addition, Sufis are falsifying the *sharīʿa*, the *ʿulamāʾ* are following their passions and violating the law, while kings, governors and judges are addicted to physical pleasures and commit injustice.

The members of group now regret that they have gone on board and wish that they had stayed in the desert. At that moment, the ship collides with an iceberg and the Day of Judgment seems to have arrived. The pious Muslims start preaching, but when their summons are not heeded, immense creatures appear with their feet on the earth and their heads in the sky. They say: 'O passengers of the ship, this is the punishment for those who have turned their backs on the Book of God and the *sunna* of His Prophet.'[12] Now storms break out, dragging the ship into whirlpools, followed by hails of stones and starvation. Some passengers repent, but the leaders persist in their sins and a black wind, pestilence and dizziness torture the travellers. Now a huge fire coming from the sea starts devouring the ship. The sea shouts: 'O fools, who are indulging in depravity, injustice, ignorance and fornication of all kinds, from your youth until your old age, now your day has come.'[13] The fishes call similar warnings. The pious Muslims seek refuge in a mosque, which suddenly breaks off from the ship and floats to a deserted island, while the ship disappears in the waves. They wait on the island until God will bring them back to their homeland.

12 Ibid., 57.
13 Ibid., 64.

The edifying tale of *Ahl al-safina* is first of all concerned with the elaboration of a moral issue, criticising the moral state of a society and juxtaposing innovation and tradition, decadence and moral values, materialism and spirituality, emphasising the central role of religion and piety. These concepts are linked to the broader concept of the 'journey', which expands the set of connotations and which enables the author to connect the moral issue to narrative experiences. The metaphoric content of the journey is first of all evoked by the separation of the author from his hometown and the endurances suffered on the way. The departure is placed into the context of religion, by quoting God's admonition to

> undertake voyages to increase their science and their knowledge, to reinforce their convictions, and to inform themselves of the state of the generations of the present times, the good things that befall them and the bad things that they endure, what is beneficial to them and what harms them, their riches and their poverty, their greatness and their pettiness, their good fortune and all uncertainties of their appurtenance to a common humanity.[14]

Travelling is a means to explore God's world, to discover the state of things. Insight can only be acquired by travelling, and whoever sets out with this aim will be recompensed for the hardships he has suffered.

However, the author perceives his departure also in a negative perspective. He leaves a town in which his message has not been heeded. He separates himself from his community, which has turned against him, and escapes the hostile environment to join a group of spiritual brothers who are united by a common vision. The journey is thus a *hijra*, a flight from a hostile, unbelieving society, with the aim of forming the core of a new, pious community, bound by a common moral and social attitude. The idea of the *hijra* has many references to the life of the Prophet, of course, and it also harbours the prospect of triumphant return, of the victory of the community governed by moral principles over the various realms of sin, perversion and ignorance. The *hijra* links the moral and social components of religious thought and determines the moral dimension of the journey. Everything that is seen on the way is judged by a moral standard which should be the basic code of a community. A

14 Ibid., 7.

journey is also a 'mission', an expedition to strengthen the moral bond to such an extent that it can be impregnated into human geography.

The journey is also meant to transcend the boundaries of the familiar and the known and to enter the realm of the unfamiliar and exotic. This crossing is of course symbolised by the boarding of the strange ship. The company is confronted with a different society which, as travellers do, is observed and described and measured by their own standards. This society is marked by many technological novelties, which are new to the travellers and inspire a sense of power, which is explicitly linked to the domination of one nation over the others and with the ability to organise society and disclose the secrets of nature. The magnificence and splendour of technology are also linked to a symbol taken from the familiar context, the city of Iram, the legendary city built by Shaddād ibn ᶜĀd as a token of his wealth and power. Shaddād rejected the call to convert to the True Faith, and his people and city were subsequently destroyed by a storm. However, the technical achievements of the '*ahl al-safīna*' are seen as an expression of materialism directed at earthly comforts and pleasures, an expression of hubris, of arrogance and pride at the human empowerment *vis-à-vis* the almighty God.

In this 'other' society the Muslims are portrayed as weak and divided among themselves. They deliver themselves to all kinds of vices, partly provided by the Europeans, allowing the Europeans to dominate them and to impose a state of permanent enslavement. Although a collection of precious old texts is present on the ship, only a few passengers appreciate this remnant of past glory, of a time when they were still part of the mainland and of the *umma*. The author here shows a futuristic vision, a kind of dystopia, as a warning against the adoption of Western influence, against the depreciation of moral values, against the dangers of foreign domination and against the fragmentation of Muslim society. The boundary between the Muslims on the land and those on the ship is partly a boundary in time, the marking off of a possible future, but it is also a moral boundary between two ethical choices, projected into space.

A third component of the concept of the journey is the traveller's exposure to the forces of contingency. Mobility entails the departure from familiar patterns and from the familiar environment, and the possibility of meeting hostile people, accidents, diseases, going astray, and so on. The ship represents a society that is afloat, that has detached itself from the safe structure of normal society; a society that has created a boundary between the mainland and itself with the aim of building a new, self-contained system of social behaviour, meanings and power. It has incorporated elements from another world, which stresses its position in between different continents that belong to neither of them. The ship has no clear destination: it is only moving to be away from the land. This lack of a solid foundation and the 'fluid' state caused by mobility expose the population to the forces of contingency, here represented by the catastrophes sent to the ship by God, first as a warning, then as castigation. The course of mobility is blocked and the vehicle is destroyed. Fate has interrupted a process of wandering which was not supported by the right context, by the moral integrity which protects societies and individuals. It is remarkable that the pious Muslims do not return to their homeland after the catastrophe, but have to await their return on a remote island. This may be a form of *reculer pour mieux sauter*, but it may also be an expression of the isolation felt by the author personally.

All these components of the 'narrative' journey come together in the ship and its complex of connotations. The ship epitomises mobility, here especially in its negative sense, as a form of dissociation from solid land. It represents a self-contained unit which is closed off from the regular social structures, and which forms a world of its own following its own rules and customs. It is detached from history and tradition and their structuring influence with regard to morality and social conduct. It is a symbol of technology and power, the container of a social model in which technical inventions have replaced the inner urge to realise a just and coherent society. Finally, the sea is the quintessential metaphor of the vicissitudes of Fate, a space without protection, without a guiding system of signs and with a permanent threat of death. The ship is the symbol of the human effort to triumph over nature and the chaos of unstructured space, and, ultimately, over the power of Fate. The sea represents the opposite forces, the recalcitrance of physical nature, the contingency of Fate and the will of God.

Tharthara fawq al-Nīl

In the second text to be discussed here, the novel *Tharthara fawq al-Nīl* by Najīb Maḥfūẓ, the ship, which is the central setting of the story, does not set out to sea: it is a *dhahabiyya*, or a typical houseboat on the Nile, which lies attached to the shore. Almost all the scenes of the story take place on this boat, and the action is almost entirely limited to conversations within this very specific setting. It should be noted that the novel was written in 1966 and reflects the spirit of a society evaluating the gains and losses of the 1952 revolution in Egypt. The protagonists belong to a generation which grew up with the slogans of the revolution and whose opportunities in life were provided, and limited, by a revolutionary regime that based itself on a combination of socialist and populist ideologies and forms of authoritarian control. There was a spirit of change, of experiments with new social and cultural ideas, but there was also disappointment about repressive methods and the failure of the regime to realise the main aims of the revolution. The novel shows that among some intellectuals revolutionary fervour had waned and that bitterness and frustration had taken its place. It is because of this context that the novel has been interpreted as a document of its time and as a forecast of the 1967 catastrophe.

Anīs Zakī, the main character in the story, lives on a houseboat on the Nile where a group of intellectuals meet regularly to smoke hashish and to make love. A civil servant, a lawyer, an art critic, a writer, a film-actor and an ex-feminist amuse themselves with small-talk, which reveals their cynical attitude towards life. They are only interested in what goes on around them if it can provide material for jokes and ridicule: 'The world does not concern us anymore than we concern it.'[15] The boat is guarded by ᶜAmm ᶜAbduh, a colossal figure, whose appearance betrays an indefinite old age and deep-rootedness. He seems to be a symbol of the defiance of death. He provides the boat with hashish and other requirements and sometimes conveys news from the 'world outside'. He is one of the all-encompassing figures that recur in the works of Maḥfūẓ and which seem to contain all kinds of contradictions in a massive and imposing personality.[16]

At one point, Samāra, a journalist, asks permission to join the group of friends. At first, her request meets with suspicion, since it is expected that she will break the intimacy of their gatherings, or, worse, will spy on them and betray their indulgences to the outside world. It turns out that, in fact, she confronts their nihilistic attitude with her own belief in the meaning of life, but she quite smoothly adapts to the spirit of the group

15 Maḥfūẓ, 18.
16 Ibid., 8, 9, 46.

when she falls in love with Ragab, the film-actor. She writes an outline of a play whose characters are based on the members of the group. Anīs steals the script and discloses the contents. Then, on a fateful evening, the friends, including Samāra, decide to take a car-ride on the shore. In their careless delirium, they hit a pedestrian, but fearing the consequences for their life and career if the police become involved, they drive on without inspecting the victim. The next day they read in the papers that the victim has died. The accident increases the tensions between the friends, and especially between Ragab, who drove the car, and Anīs, who announces that he will inform the police. This dispute leads to the dissolution of the group and the end of the smoking-sessions.

Evidently, the setting of the houseboat is first of all chosen to emphasise the distance between the group of friends and Egyptian society. The boat belongs to a different 'universe', separated from the mainland by a clear boundary. This boundary is symbolised by the gangway, which makes the boat rock whenever someone is entering. If the group is not certain who the newcomer is, the rocking causes fear and alarm, as if the outside world of the shore is intruding into their separate, self-contained domain. In spite of their trust that 'the authorities have enough to do already without bothering with the likes of us',[17] and in spite of their many cynical remarks, they are aware that they are detached from regular society, and this inspires them with a concealed sense of guilt and fear. The rocking of the boat indicates the instability of their situation, as if their self-imposed isolation has undermined the social foundations of their lives and has brought them into a precarious position without the protection of normal social structures. The boat is a refuge where the group can escape from normality, where it can enjoy a freedom that is not allowed in society, but which lacks truthfulness and security.

As a universe separated from the normal world, the boat also contains a separate system of meanings. This system is based on a kind of 're-valuation of values':

> Love is an old and worn-out game, but it is a sport on the houseboat. Fornication is held as a vice by councils and institution, but it is freedom on our houseboat. Women are all conventions and marriage deeds in the home, but they are nubile and alluring on the houseboat. And the moon is a satellite,

17 Ibid., 29.

> dead and cold, but on the houseboat, it is poetry; and madness is everywhere an illness, but here it is philosophy, and something was something everywhere else but here; for here it was nothing.[18]

On the boat the regular meanings of things and words collapse. Seriousness merges with ridicule, right and wrong become one and the same. The friends dissociate themselves from the values of mainland society and build their own values based on a profound sense of nihilism. Life on the boat is governed by an emptiness that absorbs history and the future, plunging it into a kind of timelessness unconnected with the temporal structure of the land. On the boat, the friends have no identity that is derived from the regular ideological, ethical or geographical concepts which dominate life in the outside world. They belong only to the boat.

This amoral world is not changed by the visits of Samāra, although the friends fear that her presence will be an intrusion into the introverted and meaningless atmosphere and would, so to speak, break the spell. Her intervention, claiming that life has a meaning, seems at first to lead to a confrontation. Her outline for a play, which is stolen by Anīs, reveals that according to her the community of the boat consists of empty words only, of a formal construction, as *l'art pour l'art*, as a flight from responsibility. On the boat existence is no more than a fiction, an illusion, as opposed to reality on the shore. The friends live in a realm of fantasy, constructed only for their hedonistic pleasures. However, at the same time she falls in love with Ragab and is thus slowly integrated into the nihilism of the group. As the *dénouement* approaches, it appears that she is no longer an intruder from the mainland, imbued with the values of 'normal' society, but has become one of the 'refugees', subjecting herself to the consensus within the group. Perhaps reluctantly, she has become one of the people of the boat.

It is significant that throughout the story the link with the mainland, however small, is maintained. This link is not only symbolised by the gangway, but also by the figure of ᶜAmm ᶜAbduh, who embodies everything that is connected to the land, as opposed to the boat. It is he who provides the boat with everything it needs; it is he who brings news from outside; and it is he who watches the rope with which the boat is attached to the shore, to prevent it from drifting away and going under.

18 Ibid., 107.

The detachment of the group from the mainland is thus in part illusionary. It can only exist through the protective mediation of ᶜAmm ᶜAbduh, who maintains the illusion. One can say that with the fatal accident the connection between illusion and reality, between the boat and the mainland, is restored. But the unification takes place with a bump, since the two universes are no longer compatible, the one cannot be integrated into the other without some violent concussion. The code of the boat has been internalised by the group to such an extent that they cannot combine it with the code from outside. The confrontation stirs up lingering feelings of guilt and alienation.

As in the story of *Ahl al-safīna*, the ship in Maḥfūẓ's novel is the central metaphor supporting the meaning of the story as a whole. It is used to convey a sense of separation and isolation, the image of a self-contained space, with its own system of meanings, as a place of estrangement and illusion, and as a source of catastrophes. Here, the ship is not explicitly the symbol of mobility, since it remains attached to the shore throughout the story, but it is a symbol of instability and contingency. It is not the vehicle of a journey, but it contains the possibility and constant threat of a fatal journey. When the group has dispersed, after the fight between Anīs and Ragab, ᶜAmm ᶜAbduh remarks to Anīs: 'I had made up my mind to break the moorings if he hit you again.'[19] Of course, the fact that the ship was saved from almost certain destruction leaves a glimmer of hope.

Al-Safīna

The third text to be discussed here is the well-known novel *al-Safīna*, by the Palestinian writer Jabrā Ibrāhīm Jabrā. This is the most complex text of the three treated here, and it is not possible to present an overall analysis in the context of this essay. Therefore, I will concentrate on what is obviously the main spatial component: the ship.

The story of *al-Safīna* is told by two major characters, who are taking a trip on a cruise ship from Beirut to Italy: ᶜIṣām Salmān, an architect from Baghdad, who has studied in London; and Wadīᶜ ᶜAssāf, a Palestinian businessman who lives in exile in Kuwait. ᶜIṣām has been in love with

19 Ibid., 163.

Lūmā, whom he has met in London, but whom he could not marry because she is related to a foe of the family. Without notifying ᶜIṣām, Lūmā has also booked a passage on the ship with her husband Fāliḥ, a Lebanese surgeon. Fāliḥ, in his turn, has invited an Italian friend of his, called Emilia. Wadīᶜ is travelling alone, since his friend Mahā, who also befriended Emilia, at the last moment decided not to join him. These characters constitute the company that goes on board the *Hercules* for a week's cruise on the Mediterranean, to Naples. Of course, during the journey several intrigues develop. ᶜIṣām renews his relationship with Lūmā and Fāliḥ 'escapes' with Emilia. The events consist of dialogues and contemplations, and trivial incidents which harbour the seeds of tragedy. In the end, the main characters have experienced a process of purification, but Fāliḥ has committed suicide.

The main theme of the novel, structuring the configuration of the characters and shaping the framework of their thoughts and conversations, is the journey, with its distinct phases, departure, mobility and arrival. With their departure the characters have separated from their familiar environment, leaving behind beloved ones, for some, and problematic circumstances for others. The characters have dissociated themselves from the social structures which limited their liberty of action, which imposed forms of power on them and which were connected with their relationship to the land, whether they were living in exile or not. Relationships with others are temporarily broken or taken out of the context which helped shaping them. Structures, rooted in history and tradition, are tied to the land, power is exerted over land, social relations are embedded in a context of human geography, and individual relationships are affected by all these forces. The structures on the land are presented as restrictions on emotions, contributing to a disequilibrium, an incongruence, a discrepancy between emotions and reality, between the desires of the protagonists and the opportunities provided by real life.

The second phase of the journey, the phase of mobility, is intimately linked to the sea, whose metaphoric connotations form a chain of similes through the novel. The sea is likened to 'salvation', to 'dreams', to unreality, to music, beauty and harmony. The waves of the sea are soothing, enchanting, impressive and a source of madness. The sea is a symbol of fantasy, of emotions and some hidden reality. The sea is also a symbol of eternity:

> Everything is transitory except these waves, not only metaphorically, but physically as well. They are the tunes of joy and sorrow connected with God, the angels, and the saints; tunes into which merge the wild notes of love and violent hidden sensations.[20]

And:

> The waves looked like some living thing that refused to relinquish its life and so was constantly renewing itself in a white marble wake of foam stretching away in the distance.[21]

The sea thus becomes a mythical force, a primordial space giving unity to the heart and mind and connecting them to some eternal truth. Being opposed to the symbolic system of the land, it forms a universe of its own, reaching for a deeper meaning.

For ᶜIṣām the sea is a metaphor for Lūmā, his beloved, and the journey is a form of escape from her, since, as he says, 'I could not make Lūmā my own sea, my own ship, and my own adventure.'[22] But now she is standing before him, 'like a wall, like a giant, like the sea itself.'[23] She has returned to him as from a jar fished up from the sea. For Wadīᶜ the sea is first of all a way to retain the link with the homeland. It comforts him that the waters of the Mediterranean reach the shores of Palestine, where he used to stand. It is a catalyst of memories of water, the Sulṭān's Pool in Jerusalem, baptism, and his youth. Water is the source of life and of history. For both, however, the virtues of the sea are ultimately related to the land:

> Real alienation is alienation from a place, from roots. This is the crux. Land, land, that's everything. We return to it bringing our discoveries, but as long as we hang on to the racing clouds, we remain in this fools' paradise. We are continually escaping, but now we must go back to the land, even if we are forced later to start off again. We must have *terra firma* under our feet.[24]

20 Jabrā, 22.
21 Ibid., 79.
22 Ibid., 11.
23 Ibid., 13.
24 Ibid., 74–75.

Although the third phase of the journey, arrival at a (final) destination, is not fully achieved at the end of the novel, the links between the sea and the land in the imaginations of ᶜIṣām and Wadīᶜ give us an idea of what a destination could be. Of course, the ship is bound for Europe, and the journey ends in the port of Naples. For some of the travellers, especially ᶜIṣām, Europe is an alternative homeland, where he has spent essential parts of his past and where he expects to find a future, away from the traumatic memories of Iraq. Thus, the journey on the ship is presented as a flight, which denies the bond with the land. The journey is an escape, a flight from reality. The ultimate aim for 'Iṣām is to bring 'the woman' (Lūmā), to the land, to establish a kind of reintegration that will produce a new harmony between dream and reality, feelings and their social embedding.[25] For Wadīᶜ the sea strengthens his awareness of his exile from his land, which he considers as a curse. Land is life.

In the end Wadīᶜ advises 'Iṣām to go back to Baghdad. It is in Baghdad, not in Europe, where his future lies: 'There's the lapse into inanity; there's the real defeat [...] He'll never find his freedom anywhere else.'[26] Whereas ᶜIṣām was willing to spend all his life 'at sea', as a traveller, Wadīᶜ acknowledges the necessity to return to the land, the second source of life.

As in the two previous texts, in *al-Safīna*, too, it is the ship, as a spatial setting and as a metaphoric concept, which binds the various themes together and which allows their articulation. The ship is both the symbol of detachment from the constraints of the mainland and of the impossibility of escape:

> On board a ship, it should be written as follows in letters of sun and wind: 'Abandon all memories, all ye who enter here!' For voyagers, the sea is a tremendous eraser that can wipe out the most stubborn types of ink, even images etched into the soul like wounds. But unfortunately the sea is not the river of oblivion, however much the travelers might wish it were. That only happens when it turns wild and nasty.[27]

It is still the code of the mainland which is the basis of the code of the universe of the ship, but the latter code is formed on the basis of a new

25 Ibid., 76.
26 Ibid., 198.
27 Ibid., 125.

configuration of relationships. This code is represented as imaginary, as the representation of a temporary reality. On the ship, people meet each other and become friends or enemies quickly, because they know that they will be separated soon. Contacts are established within a closed space from which the protagonists cannot escape. They are forced to deal with each other, while at the same time the surroundings and ambiance are conducive to an intensification of the senses and emotions. On the ship time has another pace, dissociated from the time on land and adapted to the pace of mobility and to the almost mythical vastness of the sea. These conditions create the opportunity for a cleansing of the souls of the protagonists, thereby preparing the way not for reaching their destination, but for meeting their destiny: the prospect of a return with a new vision of life.

Conclusions

In our discussion of the three texts, *Ahl al-safīna*, *Tharthara fawq al-Nīl*, and *al-Safīna*, we have seen how the ship is the main concept structuring the narrative, both as a spatial setting and as a coherent set of connotations which strengthen the themes of the stories. In spite of some differences, the function of the concept is quite similar in all three cases. This function is related to some more general conceptual notions related to the ship, which can be summarised as follows.

First, ships are inherently related to the concept of the journey, with its various phases, and its structural relationship to processes of initiation. A range of images and motifs connected to mobility can be used, but some new aspects are added. The departure gives the travellers a sense of freedom, since they are taken out of the environment which imposes all kinds of restrictions on their thought and actions. On the other hand, however, the ship is a closed unity without the possibility of escape. One universe of symbols is replaced by another, closed, universe, which can be equally oppressive. Therefore, in contrast to the general association of travelling and freedom, the ship rather produces a sense of claustrophobia, since escaping is impossible and the setting of the ship does not provide the same multiple perspectives as does the land. It is for this reason, too, that the maritime journey is associated with the idea of exile, an exile of a part of the community which decides to take a specific course separating it from their country; This motif comes close to the concept of *hijra* in

Islam: a self-chosen isolation of a group which separates itself from a society which seems to reject them; and the exile of those who have been displaced in their homelands, by war, occupation, defeats and traumatic experiences.

Secondly, the contrast between the ship and the land is represented in the juxtaposition of illusion and reality. The journey on board the ship is an escape from reality, an imaginary construction outside the regular spatiotemporal structures. However, these constructions are never entirely dissociated from reality and from the construction of reality on land. In the end, it always appears that the imaginary reality on the ship has been built as an enclave within reality itself and that a confrontation between the two is inevitable. There is no exile, no escape, no isolation without a return. The imaginary universe on the ship in some ways reveals a hidden meaning of reality; it becomes more real than reality itself. A truth is discovered, which can change the protagonist's place in reality on the mainland. This reconciliation between illusion and reality can never be smooth: every ship is bound for disaster. In *al-Safīna*, this disaster consists of the suicide of Fāliḥ, who can no longer endure a life filled with lies, oppression and cruelty.

Thirdly, the universe of the ship is presented as a mirror of society on land, a self-image at a distance. The universe is constructed out of several components of real society, or their antithesis, thus emphasising some constituents over others, creating a distortion which legitimises or explains the state of 'exile'. It is this mirror-function which introduces the moral component that is a very prominent connotation of the ship. Travelling on board a ship means interrogating morality, asking moral questions and evaluating moral standards. Life on ships is hedonistic, nihilistic, lascivious, subject to passions and emotions, but it is always overtaken and absorbed by the forces of morality, social responsibility, religion or intellectual and emotional sincerity.

Fourthly, a ship is a closed universe, which is built by the passengers out of the components of their life which remain attached to them after leaving their regular lives, with the aim of forming a new, coherent whole. But there is always some surplus, something that cannot be integrated into the new symbolic system that cannot be named or domesticated by the imaginary reality that is constructed. Every ship has its stowaway who, as a rule, reveals himself at the end of the story, when the catastrophe hitting the ship squeezes the truth out of the illusionary lives of the passengers. In *Ahl al-safīna* it is the group of pious Muslims which differentiates itself from the other passengers, as a kernel of piety not reconciled with the mental universe of the ship. In *Tharthara fawq al-Nīl* it is not, as could be expected, Samāra who is the intruder, since she quite easily adapts herself to the nihilism of the group, but Anīs Zakī, whose nihilism has not sprung from indulgence in hedonism, but from a deeply felt sorrow after the death of his wife and daughter. This 'kernel' of truth in the realm of illusion contributes to the final dispersal of the group after the car-accident. Similarly, in *al-Safīna* it turns out that Fāliḥ has a hidden agenda that no-one expected. He cannot decide between his two loves, Lūmā and the Italian Emilia, East and West, a life of passion and a life of the mind. It is the kernel of honesty which cannot be reconciled with a reality based on hypocrisy and mental and physical violence.

These, then, are the constituents of the 'narrative of the ship', the ship on its intertextual journey. These are the connotations of the ship that recur in the three texts that have been studied and that not only relate the texts to each other but also indicate that they are constructed around the same narrative stereotype.

There is one more aspect that remains to be mentioned: in all three texts important references to other texts can be found which are, in themselves, forms of intertextual reference. In *Ahl al-safīna* it is the Qur'ān, of course, and related texts from the religious heritage with which the story is imbued, as a justification of the journey, as a source of moral judgment, as a reservoir of similes such as the city of Iram, and finally as the common bond between the pious Muslims. Furthermore, the text is on several levels related to al-Mu'aqqit's previous work, *al-Riḥla al-Marrākushiyya*. In *Tharthara fawq al-Nīl* it is the synopsis of the play which provides an intertextual play within the story. The text, which is quoted in full, shows that the universe of the group consists of words only, as an empty shell, as a replica of itself, as an illusionary reproduction. The meetings of the group are an artificial construction, revealed by juxtaposing it to another artificial construction. Maḥfūẓ uses this episode to comment on the role of writers in a revolutionary society, in a short poem:

> You have wisdom, vision and justice,
> But you let corruption gnaw at the land.
> See how your orders are held in contempt!

> Will you order till there comes one who will tell you the truth?[28]

In *al-Safīna*, finally, there are several references to literary texts, as if the ship is a meeting-point for various literary discourses, where texts come together, mix and are dispersed again. The main reference, however, is to the *Thousand and One Nights*, especially the story of 'The Porter and the Three Ladies of Baghdad' and the Sindbād-cycle. The relevance of the Sindbād figure is obvious, since it is used in connection with the opposition between roaming and rootedness, of a life on the seas and a return to the land. The relevance of the other story, suggested by the episode of the sailor and the passenger who accuses him of having tortured him, and the suggestion to have a motto on the ship for all who enter it, is that it implies that the ship is a kind of enchanted space, or at least a space governed by an enchantment, where the lives of various persons are related to each other, where life-narratives are told to save lives, and where some mysterious secret is revealed. In the *Thousand and One Nights*, all characters, except the porter, have a double identity, which is gradually unmasked. In the end, the identities are reconstructed and brought into harmony. Likewise, the ship is an enchanted space; it is filled with false identities, it is full of tales, it is a place where lives meet and are driven off course, only to collide with destiny.

28 Maḥfūẓ, 108.

D'arbres et de lunes : parcours intertextuel dans la littérature arabe contemporaine

Luc-Willy Deheuvels
INALCO (Paris)

Dans quelle mesure la littérature arabe moderne fait-elle appel pour se dire à la sphère littéraire arabo-islamique classique ? Quelle y est la part de renouvellement, et peut-on y déceler une périodisation nette qui installerait un *avant*, et un *après* 1967 ? Cette date importante de l'histoire internationale, marquée par la guerre israélo-arabe, est-elle une date de rupture, dans la littérature arabe, et d'apparition de nouvelles esthétiques ? Ces questions surgissent, dès lors que l'on entend s'interroger sur l'intertextualité[1] dans la littérature arabe après 1967, thème du sixième colloque de l'EMTAR. Quelques éléments de réponse en seront recherchés ici, à travers l'étude du motif de l'arbre et des *topoï* d'ordre dénotatif et connotatif auxquels il est associé.

La présente analyse s'attachera dans un premier temps à établir les constantes et les permanences, sur la base d'un corpus de textes arabes du vingtième siècle montrant notamment à quel point le motif de l'arbre reste fortement marqué par les connotations sacrées et mythiques qui lui sont attachées dans la culture arabo-islamique classique.

Puis l'étude de la répétition intertextuelle des motifs associés de l'arbre et de la lune dans des écrits arabes postérieurs à 1967 conduira à éclairer une voie de renouvellement, à travers la formation d'un *topos* dont il sera montré qu'absent de la culture arabo-islamique classique, il fait son apparition dans la littérature arabe avec force dans les années 60, au confluent d'esthétiques littéraires marquées tantôt par l'existentialisme et un appel à l'engagement de la littérature au sens politique, tantôt par le

1 Deux formes d'intertextualité seront envisagées dans cette étude. D'une part l'intertextualité stricte, marquée par la présence effective d'un texte dans un autre texte (citation, emprunt, plagiat, allusion), et le jeu de renvois d'un texte à un énoncé antérieur; d'autre part, la reprise dans un texte de *topoï*, marques littéraires conventionnelles (marques lexicales, syntaxiques, rhétoriques, motifs etc.) caractéristiques de démarches esthétiques particulières.

théâtre de l'absurde, et la littérature du solipsisme, combiné dans ce second cas avec le thème de la métamorphose.

Le motif de l'arbre est marqué par des permanences très fortes, tant du point de vue des connotations qui lui sont attachées, souvent liées à des mythes, que de la façon dont le lexique est mobilisé dans les différentes époques et esthétiques.

La littérature arabe a une façon bien à elle d'user des termes liés à l'arbre. On conçoit, en général, que l'utilisation d'hyperonymes (de termes désignant le genre, comme *arbre*) dénote la recherche d'une stylisation et peut donner au texte une portée symbolique ; on considère aussi couramment, dans les analyses stylistiques prenant appui sur les littératures occidentales, que le passage du général au particulier (par exemple d'*arbre* à l'hyponyme *pommier*) est en revanche un mode de présentation caractéristique des énoncés descriptifs didactiques, et un procédé très courant dans l'esthétique réaliste. Or, l'examen des occurrences des noms de genre et d'espèce liés à l'arbre dans la littérature arabe révèle une différence notable : dans les textes arabes anciens comme modernes, la déclinaison du terme générique *shajara* (*arbre*) en termes d'espèces particulières (pommier, palmier, oranger, olivier ...) ne procède pas du tout de la même démarche. Ainsi dans *Zaynab* (1913) de Muḥammad Ḥusayn Haykal, roman paysan ancré dans les réalités des campagnes égyptiennes, sur 73 occurrences du lexique de l'arbre dans le roman, 65 (soit près de 90%) se rapportent au genre, et sont lexicalement partagées entre الشجر, الشجرة, الأشجار, شجرة, شجيرات et الشجيرات. Les quelques emplois d'hyponymes (huit occurrences de *palmier*, *mûrier*, *sycomore*, *acacia*) n'y relèvent pas de *topoï* descriptifs visant à susciter un effet de réel, dans le cadre de ce qui serait une esthétique réaliste. Ils y sont toujours liés à un engagement affectif marqué de la narration (euphorique / dysphorique), l'arbre devenant le lieu d'une projection de la passion de Zaynab, de son déclin physique et de sa mort.[2]

Dans le cas de la poésie, on pourrait penser à une plus importante hypéronymie, favorisée par la tendance du discours poétique à la stylisation et au symbole. L'examen de deux recueils récents de Maḥmūd Darwīsh, *Arā mā urīdu* (1990) et *Aḥada ᶜashara kawkaban* (1992), prouvent qu'il n'en est rien. Poétisation du réel, symbolisme d'une nature

2 Un tel constat corrobore l'appartenance de *Zaynab* à une écriture très influencée par l'esthétique romantique.

palestinienne chargée émotivement et idéologiquement jusqu'à saturation caractérisent l'écriture de Maḥmūd Darwīsh, le grand poète de la résistance nationale du peuple palestinien. Un relevé des occurrences du lexique de l'arbre dans ces deux recueils conduit aux observations suivantes :

➢ Dans *Arā mā urīdu* (1990), face à 12 occurrences de *shajar*, on trouve 55 hyponymes (*amandiers*, *bananiers*, *sureau*, *châtaignier*, *chêne et chêne vert*, *citronnier*, *cognassier*, *cyprès*, *dattiers*, *lilas de Perse*, *mûriers*, *néfliers*, *noisetiers*, *figuiers de barbarie*, *oliviers*, *orangers*, *pêchers*, *pins*, *pommiers*, *pruniers*, *vigne*, *saule*).

➢ Dans *Aḥada ᶜashara kawkaban* (1992), la proportion est rigoureusement la même : 14 hypéronymes pour 60 hyponymes.

Que retirer de ces analyses ? Le texte le plus prosaïque, celui en qui certains ont cru voir le premier roman arabe, salué ainsi au nom d'une grande adéquation au référentiel réel (celui de la campagne égyptienne), est aussi lexicalement celui qui est le plus pauvre pour l'arbre. Il ne s'enrichit que lorsque le texte se charge affectivement. Le texte poétique a une palette lexicale d'une très grande richesse, alors même que la charge connotative et symbolique y est très forte. Ces deux exemples ne sont en rien des exceptions. Ils mettent à jour une réalité. En fait, une tendance si forte qu'on peut l'élever en règle se révèle, quant au lexique de l'arbre dans la littérature arabe : plus l'engagement affectif et axiologique est important, plus la valeur connotative est forte, plus l'écriture favorisera le passage du genre à l'espèce.

On peut même considérer que, quand il est question d'arbre dans la littérature arabe, le passage du genre à l'espèce contribue à orienter la perception. L'horizon d'attente créé par le texte s'installe en un jeu intertextuel fondé sur la reprise de tournures d'hypercodage rhétorique, de *topoï* caractéristiques de la littérature arabe, parfois même de scénarios entiers. C'est particulièrement le cas des exemples reliant l'arbre au mythe. La littérature arabe moderne s'inscrit à cet égard dans une continuité notable avec la sphère littéraire et culturelle classique, y compris dans la façon d'assumer un héritage mythique largement antéislamique. De nombreux exemples peuvent en être donnés, allant de l'arbre cosmique,[3] à l'association entre l'arbre et la course du soleil,[4] au palmier et aux connotations mythiques qui continuent à y être rattachées, l'associant analogiquement à l'homme.[5] Il en est d'autres, directement liés à des représentations paradisiaques. Nous nous attacherons ici à un exemple précis, celui de l'association fréquente entre arbres et murailles, dans la littérature arabe moderne.

L'association *arbre* et *muraille* (*sūr* et mention précise d'un certain nombre d'espèces, notamment d'arbres fruitiers) fonctionne intertextuellement dans la littérature arabe comme un *topos* renvoyant à des représentations paradisiaques portées par les textes classiques. Ainsi, dans le dictionnaire géographique de Yāqūt, parvenu aux sources du Nil, Hā'idh se trouve devant la muraille (*sūr*) du paradis[6] qu'il lui est interdit d'escalader pour admirer toutes les merveilles qu'il renferme. Bien des siècles plus tard, en 1975, la première des « histoires de notre quartier » de Naguib Mahfouz s'ouvre sur un enfant dont le plus grand rêve est de parvenir de l'autre côté de la muraille du monastère, inaccessible « lune vers laquelle se tendent les mains »,[7] seul lieu de verdure du quartier, là où poussent arbres et mûriers. La même configuration présidait déjà à la description de la maison de Gabalāwī, allégorie du paradis perdu et inaccessible, dans le roman *أولاد حارتنا*, que le romancier égyptien publia en 1959. Un tel réinvestissement n'a rien de limité à cet auteur. De Yūsuf Idrīs à Yaḥyā al-Tāhir ᶜAbd Allāh, Ibrāhīm ᶜAbd al-Majīd et de très nombreux autres, la liste est inépuisable de textes où l'association *arbre* et *muraille* traduit un engagement affectif euphorique très fort, et une reprise intertextuelle renvoyant à des représentations paradisiaques.

3 L'arbre cosmique : cet arbre, largement présent dans les textes classiques d'auteurs mystiques pour qui il est le symbole de l'homme parfait, se retrouve parfois dans des textes contemporains, comme chez Neguib Mahfouz (حكايات حارتنا, 1975) ou al-Ṭayyib Ṣāliḥ (بندرشاه et دومة ود حامد).

4 Voir aussi, Luc-Willy Deheuvels, « Le Caire comme contre-utopie », Dossier spécial sur Le Caire de Mahfouz, *Qantara*, Institut du Monde Arabe, n° 50–51 (hiver 2003–printemps 2004), 56–58.

5 cf. Ibn al-Wardī, *Kharīdat al-ᶜajā'ib wa-farīdat al-gharā'ib*, Beirut, n.d., 200, and Muḥammad 'Ajīna, *Mawsūᶜat asāṭīr al-ᶜarab ᶜan ᶜaṣr al-jāhiliyya wa-dalālātihā*, Beirut : Dār al-Fārābī, 1994, 279–280.

6 Yāqūt al-Ḥamawī, *Muᶜjam al-buldān*, Beirut, 1979, vol. 5, 339.

7 Najīb Maḥfūẓ, *Ḥikāyāt ḥāratinā*, Cairo: Dār Miṣr lil-Ṭibāᶜa, 1975, 3.

Si l'association *shajara* (*arbre*) et *sūr* (*muraille*) constitue un cas d'hypercodage renvoyant intertextuellement à des pans entiers de la sphère littéraire arabe ancienne et moderne, celle entre *arbre* et *lune* est, elle, très différente. On peut dater des années soixante son intrusion dans la littérature arabe, où elle a eu tendance, par jeu d'intertextualité explicite, à constituer un *topos* lié à des esthétiques contemporaines.

Nous partirons d'une analyse de cette association en situation dans un premier exemple, celui d'un court texte du syrien Zakariyyā Tāmir. Inséré dans une nouvelle du recueil *النمور في اليوم العاشر* [Les Tigres le dixième jour] (1969), il porte le titre de *شجرة الأقمار الحمراء* [L'Arbre aux lunes rouges].

Résumé : Des étrangers envahissent le champ bien vert d'une plantation d'orangers. Ils ouvrent le feu sur une femme, lui arrachent son enfant à qui elle donnait le sein, et le conduisent pour lui faire subir un interrogatoire. Ses pleurs sont interprétés comme l'expression de ses regrets d'être arabe. Les juges, persuadés que, quand il sera grand, il prendra les armes pour les tuer et récupérer son champ, le condamnent à mort. Ils l'enterrent vivant dans un trou au milieu des orangers. Arrosé par le sang de sa mère, au printemps, il se transforme en arbre, un oranger dont les fruits sont des lunes rouges, éclairant une nuit dont l'aube tarde à venir.

Ce texte à l'esthétique symboliste s'intègre dans une littérature engagée offerte à une réception qui le décode en fonction de la réalité palestinienne (les étrangers = les Israéliens, le champ envahi = la terre palestinienne, la mère assassinée = la Patrie, l'enfant = le futur combattant). Cette écriture allégorique obéit strictement à la règle que nous avons mise à jour ci-dessus, concernant le lexique de l'arbre. Ici aussi, l'hyponymie n'a pas pour but de marquer un effet de réel ; au contraire, la mention de l'oranger s'inscrit dans une symbolique d'époque. Au même titre que l'olivier et le figuier de barbarie, il renvoie constamment, dans la littérature de résistance, à la terre palestinienne perdue. L'intertextualité joue par exemple pleinement entre les orangers de Zakariyyā Tāmir et ceux de Yaḥyā al-Ṭāhir ^{c}Abd Allāh : dans la nouvelle *ثلاث شجرات كبيرة تثمر برتقالا* [Trois grands arbres qui donnent des oranges] (1970), une fillette de six ans, orpheline de père, questionne sa mère sur l'absence du frère aîné, sorti du camp de réfugiés de Jaffa. La mère lui dit qu'il est parti là-bas, derrière les fils barbelés, chasser les étrangers pour leur permettre à toutes deux de revenir. « Là-bas, ajoute la mère, nous avons trois arbres qui donnent des oranges ». Le frère doit revenir et lui rapporter de ces oranges. L'association mur / arbres est ici modifiée par l'insertion des fils barbelés, toutefois c'est bien à l'image des arbres fruitiers d'un paradis perdu — ici la Palestine — que font écho les orangers de Yaḥyā al-Ṭāhir ᶜAbd Allāh. Avec ceux de Zakariyyā Tāmir et bien d'autres, ils constituent un élément caractéristique d'une symbolique d'époque.

Dans le texte de Zakariyyā Tāmir, la plantation d'orangers voit pousser en son milieu un arbre à lunes rouges. Si le rouge y renvoie au sang, si la lune rouge à elle seule s'affiche comme un présage, c'est l'association entre la lune et l'arbre qui retient le plus l'attention. Elle surgit chez Zakariyyā Tāmir, suscitée par le texte qui inscrit ainsi une nouvelle contribution au véritable jeu intertextuel qui s'est poursuivi durant les années soixante, dans des œuvres qui se répondaient, autour de la question palestinienne.

Le « dialogue » entre textes a très vraisemblablement été initié par Maḥmūd Darwīsh et son poème *Qamar al-shitā'* [« Lune d'hiver »], publié en 1966 dans le recueil *ᶜĀshiq min Filasṭīn* [Amant de Palestine] :

قمر الشتاء	**Lune d'hiver**
سألمّ جثتك الشهيده	*Je ramasserai ton corps martyr*
وأذيبها بالملح والكبريت	*Et le dissoudrai dans du sel et du soufre*
ثم أعبّها : كالشاي	*Puis le boirai à grands traits comme du thé*
كالخمر الردينة ،كالقصيده	*Comme le mauvais vin, comme la qasida*
في سوق شعر خائب	*Au marché de la poésie inutile*
وأقول للشعراء:	*Et je dirai aux poètes :*
يا شعراء أمّتنا المجيده !	*Poètes de notre glorieuse nation !*
أنا قاتل االقمر	*C'est moi qui ai tué la lune*
الذي كنتم عبيده !	*Dont vous étiez esclaves !*

La lune ici assassinée est celle dont les poètes arabes chantaient la beauté archétypale, idéal de perfection du visage féminin comme masculin, souligné entre autres dans des expressions rhétoriquement très marquées comme كالقمر في ليلة البدر (*comme la lune la nuit où elle est pleine*). C'est ce *topos* de la poésie lyrique et amoureuse qui est ici mis à mort par le poète assassin de la lune. Le meurtre prend la dimension d'une libération poétique, à l'heure où se développe la révolution palestinienne, celle des organisations de combat. Une poésie ancienne est appelée à mourir, une esthétique libératrice doit l'anéantir pour venir à bout de l'hiver mentionné dans le titre.

L'année même où ce poème fut composé, il reçut une « réponse », insérée dans une pièce de théâtre composée par l'auteur palestinien Tawfīq Fayyāḍ, très proche de Maḥmūd Darwīsh et comme lui fort impliqué dans la résistance ;[8] le texte en fut ensuite publié à Beyrouth dans le supplément hebdomadaire d'*al-Anwār* en août 1967, puis intégralement repris par Ghassān Kanafānī en 1968 dans *أدب المقاومة في فلسطين المحتلة* [La Littérature de résistance en Palestine occupée]. La pièce, symboliste et engagée, est caractéristique d'une esthétique du solipsisme : elle est intégralement composée d'un long monologue, qui nous fait entrer dans une conscience et suivre dans ses méandres confus et délirants le discours d'un personnage, Sāmī, professeur d'histoire et de littérature contraint au silence par les occupants de sa maison, enfermé dans une demeure de Hayfa, en bordure de mer, assailli par des cauchemars depuis que sa bien-aimée Lubnā a été métamorphosée en dragon. Dans cette écriture éclatée, il devient impossible de reconstruire la *fabula*, la déconstruction de l'écriture marquant concrètement l'aliénation du Palestinien Sāmī, victime d'une dépossession d'identité et empêché de transmettre sa culture ainsi que la mémoire collective qui y est attachée. Toutefois, comme dans le texte de Zakariyyā Tāmir, l'écriture prend des dimensions allégoriques renvoyant à la tragédie palestinienne, Lubnā se prêtant aisément à une lecture qui verrait en elle le sol palestinien occupé, vidé de sa mémoire et changé dans sa toponymie, « métamorphosé » par les nouveaux occupants, des loups qui persécutent Sāmī. Refuser la nouvelle Lubnā, ce dragon qu'il faut terrasser pour lui permettre de renaître, est l'obsession de Sāmī. Tuer Lubnā, c'est aussi tuer la lune, dit Sāmī, dont le discours fait intertextuellement sens en réponse au poème de Maḥmūd Darwīsh :

لبنى! أجل لبنى! بل التنين!! من يتصـور أن مثل هذه الحمامة الوديعة، تتحول	*Lubnā ! Oui, Lubnā ! ou plutôt le dragon ! Qui aurait imaginé que cette douce colombe se trans-*

8 Palestinien de l'intérieur, son activisme lui valut la prison quatre ans, puis l'exil après 1970.

9 بيت الجنون، المؤسسة العربية للدراسات والنشر، بيروت، 1979، ص8-9. Les passages donnés ici sont extraits du discours de Sāmī ; ils n'intègrent pas les orientations scéniques.

إلى تنين رهيب يغرس مخالبه المتوحشة في
عنقي؟
كدت أجن!!

(...)
إيه...
لا قمر في السماء!
لقد انتزعه ذلك الشاعر اللعين من الأعالي،
واغتصبه في ليلة مجنونة من ليالي الشتاء على
الشاطئ المقفر!
ثم... ثم ذوبه بالملح والكبريت!
بل وشربه !
كما لو كان يشرب خمرة رديئة في ليلة إفلاس![9]

formerait en un terrible dragon qui planterait sauvagement ses griffes dans mon cou ? C'est à devenir fou !
(...)
Eh oui... il n'y a pas de lune dans le ciel ! ce maudit poète l'a arrachée des hauteurs pour la violenter par une folle nuit d'hiver, sur une plage déserte !
Et puis... et puis il l'a dissoute dans du sel et du soufre et il l'a bue !
comme l'on boit un mauvais vin, une nuit de faillite !

Ce début de dialogue intertextuel a été prolongé par le poète syrien Nizār Qabbānī, qui composa ces vers rageurs aux lendemains de la défaite arabe de 1967, à l'encontre de ceux qui continuaient à vivre comme si rien ne s'était passé. C'est dans un dialogue intertextuel que s'inscrit à nouveau la mention de la lune, dont le poème nous dit qu'elle est encore dans le ciel :

حرب حزيران انتهت!
حرب حزيران انتهت!
فكل حرب بعدها ونحن طيبون
أخبارنا جيدة
وحالنا والحمد لله على أحسن ما يكون

وطاولات الزهر على أحسن ما يكون
والقهوة المرة بالهال على أحسن ما يكون

والقمر المزروع في سمائنا مدوّر الوجه على أحسن
ما يكون
وصوت فيروز من الفردوس يأتي : "نحن راجعون".

La guerre de juin est finie.
La guerre de juin est finie
Chaque nouvelle guerre nous voit en bonne santé. Nos nouvelles sont bonnes.
Notre santé, grâce à Dieu, est on ne peut mieux.
Les jeux de tric-trac, on ne peut mieux.
Le café amer parfumé à la cardamome va on ne peut mieux.
La lune plantée dans notre ciel avec son visage bien rond va on ne peut mieux
Et la voix de Fayrouz parvient du paradis : « Nous reviendrons ».

L'esthétique de la littérature de résistance s'impose dès le début des années soixante dans un refus de la poésie ancienne. Les lunes aux faces rebondies installées avec une stabilité millénaire dans les nuits des poèmes arabes cèdent le pas à des lunes pâles ou sanglantes, nouvelles venues qui prennent place, souvent en association avec le motif de l'arbre, et tendent à se constituer en *topos* des nouvelles esthétiques. Maḥmūd Darwīsh y revenait ainsi, dans l'un de ses plus célèbres poèmes, *جواز سفر* (« Passeport »), publié en 1970, quand il disait

لم يعرفوني... آه.. لا تتركي
كفي بلا شمس لأن الشجر
يعرفني.. تعرفني كل أغاني المطر.

لا تتركيني شاحبا كالقمر.

Ils ne m'ont pas reconnu, ah.. ne laisse pas
Ma main sans soleil, parce que les arbres
M'ont reconnu... toutes les chansons de pluie me connaissent.
Ne me laisse pas, pâle comme la lune.

L'apparition du *topos* de l'arbre à la lune est connexe de celle d'écritures nouvelles, symbolistes, parfois surréalistes, ou relevant de la littérature de l'absurde, ou encore d'écrits où l'engagement est directement en prise avec une vision marquée par l'existentialisme. Toutes ces nouvelles démarches se rejoignent dans des choix communs, ceux du fragmentaire, d'un éclatement des structures et des cadres spatio-temporels classiques de la narration, d'écritures où le thème de la folie est fort présent, en tant que manifestation de l'aliénation de l'homme ou de perte de tout repère identitaire.

Le processus de dépossession de soi est poursuivi parfois jusqu'à la métamorphose du corps. C'est le cas dans la pièce de Fayyāḍ, où Sāmī doit lutter contre une Lubnā changée en dragon ; l'enfant du texte de Zakariyyā Tāmir cité plus haut se métamorphosait aussi, après avoir été enterré sous les orangers : il se changeait en un arbre aux lunes rouges. S'il est accueilli dans ces écritures du refus et de la résistance, et associé à l'arbre et à la lune dans des textes qui tous tournent autour de la question palestinienne, le thème de la métamorphose en arbre ou après enterrement sous un arbre est apparu dans la littérature arabe, où il était inconnu, dans un premier temps avec la littérature de l'absurde. On le voit ainsi surgir dans la pièce fondatrice de cette esthétique dans la littérature arabe, *يا طالع الشجرة* [Ô toi qui montes à l'arbre] (1962) de Tawfīq al-Ḥakīm, où le corps de la femme enterré par son mari sous son arbre fruitier, dans le jardin, laisse place à un lézard vert. L'année suivante, le dramaturge libanais ᶜIṣām Maḥfūẓ écrivait une pièce, *الزنزلخت* [Le Lilas de Perse] (1963), représentée en 1968, dans laquelle le héros, Saᶜdūn, accusé d'un crime dont personne ne se souvient, pas même lui, décide d'échapper à ce monde d'amnésie et de folie en se métamorphosant en lilas de Perse.

C'est entre symbolisme et surréalisme que se positionnent les arbres liés au thème de la métamorphose, dans les textes de Zakariyyā Tāmir. Dans la nouvelle *الشجرة الخضراء* [L'Arbre vert], parue dans *دمشق الحرائق* [Damas aux incendies] (1973), un homme est fusillé. Les balles tuent en même temps l'arbre sous lequel il se trouvait, et tous deux tombent ensemble. Deux enfants, effrayés, se serrent l'un contre l'autre si fort qu'ils se changent en pierre. Dans le même recueil de Zakariyyā Tāmir, le texte وجه القمر [« Le Visage de la lune »] voit s'abattre la hache du bûcheron sur un citronnier. Quand l'arbre tombe, Samīḥa sourit car elle sait que la lune ne l'effraiera plus : elle a vu son visage sans masque.

Le thème de la métamorphose en arbre, nouvellement apparu dans la littérature arabe au début des années soixante, est aussi parfois mobilisé par certains textes en convergence avec des occurrences classiques de l'arbre dans la littérature arabe, liées à des représentations paradisiaques, ou renvoyant à ces anciens textes cultivant l'analogie entre l'homme et certain végétal. Ce rapport intertextuel est particulièrement présent dans l'écriture de Yūsuf Idrīs. Dans la pièce de théâtre *الجنس الثالث* [Le Troisième Genre] datant de 1971,[10] le héros Adam traverse en plein ciel une forêt et, franchissant une grande muraille par une porte monumentale, pénètre dans une cité extraordinaire, une utopie installée au-dessus du Caire réel, un monde où les végétaux parlent, marchent et dansent, et les arbres se métamorphosent en humains. Adam assiste aux dernières heures de ce monde mais son amour pour une femme, dernier représentant du deuxième genre humain, devrait permettre l'avènement du « troisième genre » humain, celui qu'annonce le titre de la pièce, dans un optimisme qu'on qualifierait presque de néo-positiviste.

Dans *أمّه* (« Sa mère »), nouvelle tirée du recueil *العتب على النظر*, parue en 1987, un enfant errant dans les rues du Caire trouve refuge dans le tronc creux d'un saule pleureur, qui le réchauffe et le protège comme une mère de substitution, jusqu'à ce qu'il devienne adulte. Cette analogie entre

10 Voir Luc-Willy Deheuvels (2003–2004), 56–58.

l'arbre et la mère était déjà présente dans une nouvelle publiée en 1968 par Tawfīq Fayyāḍ, dans le recueil الشارع الأصفر [La Rue jaune]. La protagoniste, dont le surnom d'Umm al-Khayr (littéralement *Mère du Bien*), fournit le titre à la nouvelle, au moment de mourir se transforme en un arbre aux dimensions allégoriques d'une *Terra Mater* palestinienne. Cet arbre verse chaque matin des larmes aux vertus thaumaturgiques, et sa taille est telle que ses branches verdoyantes enlacent toutes les maisons du village.

L'analyse du motif de l'arbre dans la littérature arabe a permis de mettre à jour une continuité au sein d'une grande sphère allant des textes les plus anciens aux plus contemporains, et un mode de fonctionnement tout à fait spécifique. Le fossé que l'on tente souvent d'établir entre littérature arabe classique et moderne s'avère décidément bien moins large qu'on ne le pense.

Par ailleurs, il est vain de chercher dans l'année 1967 une date de rupture fondamentale de l'écriture, dans la littérature arabe. Temps historique et respiration littéraire ne sont pas synchrones. La décennie des années soixante, bien avant le déclenchement de la guerre de 67, a été le théâtre d'un très important renouvellement d'écriture, et de bouleversements marqués par l'intrusion de nouvelles esthétiques. Le traumatisme de la défaite a certainement frappé les esprits, et joué le rôle de catalyseur faisant évoluer la réception, déplaçant l'horizon d'attente. Cependant, les processus de renouvellement étaient déjà à l'œuvre ; ils traduisent une ouverture de l'écriture arabe aux évolutions mondiales, avec lesquelles elle a été de plus en plus en phase, tout en développant des voies originales et en maintenant avec son patrimoine des relations d'intertextualité très denses. L'étude du motif de l'arbre, entre lunes et murailles, dans ses métamorphoses les plus contemporaines le montre bien : mémoire intertextuelle et démarche créatrice s'y conjuguent en une hybridation originale et novatrice.

Intertextuality Gone Awry? The Mysterious (Dis)appearance of 'Tradition' in the Arabic Novel

Wen-chin Ouyang
SOAS, University of London

Introduction

Imra'at al-Qārūra [The Woman of the Flask],[1] the title for which Iraqi writer-in-exile Salīm Maṭar Kāmil received the prize for the novel sponsored by the London-based Arabic literary journal *al-Nāqid* in 1990, tells the story of a woman who has been given immortality as early as the beginning of Sumerian civilisation, in the Ahwār region in what is today the southern part of Iraq. The price of her immortality is her eternal imprisonment in a bottle. The bottle, upon the death of its first owner, a Sumerian king who loved his mistress so much that he had her immortalised in the bottle, is passed down from one generation to another. The woman of the bottle becomes witness to and storehouse of Iraqi history. When the protagonist, an exiled Iraqi living in Switzerland, discovers her she becomes embroiled in two love affairs, with him and with his friend, the narrator. At the end of the novel, the protagonist and narrator find a way to release her from immortality and consequently the bottle. She fails in her application for political asylum in Switzerland, is arrested by the police and deported. She disappears and her fate is unknown. As the novel ends, the narrator, protagonist and his pregnant wife drink the liquid in the bottle, which is supposed to be the elixir of immortality, and in turn disappear as they spin out of control on the ski slope. This story is framed by a story of an Iraqi soldier who finally reaches Switzerland after seven attempts at escaping the Iran–Iraq War. As this soldier goes to his first café upon arrival in Switzerland, he is handed a manuscript by the bartender, who tells him he is the owner of the manuscript. This manuscript contains the story of the woman of the bottle.

1 Salīm Maṭar Kāmil, *Imra'at al-qārūra* (London: Riad El-Rayyes, 1990); English tr. Peter Clark, *The Woman of the Flask* (Cairo: AUC Press, 2005).

Readers of the Arabic novel will have no difficulty in identifying the woman of the bottle as a symbol of the 'past', of Iraq's long history, or in discerning the intertextual strategies of the novel. The novel rewrites the history of Iraq from Sumerian times to the present, taking us through the hegemonic rules and bloodbaths one after another in this history, evoking the atmosphere of ancient Sumerian and Babylonian mythology as well as the supernatural and labyrinthine quality of the *Arabian Nights'* story and narrative. That the 'past', whether in the form of a genie in the bottle or not, haunts the 'present' has become almost a cliché in contemporary Arabic literary and cultural discourse. The persistent presence of the 'past' in the 'present' makes it impossible for the 'present' to progress towards the 'future'. This arrested development of the 'present' in the shadow of the 'past' has come to represent the impasse that Arab intellectuals have reached with regard to modernity and the modernisation of their history, culture and literature. The stumbling block, as perceived by Arab intellectuals, is the form of political authority in place, a hegemonic force that stifles progress of any kind. In fact, the 'past' is a 'foreign country'[2] under current social, political and cultural circumstances. History itself has become elusive. As the woman of the bottle disappears, the 'past' melts into thin air as well.

Precisely because it is ephemeral, the 'past' has become the object of desire — in fact, an obsession in Arabic writing today. There is not a more expressive manifestation of this obsession than the wave of intertextuality that pervades the present Arabic literary landscape. Intertextuality with pre-modern Arabic literary texts, with varying degrees of intensity, has been a staple feature of modern Arabic fiction, whether in the form of drama, short story or novel, since the onset of what is termed the modern period in the history of Arabic literature. In hindsight, the prototypes of modern Arabic fiction, including, for example, al-Shidyāq's *al-Sāq ᶜalā al-sāq* and al-Muwayliḥī's *Ḥadīth ᶜĪsā Ibn Hishām*, already exhibited an early tendency to intertextuality which became even more pronounced in later works, especially in the writings of the post-1967 era. Intertextuality with pre-modern narratives in the Arabic novel culminated in the works of Egyptian fiction writer Jamāl al-Ghīṭānī and of his generation of writers across the Arab world. The

2 See David Lowenthal, *The Past is a Foreign Country* (Cambridge: Cambridge University Press, 1985).

success of al-Ghīṭānī's works has led to a kind of flourishing of intertextuality in the Arabic novel. Even Najīb Maḥfūẓ, the father of the Arabic novel who championed and perfected realism associated with nationalism and modernisation, has turned to 're-writing' pre-modern Arabic literary texts in an explicit fashion in his later novels, such as *Layālī alf layla* (1982) and *Riḥlat Ibn Faṭṭūma* (1983). Novels constructed on the basis of intertextuality have become so pervasive that the term, '*madrasat tawẓīf al-turāth fī al-riwāya al-ᶜarabiyya*' [the school of employing heritage in the Arabic novel],[3] has been coined to designate the type of novels that re-write pre-modern Arabic texts in an explicitly intentional fashion as a narrative strategy. In fact, close revisionist critical scrutiny reveals that even works not known for intertextuality belonging to earlier periods, such as works broadly defined within the trend of social realism, exhibit signs of intertextuality.

The proliferation of intertextuality is explained in the main as a symptom and symbol of the Arabic novel's search for identity in the postcolonial context. The Arabic novel, having borrowed its form from the West, derives its identity — authenticity — from locating its history in the Arabic cultural and literary heritage, *al-turāth*, in general, and a 'tradition' of Arabic narrative and story-telling, in particular. This so-termed 'cultural and literary heritage' is deemed the legacy of the 'past' and the Arabic novel's engagement with this legacy is deemed symbolic of the continuity, rather than rupture, between the 'past' and the 'present'. More importantly, it gives the Arabic novel an identity distinct from its 'Western' precursor. Paradoxically, the Arabic novel always seems to straddle the two poles of its perceived origins: the West and the 'past'. The quest for identity is necessarily a twofold journey, one outward bound and the other inward. *The Journey of Ibn Faṭṭuma* by Maḥfūẓ is, in part, an account of the twofold journey of modern Arabic literature couched in terms of an Arab Muslim intellectual's search for the 'Truth'. While the protagonist travels outside the 'homeland' in search for new knowledge, he too journeys inside what is defined by the novel as 'tradition', seeking authenticity.[4]

3 The term was coined by Maḥmūd Ṭarshūd in 'Madrasat tawẓīf al-turāth fī al-riwāya al-ᶜarabiyya al-muᶜāṣira', *Fuṣūl* 17 (1) (Summer 1998), 27–39.

4 See Wen-chin Ouyang, 'The Dialectic of Past and Present in *Riḥlat Ibn Faṭṭūma* by Naguib Mahfouz', *Edebiyât* 14 (1) and 14 (2) (2003), 81–107.

Modern Arabic literature's engagement with 'tradition', while interrogating its relationship with the West, has been its staple feature since the beginning of the East–West cultural exchange intensified by the European colonisation of the 'Arab World'. Intertextuality has been a strategy employed in Arabic literature to both access and assess 'tradition', as well as negotiate its role in contemporary life and, more importantly, in shaping modern literary texts. This kind of engagement is effected on the assumption that 'tradition' is a clearly defined body of knowledge constructed around an identifiable set of texts. Can this assumption be substantiated? Intertextuality found in the Arabic novel makes an ambivalent statement about this assumption. In the past decade, in the 1990s, novels fully mired in intertextuality have made this assumption a central inquiry.

This paper examines an Iraqi novel that engages in and undermines intertextuality: *Sābiᶜ ayyām al-khalq* [The Seventh Day of Creation] (1994) by ᶜAbd al-Khāliq al-Rikābī.[5] It will more particularly look at the

5 There is very little biographical information available on this important Iraqi poet, fiction writer, and dramatist. It is not known when al-Rikābī was born. There is, however, mention of his birth place as Badra, a village with a Shiᶜite majority located in central Iraq towards the east of the country and close to the Iranian borders. It is also known that he has been an invalid, in fact, bedridden since, perhaps even before, 1980. Al-Rikābī began his literary career as a poet. He may have started publishing his poems in various Arabic newspapers and literary journals in the 1970s. A collection of poetry appeared in 1976 under the title *Mawt bayn al-baḥr wa al-ṣaḥrā'* [Death between the Sea and the Desert]. Though relatively well known as a poet, al-Rikābī seems to have attracted more critical attention as a fiction writer. His first novel, *Nāfidha bi-saᶜat al-ḥulm* [A Window the Size of a Dream], was given universal critical acclaim in 1978. *A Window the Size of a Dream* launched al-Rikābī's career as a fiction writer in two ways: it put him on the literary map of Arabic fiction and it delineated his fictional trajectory. 1982 saw the publication of many of his short stories, such as 'Ḥā'iṭ al-banādiq' [Wall of Rifles], 'al-Khayāl' [Apparition] and 'al-Muḥārib' [The Warrior], which were later published in a collection of short stories under the title *Wall of Rifles* in 1983. The appearance of his short stories coincided with the publication in the same year, 1982, of his second novel, *Man yaftaḥ bāb al-ṭilasm* [Who Will Open the Talisman Gate], which gives a fictional account of life under Ottoman rule in a small Iraqi village at the turn of the nineteenth century. *Mukābadāt ᶜAbd Allāh al-ᶜĀshiq* [The Passions of Abdallah, the Lover], his third novel, appeared in the same year. It is also a historical novel concerned with the question of political hegemony covering the periods of Ottoman rule,

effects of intertextuality — as it negotiates the triangular relationship of 'authenticity', 'originality' and 'tradition' — on the shape of both the 'tradition' and the novel, and explore the following questions: Is there such as thing as 'tradition', or is 'tradition' a matter of fantasy? Has this 'tradition' disappeared, or has it simply been disfigured? What are the implications of the disappearance or disfiguration of 'tradition' in an assessment of narrative strategies — intertextuality — in the Arabic novel? Does intertextuality give the Arabic novel authenticity or rather lead it astray?

Authenticity

In a moment of creative uncertainty, the narrator-protagonist of al-Rikābī's novel confides his anxiety to his poet friend. He muses despairingly: 'What is the point of adding another novel to a pile of novels being spewed out by the printing presses every minute?' The following conversation ensues.

> The voice of the poet rang out in the darkness: 'if every novelist thought in this fashion, the novel would have become extinct since it reached the peak of its maturity at the end of the nineteenth century. Twentieth-century novelists would not have been able to challenge new forms of story-telling, such as cinema, radio and television, and create (*yabtakirū*) their novels.'
>
> I wondered aloud, laughing bitterly: 'And have these novelists left us any room for creating more?'
>
> The poet replies, 'listen, my friend! Every great novel will bear the marks of its creator (*malāmiḥ mubdiᶜihā*), just as a thumbprint implicates the identity of every human being. The question of intertextuality (*tanāṣṣ*) and similarity (*tashābuh*) worrying you now is something time has made irrelevant (*amr ᶜafā*

the British occupation and independence. These early efforts anticipated what would follow. The themes raised and the experiment with narrative techniques there would culminate in the trilogy of Iraqi history: *al-Rāwūq* [Pure Water] (1986), *Qabl an yuḥalliq al-bāshiq* [Before the Bashiq Flew] (1990), and *Sābiᶜ ayyām al-khalq* [The Seventh Day of Creation] (1994). A simple short play on the tribal custom of revenge, *al-Bayzār* [The Falconer], appeared in 1998. This was followed by another, *Nahārāt al-layālī al-alf* [The Days of the Thousand Nights]; however, it is unclear whether this has actually been published or not.

> *ᶜalayhi al-zaman*). It is not possible for novels not to read like one another in some lines or pages because the material of all novelists comes from the face of this planet; life itself. Borges once said something to the effect that no writer could claim "originality" (*aṣāla*) because they are all "translators and annotators of pre-existing archetypes". In fact, he defined "modern" literature as grounded in four basic devices (*taqniyāt asāsiyya*): work within work (*al-kitāb dākhil al-kitāb*), the contamination of reality by dream (*ᶜadwā al-wāqiᶜ bi l-ḥulm*), the voyage in time (*al-safar fī al-zaman*), and doubling (*al-mudāᶜafa*).'
>
> Would I be able to make full use of all these four devices in this novel?[6]

This passage brings together in a nutshell the disparate strands of critical thinking about intertextuality and its relationship to authenticity (*aṣāla*) in both of its meanings in the context of the contemporary Arabic novel. The reference to Borges and his 'influence' on fiction writing worldwide is important. It acknowledges the importance of Borges in integrating the narrative techniques of *The Thousand and One Nights* in modern 'Western' fiction, popularising in the process the *Nights* even more. It more significantly alludes to Borges as a precursor of the type of writing that incorporates 'the fantastic' into its world. It highlights the Borgesian understanding and use of intertextuality. There are, however, distortions of Borges, which are specific: in fact, al-Rikābī collapses the Borgesian sense of originality on the all-too-familiar Arab notion of rootedness in 'tradition', or 'cultural and literary heritage' (*al-turāth*).

For one thing, the Borgesian sense of 'originality'[7] is rendered into '*aṣāla*', rather than, let us say, '*ibtikār*', the derivatives of which appear in the passage, or '*ibdāᶜ*', as is customary in Arabic. *Aṣāla*, a more appropriate term for the novel under discussion, relates originality to intertextuality, not in the sense of Kristeva's use of the term (meaning the transposition of one or more systems of signs into another),[8] but rather in

6 *Sābiᶜ*, 164–5.

7 James E. Irby, 'Introduction', Jorge Luis Borges, *Labyrinths: selected stories and other writings*, ed. Donald A. Yates and James E. Irby (New York: New Directions Books, 1964), xv–xxiii (xv).

8 Julia Kristeva's discussion of intertextuality is diffused in her various writings. See particularly, 'The ruins of poetics', in *Russian Formalism: a collection of articles and texts in translation*, eds Stephen Ban and John E. Bowlt (Edinburgh: Scottish Academic Press, 1973), 102–19; *Desire in Language: a semiotic*

the Borgesian sense of explicit, open engagement with 'the sources of a literary work', extensively elaborated in the critical works of Bakhtin[9] and Genette.[10] For another thing, Borges's definition of 'fantastic literature', characterised by the four devices of 'work within work, the contamination of reality by dream, the voyage in time, and the double',[11] is applied to 'modern literature' in general. There are, of course, reasons for these distortions. They explain the ways in which the Arabic novel simultaneously achieves 'authenticity' and 'originality' through intertextuality with pre-existing texts belonging to diverse genres. The text of al-Rikābī's novel, *Sābiᶜ ayyām al-khalq*, exemplifies the narrative and textual strategies of this approach.

Sābiᶜ ayyām al-khalq, a novel of about four hundred pages, was published in Baghdad in 1994. Its author, al-Rikābī, who lives in and writes from Baghdad, is unknown in the West and little known in the Arab world. He came to Iraqi critical attention with his third novel, *Mukābadāt ᶜAbdallāh al-ᶜĀshiq*, published in 1982. He is said to belong to the 'generation of the sixties' (*jīl al-sittīnāt*), like al-Ghiṭānī, and is considered by Iraqi critics as one of the foremost Iraqi novelists, ranked second only to fiction 'giants' like Ghāᶜib Ṭuᶜma Farmān and Fuʾād al-Takarlī. *Sābiᶜ ayyām al-khalq* is the third of a trilogy preceded by *al-Rāwūq* [Pure Water] (1986) and *Qabl an yuḥalliq al-bāshiq* [Before the Bashiq Flew] (1990). The trilogy is in one sense an epic, a grand history of Iraq between the seventeenth century and the present told as the story of the ebbing and flowing fortunes of the Bawāshiq tribe (*ᶜashīrat al-bawāshiq*), a tribe based in the countryside. The three parts of the trilogy seem to tell one story of the disintegration of the Bawāshiq tribe as its

approach to literature and art, tr. Thomas Gora, Alice Jardine and Leon S. Roudiez (New York: Columbia University Press, 1980); and *Revolution in Poetic Language*, tr. Margaret Waller, intro. Leon S. Roudiez (London: Columbia University Press, 1984). A useful summary may be found in Graham Allen, *Intertextuality*, The New Critical Idiom Series (London / New York: Routledge, 2000).

9 Mikhail Bakhtin, *The Dialogic Imagination: four essays*, tr. C. Emerson and M. Holquist (Austin: University of Texas Press, 1981).

10 Gérard Genette, *Palimpsests: literature in the second degree*, tr. Channa Newman and Claude Doubinsky (Paris: Seuil, 1982; English translation, University of Nebraska Press, 1997).

11 Borges, *Labyrinths* (1994), xiii.

leadership is split between those who succumb to and those who resist the authority of the city. The story, as a matter of course, ends with the dominion of the city over the countryside. This history of Iraq as written by al-Rikābī is an amalgamation of the stories of the individual men and women, especially those in privileged positions, who make up the community that is the tribe. Through the stories of their loves, conflicts, transgressions and struggles, the history of Iraq unfolds as that of its people, coping with various forms of political authority imposed on them from the outside, from the Ottomans to the British, then the Baᶜthists. The beginning of the breakdown of the family is traced to the disagreement between al-Sayyid Nūr, the religious and spiritual leader of the community possessing mystical powers, and the leader of the tribe, the elderly al-Bāshiq, Muṭlaq. Al-Sayyid Nūr moves out of the protection of the tribe and establishes a hut that becomes the heart and soul of the tribesmen, and Muṭlaq builds a castle on top of the hill that becomes the symbol of his power.

The story ends with the death of Muṭlaq's sons in a confrontation with the soldiers sent by the city, except for one, and the disappearance of the tribe into the labyrinth of the city. The story in the three parts of the trilogy may be variations of the same theme, as may already be seen in his earlier novels, but the narrative techniques differ from one part to another. *Al-Rāwūq*, which deals with the Ottoman period, and *Qabl an yuḥalliq al-bāshiq*, which details life under the British occupation, both seem to have opened up new vistas for Arabic narrative and storytelling. *Al-Rāwūq*, reviewer Yāsīn al-Nuṣayr lauds, 'combines all the artistic techniques that go into the novelistic narrative: poetical, allegorical, cinematic, traditional, magical and realistic.'[12]

Sābiᶜ ayyām al-khalq, the last part of the trilogy, covers the contemporary period in Iraq's history in addition to re-telling the stories already detailed in the first two parts. It tells three stories, all three being related in first-person narrative. The first story is of the unnamed novelist's search for a new form. As the story unfolds, it transpires that the novelist is continuing work begun in *al-Rāwūq*, which recounts the circumstances surrounding the discovery of the manuscripts of an old text known also as *al-Rāwūq* (the reference to the first part of the trilogy is explicit). This old text, according to all, contains the secret history of

12 'Jadaliyyat al-qirāʾa al-thālitha', *al-Aqlām* 23 (3) (March 1988), 22–39 (24).

Madīnat al-aslāf [City of Forefathers], the subject of all the novels written by the novelist, the textualised author. The search for the definitive *al-Rāwūq* manuscript leads the novelist to the 'Museum' and its founder and director, the various manuscripts housed in the 'Museum', to Shabīb Ṭāhir al-Ghiyāth, the last transmitter of the (hi)story of the Bawāshiq, and more importantly, his love interest, Warqā'. Two processes take place at the same time: the reconstruction of the manuscript of *al-Rāwūq* and the construction of his latest novel. These searches, moreover, parallel his courtship of Warqā'.

The second story consists of accounts of two attempts at producing a definitive version or edition of the text complete with chains of transmission (*isnād*). The textualised author's attempt frames that of Shabīb Ṭāhir al-Ghiyāth: both, however, fail in the endeavour. The text, originally attributed to a saint-like Sufi, al-Sayyid Nūr, turns out to be the work of many hands through many generations. This written version of the (hi)story of the Bawāshiq, however, has oral origins. In fact, al-Sayyid Nūr begins transcribing the orally-performed (hi)story in ink onto paper only when it becomes banned by the Bawāshiq as they try to suppress the subversive elements of the story-telling. The text, and therefore the story, exists in numerous recensions. Each recension tells a different story: in fact, the discovery of a leaf of manuscript related to the work can radically change the story as well as the shape of the text. As this story unfolds, we are given to understand that at one time there existed a big black book that collated all the 'reliable' writings of those who oversaw the *Mazār* of al-Sayyid Nūr, a shrine built on the site of his hut after his death. All the versions are centred round al-Sayyid Nūr's account, or written record, of originally oral recitations of the circumstances leading to the rise of the Muṭlaq family to a leadership position (*mashīkha*) among the Bawāshiq. This big black book is torn asunder during a turbulent episode in the history of *Madīnat al-aslāf* and falls back into the original state of disarray of the 'text' — disparate fragments that tell bits and pieces of divergent stories.

The third story is the written transcript of the recorded oral version of the popular history of the Muṭlaq family known as *al-sīra al-muṭlaqiyya* [The Epic of the Muṭlaq family] sung to the soulful tunes of the *rabāb* by the poet (*shā^cir*) of the tribe. The *sīra*, structured around the conflict between the *Mashīkha* of Muṭlaq and the *Mazār* of al-Sayyid Nūr, is told in four parts, each sung by a different poet. It begins with Muṭlaq's rise to power in the Ahwār region and his parting of the way with al-Sayyid Nūr.

Muṭlaq both transforms the livelihood of the tribe from shepherding to agriculture; and turns to outsiders, soldiers and dealers from the 'city' (*al-balda*), to fortify his position and increase his and the tribe's wealth. When he succeeds he decides to build a castle (*al-qalᶜa*) as an expression of his newly acquired power and status. Mụtlaq's decision to build this castle is the straw that breaks the camel's back. As soon as work begins on top of the hill, al-Sayyid Nūr moves out of Muṭlaq's 'protection' and takes up residence in a hut (*kūkh*) across the field towards the south, withholding his almost divine grace and, more importantly, his blessings from Muṭlaq's family. Before long, disasters strike the Bawāshiq tribe. The first disaster comes in the form of a flood that destroys the harvest, and the second a plague that wipes out half of the population of the Bawāshiq tribe, including Muṭlaq's wife. Muṭlaq himself contracts the disease and in delirium crawls all the way to al-Sayyid Nūr's hut across the field, knocks on his door, and is imbued with the grace of his presence and the light shining on his face. He miraculously survives. He repents and gives up his castle. His repentance, however, does not last very long.

The second part of the *sīra* details the process of recovering his power, soon thereafter interrupted by a two-year drought. Muṭlaq return to power among the Bawāshiq tribe, and now his family acquires guns. Muṭlaq marries the wife of Mujbir, his right-hand man until he dies during the plague. Rāziqiyya gives him five sons in addition to the two he had with his first wife. Muṭlaq's eldest son, Ṭārish, falls in love with Fitna, daughter of Dhiyāb from the boat people, the al-Muᶜīdī tribe, known for their thievery. They, however, possess guns. Through the marriage of Ṭārish and Fitna, the Bawāshiq acquire guns too. The third part of the *sīra* then goes on to tell the story of the expansion of Muṭlaq's family as his other six sons — Janāḥ, Qāṣid, Khiḍr, Rabīᶜ, Nāʾif and Ḥāṣūd — marry and produce children one after another. The fourth and final part tells of their inevitable decline as their power comes to be seen as a threat to the authority of the 'city'. At the end, the 'city' sends in its troops and in a confrontation of epic proportions the era of the Muṭlaq family comes to an end as father and six sons are killed in the final battle, *Wāqiᶜat Dakkat al-Midfaᶜ*, when their guns prove inadequate to protect them from the cannons brought in by the 'city'. Ṭārish, however, escapes this fate by running away with his wife and children to his in-laws in the marshes.

Intertextuality plays an instrumental part in the telling of this story of the vicissitudes of the fortunes of the Muṭlaq family. This 'modern' (some would even say 'postmodern') text, evokes, emulates, resurrects and re-writes pre-existing texts and genres. It alludes to Babylonian myths: the flood in the first part of *al-sīra al-muṭlaqiyya* is clearly a re-enactment of the creation myth in Babylonian mythology that finds confirmation in the Biblical tradition (98). The text explicitly acknowledges its indebtedness to texts such as *The Thousand and One Nights* (98, 132, 151, 232), *al-Insān al-kāmil fī maʿrifat al-awākhir wa-al-awāʾil* by ʿAbd al-Karīm al-Jīlī (99, 248), and *Fuṣūṣ al-ḥikam* and *al-Futūḥāt al-makkiyya* by Ibn ʿArabī (99). It casts itself in the genre of popular Arabic epics, *al-sīra al-shaʿbiyya*, which serve as the vehicle for 'writing' down the oral history of a tribe. *Al-sīra al-muṭlaqiyya* is, for example, sung orally by poets first, then recorded on tape, and finally transcribed and integrated into the novel. The kind of intertextuality devised in this novel manifests itself in the form of text-shaping diverse narrative strategies and techniques inspired by Borges: work within work, the contamination of reality by dream, the voyage in time, and doubling. The innovative use of these diverse narrative strategies and techniques comes to a head here to produce one of the most profoundly intriguing and intriguingly profound Arabic novels. These clearly identified narrative strategies and techniques are necessarily framed by the search for 'originality' in the novel.

Originality

As I have already indicated above, part of the story of this novel is the novelist's search for a new form, for writing a novel unlike any previously written. The textualised author's anxiety haunts the entire text and brings to the fore the angst of his predecessors about whom stories are told and whose stories are retold. The textualised author, both as novelist and manuscript hunter, finds his doubles in two types of predecessors. The oral storytellers of *al-sīra al-muṭlaqiyya* — ʿAbdallāh al-Baṣīr, Madlūl al-Yatīm and ʿAdhīb al-ʿĀshiq — serve as his artistic precursors, especially before the epic is written down and the story becomes that of a search for the definitive manuscript. The attention al-Baṣīr pays to the making of his *rabāb* and the ways in which he organises the parts of the epic and integrates music into storytelling (40–46) remind us of the creative angst the novelist experiences. His dejection at the realisation that his pupil, al-Yatīm, has taken over the affections of his audience is even more acutely felt when al-Yatīm's innovations are highlighted as the main reason for his retirement. The transcribers or historians of this oral tradition, on the other hand — al-Sayyid Nūr, Dhākir al-Qayyim and Shabīb Ṭāhir al-Ghiyāth — are his models of scholarly attentiveness. These two sets of storytellers and historians, tellers and writers, are in turn each other's double. Doubling here must mean both mirroring and multiplying. The intersection of these two notions of doubling is the spring of the narrative in the novel, holding the narrative strands together as well as propelling their movement. The novelist's search for both an original form of the novel and the authentic manuscript opens up the textual space of the novel to two major strands of story, each with sub-strands, that in the final analysis make up the novel and the story of the novelist. The history of the Bawāshiq represented in the manuscript is so intricately woven into the story told by the storytellers that it is impossible to locate one without uncovering the other. Doubling here entails framing, one story framing another.

The novel is constructed on the principle of work-within-work at both the levels of story and text. Stories follow the frame-within-frame structure of *Alf layla wa-layla*. The story of the novelist is told in the seven chapters, each entitled *Kitāb al-kutub* followed by a subtitle made up from *sifr* (another word for book) and one of the seven letters of the word *al-raḥmān*, one of the ninety-nine names of Allāh. These chapters frame in an alternate fashion the following chapters: *Ishrāq al-asmā'*, *Kitāb al-inniyya*, *Ishrāq al-ṣifāt*, *Kitāb huwiyya*, *Ishrāq al-dhāt*, and *Kitāb al-aḥadiyya*. In the chapters entitled *Ishrāq*, *al-sīra al-muṭlaqiyya* is recounted and recorded, and in the chapters entitled *Kitāb*, the story of the manuscript is told. More significantly, the texts of *al-sīra al-muṭlaqiyya* are written on and over the texts of *al-Insān al-kāmil* (122, 248) and *Alf layla wa-layla* (151); in fact, the 'old' texts have as a result become an integral part of the 'new' texts, just as the 'old' stories are of the 'new' stories. The confluence of 'old' texts and stories with 'new' ones makes it impossible to tell them apart. Dhākir al-Qayyim's eight-page text written on the back pages of a copy of al-Jīlī's book, *al-Insān al-kāmil*, takes on the structure of the two chapters printed on those eight pages. In fact, even the titles of these chapters in the two texts are identical: *al-huwiyya* and *al-inniyya* (122, 248). More mind-boggling to the novelist is perhaps the convergence of both content and language in the two extremely divergent types of work. How could the oral story composed by an illiterate storyteller, recorded by Dhākir al-Qayyim, have adopted a Sufi world view and language belonging to a written tradition? Is it a coincidence that the parts of the history of the Bawāshiq found in these pages correspond to the two stages of the Sufi journey denoted by the two terms of the titles?

The principles of doubling and work-within-work intertwine in the game of numbers at the heart of the novel. The seventh day of creation, the title of the novel, begins as part of the Babylonian myth as well as the Biblical story of creation and ends as a narrative of the formation of the novel. It is no coincidence that the novelist is the seventh storyteller of the epic of Muṭlaq and his seven sons. The title of the chapters make up the seven letters of the word *al-raḥmān*, the numerical value of which equals that of the word *al-rāwūq*, the name given to the manuscript of the Muṭlaq epic made up of seven letters as well. Babylonian mythology, if one may think of it as a work, frames the Biblical tradition, another work that frames the Sufi numerology, yet another work that informs the structure of the novel. The narrative patterns embedded in the three kinds of cosmological articulation framing the structure of the novel take the form of history, of the journey in time that Borges speaks of. Here, the history of the Bawāshiq is only the pretext for an exploration of the development of the craft of history-making and the art of storytelling from Babylonian times to the present through the Biblical tradition and Islamic Sufism.

Narrative movements driven by historical forces are, however, guided, checked and bounded by tha geography or, more appropriately, architecture of space. The textual space of the novel mirrors the architecture of Badr Farhūd Ṭārish's 'Museum', which consists of seemingly endless corridors leading to uncountable halls named after the storytellers with no particular rhyme or reason. It also reflects the landscape of *Madīnat al-aslāf*, which is made up from interwoven winding avenues and alleys that lead everywhere and nowhere in particular. The narrative movements in the novel, driven by a search for the history of *Madīnat al-aslāf*, necessarily follow the paths set by its avenues and allies, going everywhere and nowhere. The novel, like its doubles, the 'Museum' and the 'City of Forefathers', is a geographical and historical *matāha* (respectively 143 and 153), a labyrinth of Borgesian proportions, its labyrinthine quality heightened by the contamination of reality by dream. That the storytellers all see al-Sayyid Nūr appearing in their dreams urging them to tell the story of the Bawāshiq, makes it impossible to tell for certain his role in the construction of *al-sīra al-muṭlaqiyya*. Is he merely a scribe? Is he the voice of conscience? Is he the real storyteller and historian? Or is he simply an apparition, a ghost from the past, a fantasy of origin? Similarly, the anonymous phone calls that the novelist receives from a woman contaminate his reality with fantasy. Who is she? Is she really Warqā' declaring her love without giving herself away, as the novelist imagines? Or is she a creature of the novelist's flights of fantasy, Utopian dreams? That there can be no definitive answers to these questions makes the novel an unreliable text and the outcome of its central quest uncertain.

The novel is clearly about the twofold search for history — the truth of the 'past' and the 'tradition' that can tell us this truth; and story, especially 'originality' in storytelling. The central metaphor of the novel, the state of the manuscript, *al-makhṭūṭ*, says as much. The novelist places the stake of his novel — which is presented in the form of a manuscript complete with conventional identification markings — in consolidating the manuscript known as *al-Rāwūq*, a 'text' that can purportedly tell the history of the city he lives in, *Madīnat al-Aslāf*. In the end, the dream of finding that definitive 'text' disintegrates as it comes to light that the various manuscripts form a labyrinth, the ways into and out of which are impossible to know and, more importantly, never lead to an anticipated destination. The search for the truth of the 'past', symbolised by the search for the definitive text, and the eventual outcome of the quest are explained through Ibn ᶜArabī and al-Jīlī's concepts of 'the perfect man' (*al-insān al-kāmil*)[13] and 'truth' (*al-ḥaqīqa*).

The novelist justifies his 'creative wanderlust' in his quest for both the definitive *al-rāwūq* 'text' and a new form for the novel as his knowledge of his own imperfections as an artist. The perfect man in Ibn ᶜArabī and al-Jīlī is one who realises that he is imperfect and endeavours to redress his imperfections. The Sufi odyssey culminates in a peculiar understanding of the search for the Truth. In Ibn ᶜArabī's formulation, especially in *Fuṣūṣ al-ḥikam*,[14] the Truth has myriad manifestations: however, each manifestation reflects or truthfully represents this Truth in a particular way. In other words, these manifestations, despite their seemingly irreconcilable differences, are the expressions of the same Truth,

13 Edition used: ᶜAbd al-Karīm al-Jīlī, *Al-insān al-kāmil fī maᶜrifat al-awākhir wa-al-awā'il* (Cairo: Makabat Muḥammad ᶜAlī Ṣabīḥ, 1945).

14 Edition used: Muḥyī al-Dīn Ibn ᶜArabī, *Fuṣūṣ al-ḥikam* (Qum: Initishārāt Baydar, 1999 or 2000).

and are, in their own ways, the Truth itself. Seen in this light, the various versions of the history of *Madīnat al-Aslāf* presented and represented in the novel are all true.

The form of the novel, true to its message, reflects this Sufi understanding of the Truth and its possible manifestations. This understanding matches perfectly the Borgesian labyrinth derived from his appreciation of the *Nights* narrative. Like the *Nights*, the text and narrative of *Sābiᶜ ayyām al-khalq* are labyrinthine: the text is meant to be open-ended, like the *Nights* before it became imprisoned in written forms (232); and the narrative movements are unpredictable and full of suspense. The construction of the novel in the form of various overlapping labyrinths — Borges, *Nights*, the Sufi 'Truth', the 'Museum', *Madīnat al-Aslāf*, *al-Rāwūq* — leads to one question about the novel itself: what is the story it wants to tell? More important, is the novel like the *al-Rāwūq* manuscript? Is it an unreliable text?

The ending of the story of the novelist seems to point to this course of interpretation. While conducting research on the *al-Rāwūq* manuscript(s), he falls in love with one of the Museum clerks, a woman by the name of Warqā'. He becomes certain that she returns his affections when he begins receiving phone calls from an anonymous woman who clearly knows all the details of his works. He then decides to confront Warqā' and ask her to marry him. He follows her to her bus, rides with her all the way to her house, and begins interrogation of her in his indirect ways. Even though she seems puzzled by his conjectures he comes to the conclusion that she is the anonymous woman. In the end, however, there is no way of knowing for certain whether she is the anonymous woman or not. In fact, the ending of their 'love story' is not known; that is, if there is one at all. It may have been a one-sided love affair on the part of the novelist. After all, the word Warqā' is a Sufi term for the divine book that contains the Truth, *al-lawḥ al-maḥfūẓ*, and the Truth in Sufism is, from the perspective of those looking for simple certainty, at best multiple and at worst elusive. Warqā' to the novelist is more likely a dream that cannot be attained in reality.

Most important, the three stories contained in the novel end unhappily, if one were expecting the conventional type of happy ending. There is no definitive text of *al-Rāwūq* and the true history of *Madīnat al-Aslāf* cannot be reconstructed. The story of the Muṭlaq family is known through oral storytelling but exactly how that fits into the history of the Bawāshiq or *Madīnat al-Aslāf* is not knowable. And finally the story of the textualised novelist is unreliable. In a nutshell, there is no reliable way of knowing the 'past' or, for that matter, the 'present'. If knowledge of the 'past' is unreliable, 'originality' is similarly uncertain. The search for the 'past' in the novel, as I have already explained, is parallel to the search for 'originality'. The novelist strives to write an original novel on the basis of history and the singer of tales (*shāʿir*) endeavours to transcend his predecessor and master the art of storytelling through retelling and adding to the stories they tell.

'Originality' in the Arabic novel, seen in this light, seems predicated on 'authenticity', on knowledge of and rootedness in the 'past', which is impossible, followed by transcending this very 'past', which becomes uncertain. The achievements of the novel, as a novel, seem to rest on both groundedness in and departure from the 'tradition' bequeathed by the 'past'. Intertextuality becomes a convenient narrative strategy. However, the paradox of 'authenticity' (*aṣāla*) in fact destabilises both notions of 'originality' and 'tradition'. Both become illusory and elusive, just like the definitive *al-Rāwūq* text, or the Truth in Sufism.

Tradition

Borges has, in his various short stories, lectures and essays, argued that each literary text creates its own precursors. The 'tradition' constructed through intertextuality necessarily takes a different shape in every text. Each text in effect invents its own 'tradition'. This 'tradition' is a shape-shifter; its appearance is necessarily determined by the text engaged in intertextuality with the 'tradition' it invents. In fact, it (dis)appears in the labyrinth of the intertextuality which purports to revive it, to set it as the foundation of identity, and to give it authority as the source of 'authenticity'. It is no wonder that 'tradition', and therefore the 'past', becomes untenable and out of reach. In this regard the similarities between *Imraʾat al-qārūra* and *Sābiʿ ayyām al-khalq* are difficult to miss: intertextuality, textualisation of the novelist, the frame-within-frame structure of the novel, presentation of the novel as a manuscript, and centring the narrative on the journey in search of this manuscript are some of the obvious affinities. The 'past', and the 'tradition' that is its source — roughly defined as a body of 'texts' expressive of priorities, values, practices, worldviews and histories accumulated over centuries of development — melt into thin air upon close scrutiny.

The Arabic novel's engagement with 'tradition' is, however, effected at the level of the written or printed 'text' in that it takes place in the clearly identifiable black and white pages. Intertextuality, in this kind of engagement, brings a number of 'texts' into Bakhtinian dialogism, with which theory the novelist is familiar (164), all within the borders of one written 'text'. The principles of engagement are very different from the kind found in 'orality' or 'oral literature'. Oral compositions, when dialogised in this novel, are 'textualised', written down first then integrated into the 'text' in their now written form. In other words, intertextuality is a feature of textuality of the novel, even when it pretends to mimic orality. Textualisation necessarily leads to distortions. The 'past' as embodied by oral storytelling, as in the case of the *Nights*, has a life of its own with limitless potential for growth. However, it becomes frozen at a specific juncture in time and space when it is transferred to the pages of a written or printed text with clear boundaries set by the creative agenda as well as the ideology of the author of the text.

The kind of engagement with 'tradition' pervading the Arabic novel is challenged by and responsive to a constant need for 'originality', a term associated with both 'individual talent' and 'modernity', eloquently articulated by al-Rikābī in the passage quoted above. The Arabic novel is always under pressure to express its author's ability to be uniquely innovative — to have something new to say and to say it in a new way; to be modern rather than traditional; to deal with contemporary issues, adopt new worldviews, and employ 'avant-garde' narrative techniques. ᶜAbd al-Khāliq al-Rikābī's novel, *Sābiᶜ ayyām al-khalq*, rises to these challenges internalised by intertextuality in the Arabic novel. The novelist textualised in this novel, despite his obsession with the history of *Madīnat al-Aslāf*, confesses openly that he is not a historian and is not necessarily interested in writing a true history of his city; rather, he is an artist more concerned with the 'originality' of his final product. His turn, or return to history, is a mere ploy, a way of uncovering or discovering new narrative vistas. His poet friend reminds him insistently of this fact, and of the need to take care not to link the outcome of his novel to the fate of a definitive *al-Rāwūq* manuscript. In fact, he should do the exact opposite:

> It is all very well that you should let those documents provide you with an appropriate atmosphere for your novel, but beware of making yourself a prisoner to them. Mould them in the service of your novel before you let them

> take your novel on the paths they have paved, which are necessarily not the courses of innovation. (242)

This said, the novel is inevitably haunted, even shaped by the history and geography of *Madīnat al-Aslāf*, which are in turn informed by and under the influence of the prevalent ideology determining a particular way of imagining community.

In recent nationalist imaginings of community, Benedict Anderson has acutely pointed out that 'an immemorial past'[15] — what Eric Hobsbawm and Terence Ranger would call an 'invented tradition'[16] — serves as one of the legitimating foundations of the nation. Paradoxically, the shape of the 'past' is informed and formed by the geography of the nation. The shape of the 'past' and 'tradition' in contemporary Arab political and cultural discourses is more often than not delineated by ideologies such as Arab nationalism and, above all, by the reality of the 'nation-state'. The Arabic novel writes its own (hi)story in tandem with narrating the emergence, growth and fate of Arab nation-states. The postcolonial nationalist discourses, whether critical or creative, have taken for granted that the nation-state is the framework within which the 'past' and 'tradition' may be constructed positively, and that the reconstructed 'past' and 'tradition' would in turn legitimate the nation-state.

Since independence there have been numerous stupendous projects to reconstruct the 'past' and its 'tradition' — *al-turāth* — within the framework of the modern nation-state. The assumption underlying these projects, notwithstanding the variety of ideologies framing the project and the diversity of eventual arguments made, is that the 'past' is knowable and 'tradition' tangible. The same may be said of the post-independence novels, such as those by Jamāl al-Ghiṭānī. This, however, is no longer true of the novels by al-Rikābī, as well as a number of writers who came to be formed ideologically and intellectually by the disastrous consequences of the 1967 War. The 1967 defeat is seen as a symptom of the failure of both modernisation and the nation-state. This two-fold failure seems to have undermined nationalist confidence. In post-national writings — by which I mean writings suspicious and subversive of the

15 See Benedict Anderson, *Imagined Communities: reflections on the origin and spread of nationalism* (London and New York: Verso, 1983).

16 See Eric Hobsbawm and Terence Ranger, *The Invention of Tradition* (Cambridge: Cambridge University Press, 1983).

nationalist agenda — the positivist knowledge of both the 'past' and 'tradition' becomes subject to interrogation.

The last decade and a half of the twentieth century has seen a number of works that question the legitimacy of nationalist discourses and their reconstruction of the 'past' and 'tradition'. The Libyan Ibrāhīm al-Kawnī, Iraqis Salīm Maṭar Kāmil and ᶜAbd al-Khāliq al-Rikābī, Egyptian ᶜAbd al-Jawād Khayrī, even the later Najīb Maḥfūẓ and Lebanese Ilyās Khūrī, among others, all simultaneously employ and question intertextuality and its role in reconstructing the 'past' and 'tradition'. In this they echo critic Jūrj Ṭarābīshī's scepticism in his 1993 work, *Madhbaḥat al-turāth fī al-thaqāfa al-ᶜarabiyya al-muᶜāṣira* [The Slaughter of Heritage in Contemporary Arab Thought].[17] In the zeal to reconstruct their so-called cultural heritage, the Arabs have only distorted, disfigured and butchered this heritage. Does this explain the failures of the nation-state, for what would be its fate in the (dis)appearance of the heritage perceived as the basis of its legitimacy? More important, what form does the Arabic novel take in the 'postnational' predicament? Al-Rikābī's palimpsestine, labyrinthine novel seems but one of the intriguing possibilities.

Al-Rikābī tells a fantastic tale of intertextuality gone awry, but only in the sense that intertextuality cannot serve as the mechanism for constructing the 'immemorial past' of the nation-state identified by Anderson as one of the most crucial components of the nationalist imagining of community. *Sābiᶜ ayyām al-khalq* is in part disruptive to the paradigm of both knowledge and narrative that is the nation-state. The nation-state is not the original source from which the 'past' may be derived, or the structure into which 'tradition' may be cast or, more importantly, the framework within which both may be understood. On the contrary, as an ideology, it is the straightjacket that stifles the movements of history and the developments of story. The novel is at another level an exploration of narrative possibilities outside the ideological framework set up by the nationalist discourse. The novel sets its own agenda and maps its own trajectory in and away from the shadow of the nation-state. Haunted as it is by the priorities of the nation-state — writing its history as a series of resistance to hegemonic authority imposed externally leading to the rise of *Madīnat al-Aslāf*, it forcefully reverses the

17 Jūrj Ṭarābīshī, *Madhbaḥat al-turāth fī l-thaqāfa l-ᶜarabiyya al-muᶜāṣira* (London: Dār al-Sāqī, 1993).

nationalist hierarchy. Rather than the novel serving the nationalist cause, the unruly strands of the history of *Madīnat al-Aslāf* now point to the ways forward for the novel. This novel is less engaged in imagining a community but more concerned with theorising the novel, as the textualised novelist declares: 'every theory of the novel must be itself a novel' (249). In its parody of the novel of intertextuality, it seeks to transcend the ideologies, textual patterns and narrative strategies internalised by 'the school of employing heritage in the Arabic novel' patronised by nationalism. What is, after all, the legitimacy of Iraq the nation-state that commits unspeakable atrocities against its citizens, from war with Iran, to the invasion of Kuwait leading to the Gulf war and international sanctions, not to speak of the genocide of its Kurdish population? The shift from nationalist representation of reality to search for form is a statement on the disintegration of the nation-state. In the collapse of the nation-state, the paradigm of knowledge giving shape to the novel falls apart and a search for a workable alternative begins in earnest. This said, the function of the novel has held fast. In whatever form the novel may be, story is history.

Appropriating, or Secretly Undermining, the Secular Literary Heritage?

Distant echoes of *Mawsim al-Hijra* in a Muslim writer's novel: Leila Aboulela, *The Translator*

Stephan Guth
Berne, Switzerland

This study deals with the stance a committed Muslim author takes *vis-à-vis* the secular Arabic literary tradition. This stance will be examined in the light of the intertextual relation between al-Ṭayyib Ṣāliḥ's *Mawsim al-hijra ilā al-shamāl,* or rather its English translation, *Season of Migration to the North* (as the text of reference, representing Genette's 'hypotext'), and *The Translator,* a novel written in English by the Sudanese *muslima* Leila Aboulela[1] (as the successor text, representing Genette's 'hypertext'). While al-Ṭayyib Ṣāliḥ is a well-known author and his *Mawsim*, a 'classic' of modern Arabic literature, has been widely studied,[2] Leila Aboulela's work does not belong to the literary canon, in-

1 Since the author is writing in English, I will refer to her in this article by the English spelling of her name only. In Arabic, it is Laylā Abū al-ᶜAlā'.

2 Biographical information tends to be scanty, but the novel has been investigated by many scholars and from various perspectives. Only a select bibliography can be given here (in order of appearance): *al-Ṭayyib Ṣāliḥ, ᶜabqarī al-riwāya al-ᶜarabiyya*, ed. Aḥmad Saᶜīd Muḥammadiyya (Beirut: Dār al-ᶜAwda, 1976); Mattityahu Peled, 'Portrait of an Intellectual', *MES* 13 (1997), 218–28; Jūrj Ṭarābīshī, *Sharq wa-gharb — rujūla wa-unūtha: dirāsa fī azmat al-jins wa-al-ḥaḍāra fī al-ᶜarabiyya* (Beirut: Dār al-Ṭalīᶜa, 1997), 142–85; Muhammad Siddiq, 'The Process of Individuation in al-Ṭayyib Ṣāliḥ's Novel "Season of Migration to the North"', *JAL* 9 (1978), 67–104; Mona Takieddine-Amyuni, 'Tayeb Salih's *Season of Migration to the North*: an interpretation', *ASQ* 2 (1980), 1–18; Fawziyya al-Ṣaffār, *Azmat al-ajyāl al-ᶜarabiyya al-muᶜāṣira: dirāsa fī* Mawsim al-hijra ilā al-shimāl *lil-Ṭayyib Ṣāliḥ* (Tunis, 1980); Rotraud Wielandt, *Das Bild der Europäer in der modernen arabischen Erzähl- und Theaterliteratur* (Beirut: Orient-Institut / Wiesbaden: Steiner, 1980) (=*BTS;* 23), especially pages 464–78; Rotraud Wielandt, 'The Problem of Cultural Identity

formation on her and her *œuvre* being available almost exclusively from the press, the internet, or the short epilogues annexed to editions of her novels and short stories.

A few words summarising the biographical data given in these sources and a short summary of *The Translator*'s contents may therefore be useful as an introduction.

1. The Author

Leila Aboulela was born in Cairo in 1964, of a Sudanese father and an Egyptian mother. She was brought up in Khartoum, where she learnt not only Arabic but also English in a nursery school at a very young age. From then on, the English language has been a steady companion in her life: she received her primary education from the Khartoum American School;[3] her secondary school was an all-girls' school run by Catholic nuns, and at the age of thirteen she was taken to London by her mother, who was going there to do her PhD. After their return to the Sudan a few years later Leila Aboulela enrolled in Khartoum University and graduated from there in 1985 with a degree in Economics and Statistics. She then married her husband, a man with a Sudanese father and a British

in the Writings of al-Ṭayyib Ṣāliḥ', in *Studia Arabica et Islamica: Festschrift für Iḥsān ᶜAbbās,* ed. Wadād al-Qāḍī (Beirut: Imp. Catholique. 1981), 487–515; Nada Tomiche, 'al-Ṭayyib Ṣāliḥ: le révélateur le plus sensible de l'acculturation: l'individu contre le groupe', *Ann. Islamol.* 17 (1981), 375–93; *al-Abḥāth* 32 (1984), special issue *Essays on Tayeb Salih's* Season of Migration to the North, ed. Mona Takieddine-Amyuni (contains also 'A Selected and Annotated Bibliography', 157–73); Yosif Tarawneh and Joseph John, 'Tayeb Salih and Freud: the impact of Freudian ideas on *Season of Migration to the North*', *Arabica* 35 (1988), 328–49; J.E. Davidson, 'In Search of a Middle Point: the origins of oppression in Tayeb Salih's *Season of Migration to the North*', *Research in African Literature* 20 (1989), 385–400; T.L. Liyong, 'Tayeb Salih's concluded *Season of Migration to the North*: an exercise in a subjective, development-oriented approach to African (and Third World) literary discussion', in *Perspectives and Challenges in the Development of Sudanese Studies*, eds Ismail H. Abdalla with D. Sconyers (Lewiston, Queenston and Lampeter: Edwin Mellen Press, 1993), 265–85.

3 See also Susan Miller, 'A Conversation with Leila Aboulela' (2000). <http://literalmind.com/leila.html>.

mother, and they had their first child. As her husband, a petroleum engineer, was working abroad with an oil company in Yemen, Leila was not obliged to stay in the Sudan, so she moved to the UK in 1987 for further studies. She was accompanied by her mother and brother, who enrolled himself, as Leila did, in the London School of Economics (LSE), while their mother looked after Leila's child. Aboulela graduated from LSE with a MSc and a MPhil, and when her husband found another job in Scotland in 1990, she followed him to Aberdeen, where they lived for a decade. It was there, in the 'Granite City', that she not only had two other children, but also attended creative writing courses and discovered her talent as a writer of fiction. Her first stories were apparently published in 1996.[4] *The Translator,* written in English like all of Aboulela's fiction, followed in 1999.[5] It was a great success, especially after the author had won the famous Caine Prize for African Writing in 2000 for her short story 'The Museum'.[6] The novel has been serialised for radio and been broadcast on BBC Radio 4's *Woman's Hour*;[7] it has also been translated into Dutch, German, Spanish and French.[8] Aboulela also writes short stories and radio plays. In 2003, she was living in Jakarta, Indonesia, where her husband's job again required them to move in 2000, after ten years in Scotland.

4 Four stories (*Days Rotate*, *Glass Enclave*, *The Ostrich*, *The Way Home*) have been published on the Web by the non-profit Web publisher Intangible Publications (<http://www.intangible.org>). There, they maintain that '[Aboulela's] work has appeared earlier in *Scottish Short Stories 1996* (London: HarperCollins) and *Ahead of Its Time* (Cape, 1998).' I have been unable to identify the first reference; the second might be *Ahead of Its Time*, a collection of Scottish short stories, ed. Duncan McLean (London: Jonathan Cape, 1997; 2nd ed., London: Vintage, 1998).

5 (Edinburgh: Polygon).

6 Later included in *Coloured Lights* (Edinburgh: Polygon, 2001).

7 Joanne McEwan, Review of *The Translator* (6 December 2001), *Islam Online.net,* 'The World in Crisis', <http://198.65.147.194/English/Crisis/Book Reviews/article3.SHTML>.

8 Dutch: *De vertaalster*, tr. Wim Scherpenisse (Breda: De Geus; Brussels: 11.11.11; Den Haag: NOVIB, 2001). French; *La Traductrice*, tr. Christian Surber Carouge (Genève: Éditions Zoë, 2003). German: *Die Übersetzerin*, tr. Jutta Himmelreich (Göttingen: Lamuv, 2002; Black Women Series, Lamuv TB 314). Spanish: *La traductora*, tr. Flora Casas (Madrid: Lengua de trapo / Océano, 2002).

2. The Novel

The Translator is basically a love story. It is set in the early 1990s, the first part in Aberdeen, the second in Khartoum. In a very abridged version, the plot may be summarised as follows. A young Sudanese woman named Samar, and Rae, a Scottish historian of the Middle East in his late forties, fall in love with each other in Aberdeen, but Samar, who is a Muslim believer, cannot imagine continuing their relationship without marriage and thus Rae's conversion to Islam. When she urges him to 'enter Islam' in order that they can get married, Rae feels himself put under pressure and refuses to say the *shahāda*; as she insists, the scene culminates in his shouting at her angrily to 'get out of here'. Samar, who is leaving the same day for a job as a translator in Egypt and had already planned to seize this opportunity to see her family after four years of absence from the Sudan, decides, once in Khartoum, to stay there and not to return to Aberdeen. She is still in love with Rae, but at the same time does not believe in a future for this love, at first because she feels too hurt, but then because she has come slowly to realise that it has been her own fault: it is she who has sinned both against Rae and against God; it is she who has betrayed Love as well as Islam.[9] She takes upon herself the duty of purifying her feelings and her belief by praying to God that He may show Rae the way to Islam for his own sake, not for hers — that is, not in order to be able to get married to him. In fact, she has given up the idea of marrying Rae, because she knows she has hurt him too much. But there is absolutely no need to give up this hope as, in the meantime, Rae himself has come to the conviction that he should embrace Islam, not only because he is still in love with Samar and wants to live with her, but also because, encouraged by his longing for Samar, he has opened his heart and mind to the teachings of her religion and has discovered Islam as the solution for his own problems with life. So, in the end, the two protagonists have both undergone a process of spiritual purification, a process that, in its turn, has paved the way for their more earthly happiness too. At the end of the story, they will marry within a few days

9 This notion has been noticed, among others, for example, by McEwan (2001, on-line, see above, note 6): 'In some ways her words "Just say the shahada" portrays her divergence from God, Who had been her only lifeline in her early-timed widowhood.'

and then return to Scotland, but only after visiting the tombs of Muslim saints in Umm Durmān on the other side of the Nile.

3. The Problem

It is clear that we are dealing with a piece of Islamic literature here (although Aboulela, to my knowledge, is neither a member of the World League of Islamic Literature, *Rābiṭat al-adab al-islāmī al-ʿālamiyya,* nor does she seem to be involved in the theoretical discussions going on in that organisation and related circles about the concept of Islamic literature, *al-adab al-islāmī*).[10] My problem with this text is the extent to which it is intertextually connected with al-Ṭayyib Ṣāliḥ's *Mawsim al-Hijra ilā al-Shimāl,* a novel that belongs, of course, to the *non*-Islamic, secular, Arabic literary tradition, where it holds a prominent position. According to Edward Saʿīd's rating, it even figures 'among the six finest

10 The most comprehensive and detailed investigation of Islamic literature is a study by Christian Szyska (Bonn, Germany), which unfortunately has not yet been published. For the time being, the reader may get an idea of certain specific aspects of the phenomenon from the following articles: Cihan Aktaş, 'Die "Geschichte" der islamistischen Frau', in *Die neue muslimische Frau,* ed. Barbara Pusch, Beiruter Texte und Studien, 85 (Istanbul: Orient-Institut and Goethe-Institut / Würzburg: Ergon Verlag, 2001), 123–36; Miriam Cooke, 'Zaynab al-Ghazâlî: saint or subversive?', *Die Welt des Islams* 34 (1994), 1–20; Priska Furrer, 'Propaganda in Geschichtenform—Erzählstrategien und Handlungsanweisungen in islamischen Frauenromanen aus der Türkei', *Die Welt des Islams* 37 (1997), 88–111; Priska Furrer, 'Zwischen Didaktik und Ästhetik — islamische Frauenromane in der Türkei', in *Die neue muslimische Frau* (2001), 111–21; Fedwa Malti-Douglas, 'A Literature of Islamic Revival? The autobiography of Shaykh Kishk', in *Cultural Transitions in the Middle East*, ed. Sherif Mardin (Leiden: E.J. Brill, 1994), 116–29; Christian Szyska, 'On Utopian Writing in Nasserist Prison and Laicist Turkey', *Die Welt des Islams* 35 (1995), 95–125; Christian Szyska, 'Rewriting the European Canon: ʿAlī Aḥmad Bākathīr's "New Faust"', in *Encounters of Words and Texts,* eds Christian Szyska and Lutz Edzard (Hildesheim, etc.: Olms, 1997). 131–45; Christian Szyska, 'Najīb al-Kīlānī on His Career, or: how to become the ideal Muslim author', in *Conscious Voices*, eds S. Guth, P. Furrer and J.C. Bürgel (Beirut: Orient-Institut / Stuttgart: Steiner, 1999), 221–35.
Number 23–24 (1984) of *Die Welt des Islams* is a special issue on Islam in contemporary Middle Eastern literatures.

novels to be written in modern Arabic literature.'[11] A narrow reading would suggest that although there is a direct quotation from *Mawsim / Season* in *The Translator* the connection is only a very loose one, and the function of the reference to *Mawsim* is to produce a line of harmonic affiliation with it. There are other possible readings, however, that might lead us to interpret *The Translator* as a kind of 'anti-*Mawsim*', an interpretation in which certain congruencies — for example, in the general subject of the novel — must he considered as being equivalent to literal quotation.

What are the arguments that support either of the two diverging interpretations?

4. The Quotation

The narrow reading — a very loose connection with *Season* — rests upon the fact that there is only one direct quotation from *Season* in *The Translator* and that, if other references had been intended, they would have been marked more clearly in order to initiate, or rather 'force' into operation, an intertextual dialogue. This reading looks at the intertextual aspects covered by the 'classical', minimalistic understanding of 'intertextuality' (literal quotation of, or clearly discernable allusion to, a specific pre-text or parts of it, that is, what Genette, in his typology of transtextual relations,[12] still calls 'intertextuality').

The quotation concerned reads as follows (the omissions marked with three dots being Aboulela's, not mine):

> ... the fog cleared and I awoke, on the second day of my arrival, in my familiar bed in the room whose walls had witnessed the trivial incidents of my life in childhood and the onset of adolescence ...
>
> I heard the cooing of the turtle-dove, and I looked through the window at the palm tree standing in the courtyard of our house ...
>
> I looked at its strong straight trunk, at its roots that strike down into the ground, at the green branches hanging down loosely over its top, and I

11 Quoted by the African Writers' Index (n.d.) <http://www.geocities.com/africanwriters/AuthorsS.html#salih> (viewed 03 September 2003).

12 Gérard Genette, *Palimpsestes: la littérature au second degré* (Paris: Seuil, 1982).

> experienced a feeling of assurance. I felt not like a storm-swept feather but like that palm tree, a being with a background, with roots ...
>
> TAYEB SALIH (1969)

This text has been borrowed from the first two pages of the 1969 English translation of *Mawsim al-Hijra* by Denys Johnson-Davies. In the original, the novel's first-person narrator begins his story by telling the reader that he has just arrived in his native village in the Sudan after seven years spent studying in Europe. In *The Translator,* the quoted passage has its place at the beginning of Part II, when Samar has returned from Aberdeen to Khartoum after four years of absence.

The quotation's high degree of markedness as well as its elevated position — at the crucial point of transition between Scotland and the Sudan! — leave no doubt that it is meant to open a space of intertextual significance. But what does it say?

5. *The text-analytical reading*

I am convinced that Aboulela's main motive for quoting Tayeb Salih[13] in this place was twofold:

a) on the one hand, she wanted to drop an Arab, especially Sudanese, name, thereby telling the Western reader (whom we can be quite sure she is addressing with her English narrative) that it is not only Western writers who may serve as authors of reference but that there is also a great indigenous Arab literary heritage; that there also exist Oriental experiences, values, traditions and wisdom which can he drawn upon and which are in no way inferior to their Western equivalents;

b) the second function which I believe Aboulela had in mind in quoting Tayeb Salih was to show herself as belonging to this tradition, to give the impression of a harmony between the great (though secular) tradition and her Islamic humanism. This reading rests upon the following:

First, while the above quotation from *Season* precedes Part II of *The Translator*, there is another quotation at the very opening of the novel,

13 I will use the English spelling where I am referring to the English translation.

preceding Part I, from Abū Nuwās, another representative of the great Arabic literary tradition:

> But I say what comes to me
> From my inner thoughts
> Denying my eyes
>
> ABU NUWAS (757–814)[14]

Both references, 'Abu Nuwas (757–814)' as well as 'Tayeb Salih (1969)', are explicit insofar as they mention a person's name, but either remain silent on the specific text of reference (Abu Nuwas) or give only an indirect hint to it (Tayeb Salih). The references may therefore essentially be regarded as 'name droppings'.

In the case of Abu Nuwas, the dates that Aboulela adds after the author's name — the year of his birth and the year of his death — convey the information '8th–9th century AD', that is, 'very old', 'ancient'. The reader will conclude that this Abu Nuwas is a representative of an ancient, deeply rooted, literary tradition that produced poetry and wisdom at a time which, in the European context, is usually referred to as 'Early Middle Ages'. As for 'Tayeb Salih (1969)', the average recipient will probably understand from the data given here that there is a certain Tayeb Salih, who is presumably an Arab or a Sudanese writer or thinker, and that he has written quite a number of works, among them one written or published in 1969. The title of the quoted text evidently does not matter; it is the time it was produced that it is important to tell. The quotation could easily have been referenced as 'Tayib Salih, *Season of Migration to the North*', but as is stands, it obscures the author's source rather than pointing to it, for '1969' may refer not only to (a) the Johnson-Davies translation of *Mawsim al-hijra* (in Heinemann's 'African Writers Series'), but also to (b) *The Wedding of Zein and Other Stories* (same series), a collection of translated stories that included *The Doum Tree of Wad*

14 These are the first lines of a poem which continues as follows: 'I begin to compose something / In a single phrase / With many meanings, / Standing in illusion, / So that when I go towards it / I go blindly, / As if I am pursuing the beauty of something / Before me but unclear.' Translation by Catherine Cobham, quoted from Robert Irwin, *Night and Horses and the Desert, The Penguin Anthology of Classical Arabic Literature* ([1999]; London: Penguin Books, 2002), 125.

Hamid, (c) the Arabic original of which, *Dūmat Wad Ḥāmid,* appeared with Dār al-ᶜAwda (Beirut) the very same year. When I searched for Aboulela's text of reference, I was therefore at first misled: knowing from the author's own statements that she still reads Arabic literature in the Arabic original, I dismissed the idea that '(1969)' could refer to *Mawsim al-hijra* — which had come to my mind first — since the latter had already appeared in 1966 (in the magazine *Ḥiwār)* and 1967 (book edition, Dār al-ᶜAwda). I looked through *Dūma / The Doum Tree,* not only because its 'hero' is a miraculous palm tree, but also because this story shares a lot of ideas with Aboulela's, for example, the question of the compatibility between authenticity and rootedness, on the one hand, and living with the achievements of 'modern' civilisation, on the other. There are passages in *The Doum Tree* that strongly remind of the text quoted by Aboulela, for example the following:

> Here it is: the doum tree of Wad Hamid. Look how it holds its head aloft in the skies: look how its roots strike down into the earth: look at its full, sturdy trunk (…) Look at it, my son (...): lofty, proud, and haughty as though — as though it were some ancient idol.[15]

Aboulela, however, instead of mentioning the title of the text she is quoting from, gives a date. In other cases and with other writers this could, of course, mean that it is the temporal gap, and therefore the difference between the older and the new texts, that is being stressed: look at what has been said thirty years ago, look at how things have changed in those three decades between 1969 and now (1999)! Neither here, however, nor in the case of Abu Nuwas does the text of the novel following the quotations produce a tension or contrast of this kind at all; on the contrary, it generates an essential identity of meaning. When, for example, the quotation from *Season* talks about rootedness and background, of being like a palm tree with a strong trunk, and of a feeling of assurance, this is exactly what Samar experiences on her return to the Sudan in part II of the novel which is opened by the quotation. The author shows that her heroine is repeating earlier experiences by earlier authors;

15 Tayeb Salih, *The Doum Tree of Wad Hamid,* in Johnson-Davies, *Modern Arabic Short Stories* (London: Heinemann, 1978), 83–94, here 85. First edition included in Tayeb Salih, *The Wedding of Zein and Other Stories* (London: Heinemann, 1969).

the present generation affirms the validity of the findings of their great venerable predecessors and in return gains a share in the loftiness of their quasi-eternal truths.

Secondly, that identity, not contrast or opposition, is intended becomes clear also from a close look at what Aboulela has omitted from the original. I will give here the full text of the original, italicising what has been left out in Aboulela's quotation:

> *It was, gentlemen, after a long absence — seven years to be exact — during which time I was studying in Europe — that I returned to my people. I learnt much and much passed me by — but that's another story. The important thing is that I returned with a great yearning for my people in that small village at the bend of the Nile. For seven years I had longed for them, had dreamed of them, and it was an extraordinary moment when I at last found myself standing amongst them. They rejoiced at having me back and made a great fuss, and it was not long before I felt as though I were some frozen substance on which the sun had shone — that life warmth of the tribe which I had lost for a time in a land 'whose fishes die of the cold'. My ears had become used to their voices, my eyes grown accustomed to their forms. Because of having thought so much about them during my absence, something rather like fog rose up between them and me the first instant I saw them. But* **the fog cleared and I awoke, on the second day of my arrival, in my familiar bed in the room whose walls had witnessed the trivial incidents of my life in childhood and the onset of adolescence.** *I listened intently to the wind: that indeed was a sound well known to me, a sound which in our village possessed a merry whispering — the sound of the wind passing through palm trees is different from when it passes through fields of corn.* **I heard the cooing of the turtle-dove, and I looked through the window at the palm tree standing in the courtyard of our house** *and I knew that all was still well with life.* **I looked at its strong straight trunk, at its roots that strike down into the ground, at the green branches hanging down loosely over its top, and I experienced a feeling of assurance. I felt not like a storm-swept feather but like that palm tree, a being with a background, with roots,** *with a purpose.*[16]

16 Tayeb Salih, *Season of Migration to the North*, tr. Denys Johnson-Davies, African Writers Series ([1969]; Oxford: Heinemann, 1991), 1–2.

Tayeb Salih's narrator returns 'with a great yearning' for his people while Samar is not totally happy to return to Khartoum; in Salih's text people 'rejoiced' at having the narrator back 'and made a great fuss' while for Samar her coming back also means to be confronted with a number of problems; therefore, Aboulela leaves out also the passage saying 'I knew that all was still well with life', as well as the last three words of the final paragraph: while Salih's narrator feels again like a being 'with a purpose', Samar's existence is characterised, for the moment at least, by a lack of purpose. Even the metaphorical 'fog' which, in Salih's novel, has risen between the narrator and his people because he has 'thought so much about them' during his absence, by way of omission of the preceding sentences in Aboulela's text becomes a real fog that clears before the narrator awakes — for Samar has not transfigured her people during her absence as had Salih's hero. What is left after all these omissions is a profile of the person speaking in the quotation that is identical to the profile of Aboulela's protagonist. The text of reference has been cut down so as to agree with Aboulela's text.

Thirdly, when I happened to attend a public reading by Leila Aboulela in Berne in June 2002 where she also read some passages from *The Translator*, the author answered a listener's question saying that, although she writes in English, she considers herself a Sudanese writer, that *The Translator* should, in the first place, be read as a piece of *Sudanese* literature, and that she feels indebted, among others, to al-Ṭayyib Ṣāliḥ.[17] It goes without saying that modern authors, for some reason or other, do not always tell the truth when they are asked this kind of question, and that one has to handle their own statements carefully and with some reservation. However, if Aboulela really meant what she said then, I think that the expression 'feeling indebted' would testify to a wish to be seen as a writer who is in line with the tradition rather than rebelling against it (although the one does not, of course, necessarily exclude the other).

Fourthly, a last, and perhaps the most important, point is that had Aboulela wanted her novel to embark on a serious critical dialogue with

17 When asked in an interview about the authors that she most admires, Aboulela did not mention al-Ṭayyib Ṣāliḥ but rather Jean Rhys ('because of the transparent way she writes about feelings') and Anita Desai ('because of her intelligent insight into the life of ordinary people'). She named Charlotte Brontë's *Jane Eyre* as the book that she would like to have as a first edition. See Miller (2000, cf. note 3 above).

Mawsim al-Hijra / Season of Migration, there should have been more, and other, references to that text, not simply a single quotation from which the average Western reader is unable to deduce the complexity of problems that Ṣāliḥ's narrative raises. Instead, however, the author abstained, for example, from arranging a conversation between Samar and Rae about Ṣāliḥ's book, which one or both of them could have read, or of leaving some other traces that could have opened up the intertextual space on other occasions: one will search in vain for the name of *Mawsim*'s central character Muṣṭafā Saᶜīd, for instance.

6. Other readings

As I have already indicated, the above reading focuses more on the author and her possible intentions than on the work itself and the life of its own that it starts to live once its creator has released it into independence. Let us now look at the text regardless of what Aboulela might have intended, and turn to the recipients. In spite of the fact that there is only one direct quotation and that nowhere else in the text is to be found anything that could be described as an allusion, many people with a background reading of *Mawsim al-Hijra* feel themselves reminded of Ṣāliḥ's novel when reading *The Translator:* Ferial Ghazoul, for example, called *The Translator* 'Aboulela's "Season of Migration to the North".'[18] They do so, however, not so much because Ṣāliḥ's name is mentioned and the opening passage of *Season* is quoted, but rather because (a) both authors are Sudanese, and (b) both novels revolve round the same general problem, that is, the East versus West conflict. We are faced here with the well-known phenomenon that intertextuality is established not only by the author but also — or, as some say, even completely — by the recipients. If this is true, and if we also allow non-literal, indirect and probably unintended correspondences to pass as 'quotations' or 'allusions', then a surprisingly dense net of correspondences between *The Translator* and *Mawsim / Season* may be detected (or, as I would prefer to say, constructed).

18 Ferial Ghazoul, 'Halal Fiction' (review of L. Aboulela, *Coloured Lights* and *The Translator*), *Al-Ahrām Weekly Online* 542 (12–18 July 2001). <http://weekly.ahram.org.eg/2001/542/bo4.htm> .

➢There is, for instance, the fact that *The Translator* is written in English, that is, in exactly that language which in *Mawsim* Muṣṭafā Saᶜīd still had to ban to a secret room, wanting to conceal its everlasting influence upon him. For Aboulela, using the English language is natural; nor does the author show her heroine Samar suffering from inner conflicts because she uses the former colonisers' language.

➢ The 'indirect', 'implicit' intertext is also gendered. While *Mawsim* has a male author as well as a male narrator and another male central character (Muṣṭafā Saᶜīd), the hypertext's author and heroine are both women. A possible meaning of this divergence could be: thirty years after *Mawsim*, women have taken over the role formerly occupied by men.

➢ There are further divergences, in structure as well as in contents. Among the structural ones is the fact that, whereas *Mawsim al-Hijra* has two protagonists with two corresponding layers of events, one plot (the narrator's) being skilfully woven into the other (Muṣṭafā Saᶜīd's), the situation in *The Translator* is much less complex: there is, for instance, only one central character (Samar), and only one temporal dimension (the novel's events are told in natural, chronological order), in contrast to the complex time structure and the intricate interweaving of past and present in *Mawsim*. If Aboulela has intended this divergence, the 'plain', explicit version of this implicit, structural comment on *Mawsim* might be a statement like: 'For me, the past has ceased to he such a heavy burden as it seemed to be for al-Ṭayyib Ṣāliḥ some thirty years ago; it no longer intrudes into my present with the same fatal effects.'

➢ Approximately two thirds of Aboulela's novel (which the author wants to be considered as a piece of Sudanese literature) consists of events that take place in Britain whereas in *Mawsim al-Hijra* Europe figures only indirectly, through Muṣṭafā Saᶜīd's narration and the scattered pieces of information which the narrator happens to obtain about Muṣṭafā's former life. By contrast, most of the events in *Mawsim* unroll in the Sudan. Possible meaning: 'Life in Britain has, or should, become a theme of Sudanese literature because it has become part of Sudanese life.'

➢ *The Translator*'s second part opens with a quotation from *Mawsim*'s very beginning, and the quotation likens Samar to *Mawsim*'s narrator, not to Muṣṭafā Sa^{c}īd. Could that mean that part I of *The Translator* corresponds to Muṣṭafā Sa^{c}īd's experience in England while Part II is pointing more to al-Ṭayyib Ṣāliḥ's narrator, who no longer suffers under the conflict between East and West as severely as Muṣṭafā Sa^{c}īd did?

➢ As for the correspondences between elements of the works' contents, it may be sufficient to mention only two of them. If in *Mawsim* Jean Morris becomes Muṣṭafā Sa^{c}īd's victim because she does not surrender to his attempts to take revenge on the colonisers by seducing their women, a parallel to this in *The Translator* could be the idea that Rae becomes *Samar*'s victim because he refuses to accept Islam. *The Translator* at least dwells upon the idea of a guilt, a sin for which Samar, the *muslima,* is to be blamed and for which she has to do penance. But whereas Muṣṭafā Sa^{c}īd was unable to find peace with himself and has to die, Samar is saved through her strong belief, and lives on in happiness. Possible meaning:

> Trying to bring about 'by force' a non-Muslim's conversion to Islam is equivalent to a crime like the violation and murder of Jean Morris: like this violation and murder, it does not remove the East–West dichotomy, and does not solve the problem, since the murderer / 'murderer' loads upon himself a guilt; but whereas an unbeliever like Muṣṭafā Sa^{c}īd cannot (or the unbelieving Arab intellectual of the late sixties could not) be saved, Islam offers the possibility of repentance and eventual salvation.

➢ A close look at the ending of *The Translator* may also be meaningful. In the last scene of *Mawsim* the narrator is close to drowning in the middle of the Nile, between North and South, but eventually decides to go on living for the sake of some good people and manages to reach the bank of the river (the text remains silent about whether it is the northern or the southern bank). At the end of *The Translator*, there is no drowning but a reference to the Nile: before Samar and Rae leave for their honeymoon they want to go to Umm Durmān on the other side of the river in order to visit the tombs of holy men.

The divergences of *The Translator* from *Mawsim* revealed by the above comparisons are all highly significant and very meaningful, and it is obvious that they add to Aboulela's novel the quality of a *mu^{c}āraḍa* of Ṣāliḥ's. By contrast to the first reading, the relation between the two texts is now a relation of difference, of opposition, or discrepancy rather than of successorship and harmony. This is the reading, for example, of Jamāl Muḥammad Ibrāhīm, Sudan's ambassador in London, and Ferial Ghazoul. The first called *The Translator* 'a dialogue of civilisations' in contrast to Ṣāliḥ's *Mawsim,* which according to him depicts the 'clash of civilisations'.[19] The latter expressed her opinion that *The Translator* is 'radically different' from *Mawsim,* for al-Ṭayyib Ṣāliḥ in his novel shows

> — through the exploits and tragedy of his protagonist Mustafa Saᶜeed — the impossibility of achieving a meaningful rapport between the colonised and the coloniser, between North and South. While Aboulela's protagonists also suffer in a culture that is by no means colour-blind, the author makes it possible to join South to North under the emblem of a universal quest, that of Islamic humanism.[20]

7. *Conclusion*

It is clear that the less an intended intertextual reference is marked explicitly, the greater becomes the possibility of non- or misunderstanding.[21] In *The Translator,* the only reference which is clearly marked suggests that Aboulela tries to appear in harmony with her non-Islamic literary tradition. Since all the other correspondences have no marking at all it may be wrong to read them as 'references marked zero' or allusions to *Mawsim,* and it is possible that one 'reads into' the text something which the author herself has not intended. However, given the fact that the second reading does not twist the text to suit a certain argument and that, from a linguistic point of view, it is therefore not at all illegitimate; we cannot exclude the possibility that Aboulela, when writing *The Translator,* was well aware of the points in which her novel differs from Ṣāliḥ's *Mawsim.* In this case, we would have to conclude that her position

19 Quoted in Ghazoul (2001, cf. note 17 above).

20 Ibid.

21 See also, for example, the diagram ('Progressionsskala intertextueller Markierung') given in Jörg Helbig, *Intertextualität und Markierung: Untersuchungen zur Systematik und Funktion der Signalisierung von Intertextualität*, Beiträge zur neueren Literaturgeschichte, Folge 3; 141 (Heidelberg: C. Winter, 1996), 183.

vis-à-vis the secular literary heritage oscillates between, on the one hand, reverence and the desire to be seen to be in line with it and, on the other, the wish to break with it. Her opposition would, however, then be a non-explicit one, leading us to ask: why so? Would inexplicity, or unmarkedness, be part of a literary programme? Would it testify to a very skilful, very subtle, very cautious approach to tradition here, perhaps out of simultaneous reverence in spite of basic opposition, an approach respectful of the secular or the non-believer, and 'with pure moderation'?[22] Or would it be a kind of conscious disguise, the author wanting her opposition to the secular tradition to remain unrecognisable, or at least not clearly identifiable? And would not that then be a kind of *taqiyya* in order to avoid criticism on the part of the secular literary establishment, or perhaps even a cunning strategy to undermine *Mawsim al-Hijra* without secular readers becoming aware of it?

Any definitive answer to these questions remains highly speculative. What can be said, however, is that for reviewers of *The Translator* the one marked intertextual reference passes completely unnoticed, while it is the novel's general theme, the East–West dichotomy, that makes them relate it to other works and in this way opens the intertextual dimension. For an educated Arab readership the text that comes to mind almost immediately is Ṣāliḥ's *Mawsim,* and *The Translator* is seen as an 'anti-*Mawsim*'. Western readers without that background however are not equipped to receive *The Translator* as a new contribution to an old inter-Arab debate; they read it against their own backgrounds. In their readings, Aboulela's novel becomes related to other *texts* only very rarely; Joanne McEwan's comment that, in contrast to Western novels depicting the Orient '[t]his time the Orient visits the Occident'[23] or Sabine Berking's observation that *The Translator*'s happy ending represents a 'postcolonial reply to the colonial narratives'[24] are rare exceptions here. The majority of Western reviewers relate the novel to an extra-literary context, which in most cases is Islamic extremism. They praise Aboulela's 'serious'-ness and 'moderation' in contrast to the discourse of 'fundamentalist' rad-

22 McEwan (2001, cf. note 6 above).

23 McEwan (2001).

24 'postkoloniale[.] Antwort auf die kolonialen Erzählungen', Sabine Berking, 'Liebe geht auf die Knie' (review of *The Translator*), *Frankfurter Allgemeine Zeitung,* WWW edition (6 November 2001), <http://www.literaturpreis.org/aktuell/uebersetzerin.html>.

icals.[25] Although the reader is introduced, throughout the book, to the 'dictates of Islam', Aboulela's '*da^{c}wah* or propagation of Islam' is obviously not too difficult to digest for non-Muslims, because she does not 'exceed the limits'[26] — an attitude which for many reviewers seems to be mirrored also in her style, which they describe as 'lyrical'[27] and 'quiet',[28] a 'rhythmic prose',[29] 'full of poetry' and 'wonderful, unobtrusive lyrics'.[30]

As a Sudanese living in Scotland, an 'Oriental' in the West, a Muslim believer in a Christian or unbelieving environment, as an Arab having read Arabic as well as Western literature, and writing in English, Aboulela participates in a multitude of discourses that are potentially conflicting because of different standards and norms. When writing *The Translator* she was without doubt quite aware of the contexts, literary as well as extra-literary, that form the folio against which she was producing her text and against which that text would he received. It is very likely that this participation, simultaneously, in a great number of different discourses lies at the ground of her novel's ambiguous outlook towards *Mawsim al-Hijra.* It is perhaps also the reason why she did not shy away from quoting Abū Nuwās and al-Ṭayyib Ṣāliḥ in a way that attempts to appear as their successor and equal — an attempt that runs the risk of being judged naïve, as her work would not of course stand any comparison with those two 'great classics'. Most reviewers hold that, from the point of narrative skill, *The Translator* is a rather weak story,[31]

25 McEwan (2001), summarising earlier reviews.
26 Ibid.
27 Ghazoul (2001, cf. note 17).
28 Berking (2001, cf. note 23).
29 McEwan (2001).
30 'Voll Poesie, in wunderschöner zurückhaltender Lyrik', Ellen Ismail, 'Von Exil und Heimat, von Liebe und Glauben' (review of *The Translator*), *epd-entwicklungspolitik* 18 (2001) <http://www.literatur-preis.org/aktuell/ uebersetzerin.html>.
31 See, for example, the following statements: 'This novel is written in a simple, lyrical way' (Dorset County Council: Open Books, Summary of *The Translator,* Extract, Interview Q&A with Leila Aboulela. <http://www.dorset-cc.gov.uk>, (2000?); 'it is well told and not without realism, but altogether not much more than a "pretty tale"' (Miller, 2000): Rae's conversion to Islam is seen as an 'unexpected reversal' which is 'unconvincing' and 'somewhat contrived', so that '[t]he ending of the novel constitutes a contemporary use of the classical *deus ex*

its strength lying mainly in its 'emotional honesty',[32] in the power with which a woman is struggling here 'for peace, happiness, and a return to oneself,'[33] in the 'sophisticated commitment to an Islamic worldview' and 'a certain narrative logic where faith and rituals become moving modes of living'[34] as well as in the 'quiet, free and easy, naive way' in which the story 'demystifies words like "integration" and "assimilation", for the West always meant nothing but an adjustment to its own worlds and values.'[35] One reviewer cannot but smile even at such achievements: 'In the end our hero finds her true self and we are even inclined to feel that she will make peace with the Scottish weather.'[36]

machina' (Ghazoul, 2001), and this is also detrimental to one of the book's basic ideas: 'Die [...] Absicht, dem westlichen Leser die Offenheit und die Schönheit des Islam zu vermitteln, wird letztlich der Bekehrungsgeschichte geopfert' ('the intention to impart to the Western reader the openness and beauty of Islam becomes sacrificed in the end to the story of conversion': Berking 2001).

32 (Dorset County Council: Open Books, 2000?).

33 McEwan (2001).

34 Ghazoul (2001).

35 Berking (2001): 'Aboulela entmystifiziert mit ihrem leisen, zwanglos-naiv erzählten Buch Vokabeln wie Integration und Assimilation, denn der Westen meinte immer nur eine Angleichung an seine Welten und seine Werte.'

36 McEwan (2001).

Intertexte et mémoire dans l'écriture romanesque de Rabī[c] Jābir : Essai sur le roman *Ralph Rizqallah fī al-mir'āt*

Sobhi Boustani
INALCO – Paris

I. Introduction

Rabī[c] Jābir est né à Kfarnabrakh (chouf) au Liban en 1972. Il a entamé des études d'architecture, mais il les abandonne pour une licence de physique qu'il obtient en 1993. Son nom figure actuellement sur la page culturelle du journal *al-Ḥayāt*. Rabī[c] Jābir a publié dix romans et a obtenu le prix de la revue *al-Nāqid* pour son premier roman S*ayyid al-*[c]*atma* [Seigneur de l'ombre] (1992).[1]

Rabī[c] Jābir se réfère aisément aux cultures européenne et extrême-orientale pour trouver matière à ses romans. *Kuntu Amīran* [J'étais prince], par exemple, doit son sujet à la culture européenne. Les événements du récit se déroulent en Italie, au XIII[e] et XIV[e] siècles, où des événements historiques, des traditions littéraires et des légendes populaires sont régulièrement sollicités.[2] La Chine ancienne, sa culture, sa

1 Les romans de Rabī[c] Jābir : *Sayyid al-*[c]*atma* [Le Seigneur de l'ombre] (London : Riyāḍ al-Rayyis, 1992) ; *Shāy aswad* [Thé noir] (Beirut: Dār al-Ādāb, 1995) ; *al-Bayt al-akhīr* [La Dernière Maison] (Beirut: Dār al-Ādāb, 1996) ; *al-Farāsha al-zarqā'* [Le Papillon bleu] (Beirut : al-Markaz al-thaqāfī al-[c]arabī, 1996) ; *Ralph Rizqallah fī al-mir'āt* [Ralph Rizqallah dans le miroir] (Beirut: Dār al-Ādāb, 1997) ; *Kuntu amīran* [J'étais prince] (Beirut: al-Markaz al-thaqāfī al-[c]arabī, 1997) ; *Naẓra akhīra* [c]*alā Kīn Sāi* [Dernier regard sur Kin Sai] (Beirut : al-Markaz al-thaqāfī al-[c]arabī, 1998) ; *Yūsuf al-inklīzī* [Joseph l'Anglais] (Beirut: al-Markaz al-thaqāfī al-[c]arabī, 1999) ; *Riḥlat al-Ghurnāṭī* [Voyage d'un citoyen de Grenade] (Beirut : al-Markaz al-thaqāfī al-[c]arabī, 2002) ; *Bayrūt madīnat al-*[c]*ālam* [Beyrouth, cité du monde] (Beirut : al-Markaz al-thaqāfī al-[c]arabī — Dār al-Ādāb, 2003).

2 Hartmut Fähndrich, « Quelques réflexions sur le roman-conte de fées *J'étais une fois un prince* de R. Jābir », in *Romanciers arabes du Liban* (Toulouse :

mythologie et sa *sagesse* constituent le thème et le théâtre des événements du roman *Naẓra akhīra ᶜalā Kin Säi* [Dernier regard sur Kīn Sāi]. Romancier prolixe et fécond, Rabīᶜ Jābir frappe par la diversité de ses thèmes ainsi que par l'indéniable innovation de sa technique narrative. Dans cet article, je m'arrête sur un exemple de cette écriture. Il s'agit du roman *Ralph Rizqallah fī al-mir'āt* [Ralph Rizqallah dans le miroir] où la tradition européenne laisse inexorablement ses empreintes. J'y étudie le phénomène intertextuel, en suivant ses manifestations, analysant sa fonction et en tentant d'y déterminer le rapport de l'intertextualité à la mémoire personnelle de l'auteur et à la mémoire collective de son milieu.

II. Sujet du roman

Le roman débute en annonçant un fait divers réel: « il s'appelait Ralph Rizqallah. Le samedi 28 octobre 1995, il arrêta sa voiture en face de la grotte aux pigeons *al-Rawsha*, et, laissant Beyrouth derrière lui, sauta d'une hauteur de 45 m. sur les rochers. Il avait 45 ans. » Cette annonce est suivi du faire part tel qu'il est publié dans le journal libanais *al-Nahār* du lundi 30 octobre. La présentation de la victime correspond parfaitement à la réalité : professeur à l'université libanaise, journaliste à *Mulḥaq al-Nahār* [Le Supplément d'*al-Nahār*], marié et père de trois enfants. Les lieux mentionnés figurent précisément sur la carte de Beyrouth. Le roman n'a pas d'intrigue au sens classique du terme et l'état initial du récit : «il sauta ; il se jeta ; il tomba… » (9) est identique à son état final : « et puis il sauta », dernière phrase du récit (182). Toute la dynamique du narrateur homo-diégétique qui n'est autre que l'auteur Rabīᶜ Jābir, désigné explicitement à deux endroits du roman (53, 160), consiste, sur un premier plan, à effectuer des recherches concernant le héros *in absentia* Ralph Rizqallah (désormais désigné par les initiales (R.R.) dans cette étude) : « j'ai décidé de faire des recherches sur ce personnage » (35) ; deux pages plus loin il réaffirme cette décision prise en juin 1996, huit mois après sa mort, et puis à la page 92, parlant du père de R.R., il réitère sa volonté de « pénétrer dans le cœur de son fils R. ». Ce voyage dans la vie du héros, qui constitue effectivement l'objet du sujet Rabīᶜ Jābir, n'aura en réalité que des adjuvants : Halā, la femme de

CEMAA, 2002), 131–41.

R.R., sa famille (père, mère et sœur) et ᶜAbīr, une amie du narrateur qui travaille au ministère de la justice. Nous constatons, par conséquent, l'absence des opposants. Quant aux destinateur et destinataire, ils ne sont que le narrateur lui-même. Le schéma actantiel se trouve de ce fait réduit essentiellement à un sujet et à un objet, un héros narrateur et un héros *in absentia :* un héros explorateur et un héros à explorer.

III. Hétérogénéité d'un texte

Le lecteur de ce roman constate, sans peine, l'exploitation de l'intertextualité comme support principal de la narration. L'intertexte est abondant : textes du poète portugais Fernando Pessoa (1888–1935), tirés de son livre *The Book of Disquiet* [Le Livre de l'inquiètude] que le narrateur traduit par *Kitāb al-lā-hudū'* (26), des articles de R.R. publiés dans *Mulḥaq al-Nahār* (20, 22, 30, 131…), des articles d'Ilyās Khūrī, écrivain et journaliste libanais contemporain, publiés dans le même magazine, le rapport officiel du médecin légiste qui a pratiqué l'autopsie (141), le procès verbal de la gendarmerie lors de la découverte du corps (162), et enfin et surtout les deux ouvrages : *Alice's Adventures in Wonderland* [Alice au pays des merveilles] et *Through a Looking-Glass* [De l'autre côté du miroir] du célèbre écrivain anglais Lewis Carroll (1832–1898). Ces deux ouvrages constituent la moelle épinière de la structure narrative du roman. Je limite cette étude à cet intertexte précis : Le titre du roman nous renvoie directement à l'œuvre de Lewis Carroll. Par le choix du titre *R.R. dans le miroir*, l'auteur nous met dans les mêmes conditions qu'Alice regardant avec son chat le miroir. Il y a la volonté de découvrir un univers qui échappe aux lois conventionnelles, découvrir un monde qui n'est pas étouffé par les lois apparentes de la raison.

Rabīᶜ Jābir use dans son roman de presque toutes les formes d'intertextualité, répertoriées dans *Palimpsestes* de Gérard Genette:[3] il y a des formes explicites et implicites :

3 Gérard Genette, *Palimpsestes, la littérature au second degré* (Paris : Seuil, 1982).

a) Les formes explicites sont les plus fréquentes :

1. La citation la plus simple où l'auteur insère un texte dans un autre en se servant des caractères typographiques distincts :

> Humpty Dumpty sat on a wall
> Humpty Dumpty had a great fall
> All the King's horses and all the King's men
> Couldn't put Humpty Dumpty on his place again.

Ce passage tiré du chapitre « Humpty Dumpty » du livre *De l'autre côté du miroir* est cité en anglais à deux reprises dans le roman. Il est en italique et en caractères gras, mais sans guillemets et sans indication de la source (24, 51). Mais d'autres citations sont mises entre guillemets avec une référence explicite à l'auteur et à la source. C'est le cas par exemple des différents articles de R.R. cités dans la fiction, des faire parts de sa mort, des documents officiels… Explicite aussi est l'appel fait à Fernando Pessoa et à son ouvrage *The Book of Disquiet* pour répondre à sa place :

> « Souffre-t-il [R.R.] de la migraine ? »
> Pessoa : « J'ai une forte envie de mourir car je souffre de la migraine ».

Et pourquoi ne pouvait-il plus supporter le monde ?

> Pessoa : « ma tête me fait mal, et le monde entier me fait souffrir aussi » (26).

2. Comme type d'intertextualité dans le roman, nous observons aussi la relation dite *in absentia.* Sans toutefois insérer un texte dans un autre comme c'était le cas précédemment, l'auteur interpelle explicitement une référence source. Cette forme d'intertextualité est particulièrement foisonnante dans le roman étudié, dans la mesure où l'auteur s'évertue à nouer solidement les liens entre son texte et les deux ouvrages cités de Lewis Carroll. Cette relation avec un texte *in absentia* rompt parfois brusquement l'ordre de la narration. Observons, par exemple, le passage impromptu d'un sujet à un autre dans ce paragraphe :

> J'ai pensé, dit le narrateur, que Ralph avait la possibilité d'écrire des contes…Et je me suis demandé pourquoi il ne l'avait pas fait. Après la publication du deuxième tome des Aventures d'Alice en 1872, sous le titre *De l'autre côté du miroir*, les journalistes demandèrent à Lewis Carroll s'il

> comptait en publier un troisième. L'auteur qui avait 40 ans à l'époque répondit qu'il ne pensait pas le faire… (69, 70)

Le changement de registre est une claire invitation à chercher la réponse dans cet intertexte.

Il y a aussi des renvois directs et explicites à la source sans pour autant rompre la narration : « Assieds-toi comme Humpty Dumpty au bord d'un mur et joue avec les mots. Sans bouger, joue seulement avec les mots » (31). Là aussi, même si le texte source, l'hypotexte, n'est pas cité intégralement, son évocation est inéluctable pour la signification du nouveau texte, de l'hypertexte selon la terminologie de Genette.

3. Il y a aussi le pastiche, non dans le sens « de déformer un texte précis », comme souligne N. Piégay-Gros dans son ouvrage *Introduction à l'intertextualité*, mais imiter un style. « Le choix du sujet est donc indifférent à la réalisation de cette imitation ».[4] Le dialogue entre le narrateur et R.R. nous en fournit une bonne illustration. R.R. apparaît soudainement dans la chambre du narrateur: « La porte bougea et R. apparut derrière elle. Il me regarda et me demanda : « pourquoi es-tu seul ici ? » « Pourquoi, parce que il n'y a personne avec moi », dis-je, « as-tu pensé que je ne sais pas répondre à une telle question ! Vas-y poses en une autre ». « Tu parles comme Humpty Dumpty, dit-il en souriant ». « Et toi tu parles comme Alice, lui répondis-je » (96). Nous lisons dans *De l'autre côté du miroir* le dialogue suivant :

> « Pourquoi restez-vous perché tout seul sur ce mur ? », s'enquit Alice, peu soucieuse d'engager une controverse.
>
> « Ma foi, parce qu'il n'y a personne avec moi ! », s'écria Humpty Dumpty. « Pensiez-vous que je ne connusse pas la réponse à cette question-là ? Posez-en une autre. » (276)[5]

4 Nathalie Piégay-Gros, *Introduction à l'intertextualité* (Paris : Nathan, 1996), 65.

5 Concernant les ouvrages de Lewis Carroll, nous nous référons à deux éditions : *Tout Alice,* tr. Henri Parisot, chronologie, préface et bibliographie par Jean-Jacques Mayoux (Paris : Flammarion, 1979) ; *Alice aux pays des merveilles et De l'autre côté du miroir,* traduit de l'anglais par André Bay. Préface de André Maurois (119ème éd. ; Paris : Livre club du libraire, 1961). Toutes les citations et les pages indiquées dans le contenu se réfèrent à ces deux éditions qui seront distinguées : (*Tout Alice* + page) pour le premier ; (*Alice,* + page) pour le second.

b) Les formes implicites

1. Le type d'intertextualité implicite le plus répandu dans le roman est sans doute l'allusion littéraire : sans aucune marque explicite, plusieurs paragraphes renvoient le lecteur au texte référence. Ainsi, une réflexion du narrateur comme la suivante : « c'est ainsi qu'à un moment donné tu me voyais regarder le reflet de mon visage dans le miroir et me dire : j'enquêterai sur sa propre personne » (37), ne peut que rappeler la situation d'Alice dans *De l'autre côté du miroir.* Des comparaisons comme : « Comme si je m'enfonçai dans la terre...Je fonds comme une bougie et je me tasse dans ma chaussure... » (88), rappellent *Alice aux pays des merveilles.* Les allusions littéraires sont trop fréquentes pour être exhaustivement recensées, nous y reviendrons d'ailleurs en plusieurs endroits de notre analyse.

IV. Protocole d'une lecture

En faisant des deux ouvrages de Lewis Carroll un support principal de la narration et une plate forme sous-jacente sur laquelle se greffe le roman *R.R. dans le miroir*, l'auteur impose à son lecteur un protocole de lecture. Tout protocole est, certes, une contrainte, mais il peut être aussi, en aval, une ouverture : contrainte dans la mesure où il détermine le cadre général d'une approche et trace *à priori* une voie de lecture, mais aussi ouverture en ce sens qu'une fois engagé sur cette voie, une porte s'ouvre sur un large domaine d'interprétation et de suggestion. Comment pénétrer dans l'univers de cet hypertexte : le roman, sujet de notre étude, en empruntant la voie tracée par l'hypotexte : les deux ouvrages mentionnés de Carroll ?

Notons, de prime abord, que la structure narrative du roman et la démarche entamée par le narrateur en vue de ses recherches semblent répondre à ce phénomène d'optique qu'est le reflet dans le miroir. Une symétrie inversée, qui fait évoluer les actions de l'événement le plus proche : le suicide de R.R. vers l'élément le plus éloigné : vie et enfance.

Alice au pays des merveilles et *De l'autre côté du miroir* opèrent dans le roman de Rabīᶜ Jābir comme une métaphore géante en y établissant toute une série successive d'analogies. Les deux ouvrages y seront particulièrement exploités comme un terrain d'entente, un lieu de rencontre où s'établit tout un réseau d'équivalence entre les différents protagonistes de la fiction.

a) 1e équivalence : R.R. = Rabīʿ Jābir

Le premier rôle donné à *Alice au pays des merveilles* est d'établir l'adéquation entre Rabīʿ Jābir et R.R. Cette œuvre introduit d'emblée un pont liant les deux héros, un lien perçu à la fois sur le plan de l'énonciation et sur le plan de l'énoncé. Nous lisons (23) : « Si je savais qu'il aimait *Alice aux pays des merveilles* ! Si ! …Je tournai le dos au miroir, revins à mon lit et pour ne pas couper les ponts entre nous, je chantai d'*Alice aux pays des merveilles :* Humpty Dumpty sat on a wall… ». Cette scène dans laquelle le narrateur dévoile ses sentiments et affiche sa stratégie nous permet de déduire les équations suivantes :

> R.R. aime Alice aux pays des merveilles et de facto le personnage d'Alice
>
> Rabīʿ Jābir aime Alice aux pays des merveilles et de facto le personnage d'Alice

Donc, un premier signe de rapprochement entre les deux héros pourrait être retenu: R.R. = Rabīʿ Jābir.

b) 2e équivalence : R.R. = Rabīʿ Jābir = Lewis Carroll

Le rapprochement qui s'est effectué entre les deux héros à travers *Alice au pays des merveilles* prépare une 2e équation à trois éléments : les deux héros et Lewis Carroll, auteur de cette œuvre. En effet, à la question : « pourquoi Ralph n'avait-il pas écrit des romans ? » citée ci-dessus et répétée à la page 71, le narrateur fait appel pour répondre, comme nous l'avons déjà souligné, à l'univers de L. Carroll. Puis, le narrateur se lance dans une opération de calcul qui conduit au résultat suivant : Lewis Carroll avait vingt-quatre ans quand il a rencontré Alice pour la première fois ; le narrateur, Rabīʿ Jābir a vingt quatre ans au moment de l'écriture de ce roman ; R.R. avait vingt quatre ans quand il s'est marié (71–72). Cet élément commun : « à l'âge de 24 ans » joue le rôle d'un catalyseur unissant sous la même enseigne la vie de R.R., notamment son mariage, et les deux projets littéraires de L. Carroll et de Rabīʿ Jābir, ce qui justifie une adéquation entre les trois éléments :

R.R. = Rabīʿ Jābir = Lewis Carroll

c) Le miroir : symbole et métaphore

Le miroir, élément dominant, est évoqué plus de cinquante fois dans la fiction. En plus de son potentiel suggestif, le miroir est exploité métaphoriquement par le narrateur pour établir la similitude entre trois voyages : celui d'Alice, celui du narrateur sur les traces de R.R. et celui de ce dernier, à travers son suicide, vers l'au-delà. Cette ressemblance est accentuée par une série de comparaisons. La première est entre le miroir et la surface de l'eau. La « Maison du Miroir » d'Alice est équivalente à « la maison d'eau » de R.R. : évoquant les deux ouvrages de Carroll, le narrateur dit : « Dans le premier roman, Carroll a inventé un monde souterrain, mystérieux dans le deuxième livre, nous n'accédons pas à ce monde par un terrier creusé dans le sol mais à travers une plaque de verre qui ressemble à l'eau. Car, dans la glace, nous pouvons voir notre visage et dans l'eau aussi » (73). Cette analogie entre surface d'eau et miroir est l'une des comparaisons maîtresses dans la fiction. En voici quelques-unes : « dans mes rêves je vois Ralph tomber vers une surface d'eau limpide comme un miroir » (32) ; et quelques lignes plus loin : « comme un fantôme, il passait au travers d'une plaque en glace » (33). Une fois la ressemblance entre les deux éléments concrets (miroir, eau) établie, les voyages entrepris deviendront parfaitement identiques malgré la dissemblance de leur fin. C'est l'entreprise en tant que telle qui est visée, c'est-à-dire le voyage vers l'inconnu, vers un univers imperceptible par notre raison. Il dit : « Alice sauta dans la chambre qui était dans le miroir. Ceci fut raconté dans un livre paru pour la première fois en 1872. 123 ans plus tard, le même phénomène se reproduit, mais pas dans un livre et sans avoir la même fin. Alice revient parce qu'elle a ouvert les yeux. Ralph ne revient plus » (34).

Quant au voyage du narrateur, le miroir faisant partie du décor de sa chambre est là pour rappeler le miroir d'Alice. Une nette focalisation sur cet élément le met en évidence et contribue à lui attribuer le rôle d'un personnage à part entière dans le roman. En décrivant sa chambre modeste et lugubre, il s'attarde sur le miroir accroché au-dessus du lavabo (14). Une autre scène, plus significative encore : prenant l'ascenseur dans l'immeuble où habitent les parents de Ralph, la seule chose qui le frappe est le miroir accroché au mur : « je regarde le miroir, dit-il, il est petit et rectangulaire et ne ressemble en rien aux miroirs habituels des ascenseurs. Je n'y vois que la partie supérieure de mon corps, en plus de mon visage.

Comme si quelqu'un avait pris le miroir d'un lavabo pour le fixer dans l'ascenseur » (53).

Alice avait donc son miroir, Ralph avait le miroir de l'eau et Rabīʿ Jābir avait également le sien. Les conditions identiques du voyage sont réunies. Dans *De l'autre côté du miroir,* la porte grande ouverte du salon laisse entrevoir un bout du couloir de la « Maison du Miroir » d'Alice. Ce couloir incite l'héroïne à aller découvrir ce qui pourrait être différent de l'autre côté : « on peut tout juste avoir un petit aperçu de ce qu'est le couloir de la Maison du Miroir ... Plus loin ... il est peut-être tout différent », dit-elle à Kitty.[6] Le narrateur, en plus du miroir, souligne dans la description de sa chambre la présence d'une porte noire fermée avec des clous dans laquelle le propriétaire prétend avoir entassé les meubles d'une famille partie en Amérique. La chambre derrière cette porte reste malgré tout un espace inconnu pour le narrateur.

d) Le miroir : de l'équivalence à l'identification

Quand Rabīʿ Jābir, le narrateur, regarde dans le miroir, il y voit son image, ce qui est normal. À plusieurs reprises dans le roman, il se dirige vers le miroir et s'adresse à Rabīʿ Jābir qui est en face de lui: « la nuit, je me suis mis devant le miroir et lui ai dit : 'désormais j'oublie tout' » (12). Mais ce même miroir reflète aussi, dès les premières pages du roman, l'image de R.R. En effet, l'image de R.R. se superpose dans le miroir à celle du narrateur. L'objectif du narrateur, annoncé au début du roman et qui consiste à explorer l'univers abscons et mystérieux de R.R., pourrait toucher également le propre univers du narrateur et à travers lui celui de l'être humain. L'identification complète des deux personnages serait alors à l'origine de leur communication spirituelle même si auparavant ils ne se sont jamais adressés la parole. Dans l'un de ses articles publiés à *Mulḥaq al-Nahār*, R.R. exprime ses idées en s'adressant à un destinataire virtuel (20). Le narrateur lit quatre fois l'article et, troublé par ces propos, conclut, sans le moindre doute, que c'est bien lui ce destinataire virtuel. Étonné, il s'interroge : « pourquoi me dit-il : « ton appartement humide » ? Et comment a-t-il su que je possède une chaise ? Je me suis dirigé vers le miroir et lui ai fait part (*ṣarraḥtu lahu*) de ces réalités » (21). L'interprétation de cette phrase ne laisse aucun doute :

6 *Tout Alice*, 217.

quand il se regarde dans le miroir c'est aussi l'image de R.R. qu'y est reflétée.

e) Fusion des deux personnages

Les indices qui indiquent une fusion des deux personnages sont multiples dans le roman. Dans sa quête, le narrateur se rend à la maison des parents de R.R., il en décrit les meubles. Cette description évoque en permanence la maison des grands parents du narrateur. Le parallélisme entre les deux espaces dépasse la simple similitude pour atteindre l'identification. La table sur laquelle sont posés le poste de télévision et le « vidéo », lui paraît familière : « où l'ai-je vue ? », se demande-t-il, et la réponse ne se fait pas attendre : « en face de moi il y a un poste de télévision et un « vidéo » posés sur une table avec deux étagères, en aluminium et verre. Où ai-je vu cette table auparavant ? La rouille qui couvre ses pieds ? Les fils électriques qui s'entrelacent autour d'eux ? Est-ce dans la maison de mon grand-père ? » (54).

Ce n'était qu'un début. Le buffet dans la salle à manger est le même que celui de la maison de son grand-père où on mettait le panier de dragées à l'intérieur sur l'étagère inférieure, caché derrière les nombreuses assiettes (56). La montre du père de Ralph, avec son grand cadran bleu et son bracelet métallique argenté, attire aussi son attention. Il s'interroge sans dissimuler son étonnement : « mon grand-père, n'en avait-il pas une pareille ? » (58). Le père revient avec une cafetière bleue, la vapeur s'en dégage exhalant l'odeur de cardamome. Cette scène renvoie immédiatement au grand-père: « j'ai pensé immédiatement à mon grand-père », dit-il (85).

L'identification qui se construit entre les deux personnages est également perçue dans le regard des autres, et plus précisément dans le regard des parents de Ralph. Ces derniers se comportent avec le narrateur avec une familiarité telle qu'on croirait qu'ils le connaissent depuis très longtemps, depuis son enfance (76).

Les scènes montrant sa place par rapport à la famille sont multiples. Le narrateur regarde le balcon dans l'appartement des parents et voit le mégot d'une cigarette. Il se demande si le père l'a fumée en l'attendant sur ce balcon. Une série de questions s'égrènent : « le père s'assoit-il chaque matin sur cette chaise ? » ; « est-ce qu'il m'a attendu ce matin même ? » Le questionnement cède la place à une certitude : « seulement, je sais que sur ce balcon il attendait Ralph » (77).

Le processus fusionnel des deux héros aboutit. Le narrateur quitte l'appartement des parents de Ralph et prend l'ascenseur. Il nous révèle ces détails : plus il descend, plus la silhouette du père disparaît derrière la fenêtre vitrée de l'ascenseur. Il se retourne et se trouve face au miroir, il est effrayé : « sur l'instant j'étais pris de panique » précise-t-il (60). La raison de cette frayeur réside sûrement dans ce petit miroir de l'ascenseur. L'allusion à une certaine analogie glissée implicitement dans la narration guidera le lecteur dans son investigation. En effet, avant de quitter l'appartement, le narrateur demande au père de Ralph : « depuis quand habitez-vous cet immeuble ? » Et le père de répondre : « depuis 29 ans ». Dans l'ascenseur Rabīᶜ Jābir regarde sa montre: entre le moment où il y est rentré pour monter dans l'immeuble et le moment de sa sortie, il y a vingt-neuf minutes (60). L'effet de miroir est doublement investi : d'un côté, les vingt-neuf minutes sont le reflet de vingt-neuf ans ; le reflet du narrateur dans le miroir est parfaitement le reflet de l'image de Ralph, d'un autre. Il revit alors le parcours de son héros qui, pendant vingt-neuf ans, a pris le même ascenseur et s'est regardé dans le même miroir rectangulaire. Cette abolition des frontières entre personnages justifie le passage sans transition à la description de Ralph dans cet espace et sollicite à cette fin l'intertexte. L'histoire de Ralph dans l'ascenseur rappelle l'histoire d'Alice dans la Maison du Lapin. Comparons les deux textes : « Cet ascenseur l'étouffait. Ralph grandissait et imaginait qu'il était devenu plus fort … sans pouvoir bouger ses bras, il ne voyait dans le miroir que son tronc. Comme si les murs se refermaient sur lui. Plus les jours passaient, plus il grandissait et plus les murs se refermaient sur lui » (61).

Dans *Alice au pays des merveilles* on lit : « avant d'avoir absorbé la moitié du contenu du flacon, elle constata que sa tête se trouvait pressée contre le plafond, et elle dut ployer l'échine pour éviter de se rompre le cou … Elle continuait de grandir, de grandir tant et si bien qu'elle dut s'agenouiller sur le plancher : un instant plus tard elle n'avait même plus assez de place pour y demeurer à genoux, et elle s'efforçait de se coucher, un coude contre la porte et l'autre bras replié sur la tête. Elle n'en continuait pas moins de grandir ».[7] Le chiffre « 29 », commun à deux situations ainsi que le rapprochement intertextuel mentionné, nous permettent d'évoquer une autre analogie, spatiale cette fois-ci: Maison du Lapin = espace de l'ascenseur = espace de l'appartement des parents.

7 Ibid., 120.

Nous pouvons, sans trop risquer, étendre cette analogie à la chambre du narrateur.

La réaction du narrateur dans l'ascenseur et la sensation de frayeur qui l'a envahi ne sont-elles pas une preuve supplémentaire de la fusion spirituelle entre R.R. et Rabīᶜ Jābir ?

Dans son article « al-Farawila al-akhīra » [« Le dernier panier de fraise »] publié dans *Mulḥaq al-Nahār* du 15 avril 1995, Ralph Rizqallah, une fois dans l'appartement de ses parents, se qualifie de *zā'ir* (visiteur) (68). Or, Rabīᶜ Jābir se retrouve dans cette situation lors de sa visite à Halā, la femme de R.R. ainsi que dans sa visite aux parents de Ralph. Ce vocable, répété trois fois de suite à la page 56, est mis en évidence par l'auteur pour accentuer une fois de plus l'identification des deux personnages. La frayeur du narrateur dans l'ascenseur est alors justifiée. L'écrasement de R.R. sous le poids de cet espace est aussi l'écrasement du narrateur.

Le narrateur sort de l'appartement d'Ibrāhīm Rizqallah, le père de Ralph, quitte l'ascenseur et emprunte une rue mouillée par la pluie : « je marchais dans une longue rue mouillée par la pluie », dit-il (88). Un phénomène étrange, contraire à celui survenu dans l'ascenseur, se produit. Il décrit ce phénomène en se référant encore une fois au texte d'origine de L. Carroll : « Mon corps se rétrécit et diminue comme un chiffon dans une eau bouillante, je me transforme en un nain, je fonds comme la cire et je me tasse dans mes chaussures » (88).

Alice vit la même scène : « Quelle drôle de sensation ! fit Alice. On dirait que je rentre en moi-même comme un télescope. » C'était exact : elle ne mesurait plus maintenant que vingt-cinq centimètres … Pourtant, elle attendit un instant encore pour voir si elle allait continuer de rapetisser : cela l'inquiétait un peu : « Car, voyez-vous, se disait Alice, je pourrais bien finir par me réduire à néant, telle une bougie ».[8]

L'aventure du narrateur continue, exactement comme continue l'aventure d'Alice dans son monde merveilleux. Il regarde ses pieds et, stupéfait, il découvre la raison de son rapetissement. Il remarque que ce ne sont plus les siens, il marche sur deux pieds couverts de boutons et de taches bleues et rouges. Il marche sur les pieds d'Ibrāhīm Rizqallah, le père de Ralph (89). Sans négliger le poids oppressif du système patriarcal et des liens familiaux dans la société orientale que suggère ce texte, peut-

8 *Tout Alice*, 100.

on voir aussi, par cette métamorphose, un autre signe de fusion entre les deux héros, saisi à travers le père cette fois ?

Dans son enquête, le narrateur regarde des photos traçant la vie de R.R. Un dialogue entre Rabīᶜ Jābīr et R.R. inspiré du chapitre *Twideuldeume et Twideuldie* de *De l'autre côté du miroir* se déroule entre eux. Twideuldie dit à Alice : « vous ne seriez nulle part. Vous n'êtes qu'une espèce d'objet figurant dans son [le Roi Rouge] rêve »,[9] et à l'une des réflexions du narrateur, le héros R.R. répond : « comment puis-je te détester alors que je n'existe pas ! Je suis seulement un personnage dans ton rêve, un simple fantôme » (97). Le narrateur, intrigué par ces propos, continue à regarder les photos :

> Je regardai les photos, je ne vis pas son visage. Je vis, en revanche, les visages de ses parents, de sa famille, de sa femme et de ses camarades. Son visage n'était pas sur les photos.
> — Pourtant… dis-je, étonné !
> — Regarde encore une fois me dit-il, c'est la réalité.
> — Je regardai à la place de son visage, je vis le mien (98).

Il est clair que le visage de l'un est le visage de l'autre et que la fusion est complète.

Dans le rapport du médecin légiste on lit : « une plaie de 5 cm au dessus de la tempe droite » (141). Le chapitre suivant décrit le narrateur qui marche dans Beyrouth dans un cadre mariant le réel et le surréel. L'expression « je marche », répétée cinq fois, situe l'action dans un espace géographique réel. Des rues de Beyrouth sont explicitement citées : « la Voie du Ministère des affaires étrangères, rue Evêque Msarra … » (143). Cet espace est couvert de neige comme au pôle nord. Sachant que la neige est extrêmement rare à Beyrouth, et certainement pas de la neige rappelant le pôle nord, nous pensons que cette description fait écho aux pages 110 et 111 du roman où il est question des ours polaires étudiés et vus par R.R. à Toronto. Dans les rues de Beyrouth, le narrateur suit les traces de quelqu'un : les traces d'un être humain ou d'un ours polaire, pense-t-il — on comprend la raison du choix du cadre. Brusquement, il aperçoit un homme le devançant de 10 mètres. Cet homme, ressemblant au grand-père du narrateur, se retourne, Rabīᶜ Jābir le voit de face. Pas de

9 *Tout Alice*, 256.

doute, c'est R.R. en personne, mais la cicatrice de cinq centimètre de long est au dessus de la tempe gauche (144).

Un ultime retour à l'hypotexte s'impose. Quand Alice s'adresse à Kitty pour lui exposer « toutes ses idées sur la Maison du Miroir », elle lui précise : « d'abord il y a la pièce que tu peux voir dans la glace ... Elle est exactement semblable à notre salon, mais les objets y sont inversés ».[10] La scène décrite ci-dessus confirme d'un côté que le chemin des deux personnages est identique et de l'autre que l'un est parfaitement l'image de l'autre. Le narrateur voit R.R. comme s'il se voit lui-même dans le miroir.

Ceci étant, le critique serai-il tenté de parler d'une certaine métempsychose ? Le narrateur est né certes, bien avant la mort de R.R., mais l'identification des deux personnages et la substitution de l'un à l'autre ne l'autorisent-elles pas à penser à ce phénomène ?

f) L'irrationnel à la rescousse

Les deux œuvres de Carroll sont indiscutablement un passage obligé à la compréhension de l'identification des deux héros ainsi qu'à leur parcours. Par son voyage au-delà de la surface d'eau, R.R. a mis terme à un monde confus, oppressant et ingrat. La rationalité de la vie ne lui a rapporté que déception : le chemin parcouru a abouti tout à fait à l'inverse de ce qu'il attendait. Tout est inversé comme dans un miroir. Le chemin censé conduire au bonheur mène au malheur (30). Le dicton *man jadda wajad* qu'on peut traduire par : « travaille, applique-toi, tu récolteras le fruit de ton effort » est inversé : « tu fais les choses dans l'intention d'aboutir à un résultat, mais soudainement tu découvres que tu es arrivé à son contraire » (30). Les recherches entreprises par le narrateur ne sont pas étrangères à ces données. Saisir « le cœur de R.R. », saisir le mystère de sa vie c'est voyager dans un univers qui ne sera pas gouverné par la raison. C'est pourquoi le narrateur était conscient qu'il rentrait dans un labyrinthe sans fin (38). Ce labyrinthe est la preuve de notre ignorance et de l'incapacité de la raison d'appréhender l'âme des choses. Appeler l'irrationnel à la rescousse serait, à l'instar de la démarche d'Alice, reconnaître la connaissance intuitive aux dépens de la connaissance acquise. Évoquant cette connaissance le narrateur dit : « ceci ressemble à quelque chose que je connais bien, quelque chose que je connaissais bien,

10 Ibid., 217.

il y a longtemps, depuis l'école et avant que les livres ne m'aient pollué et ne m'aient transformé en un loup détestant les hommes. Ceci ressemble à la vie » (38). Le narrateur est pris à son jeu comme l'était Alice. Cette dernière, dans son nouvel univers, désire arriver au carré huit « avant qu'il fasse nuit » pour être Reine ;[11] lui aussi désire arriver au lieu dit Rawsha (la Grotte aux pigeons) pour découvrir ses mystères, pour dévoiler le secret de R.R. La dernière partie du roman est focalisée sur ce lieu qui devient l'objectif obsessionnel du narrateur : « mardi 25 juin 1996 ... Je suis en route pour Rawsha », précise-t-il (148). Dans cette dernière partie, le narrateur introduit un nouveau personnage, la tante de R.R., qui s'est suicidée elle aussi quand Ralph avait seize ans, ouvrant ainsi le chemin à son neveu. La solitude est le trait commun liant les deux personnages. Un parallélisme s'établit entre la solitude de R.R. et celle de sa tante. Avant de se suicider le héros se sentait seul, à l'université, lieu de son travail, à la maison et dans toute la société (175). La tante, de son côté, vit la solitude de ses rêves. Plusieurs scènes nous renvoient également à l'ouvrage de Lewis Carroll *De l'autre côté du miroir*. La tante répète à deux reprises : « je cours, je cours, mais je reste à la même place ». On lit dans le texte d'origine : « C'est un pays bien lent ! dit la Reine. Ici, voyez-vous, il faut courir de toutes ses forces pour rester à la même place ».[12] Le jeu d'échec est aussi une élément commun entre les deux textes : la tante jouait avec un jeune homme qu'elle connaissait il y a quelques années, elle avait les pions noirs et lui les blancs. En tout cas, le nombre de pages limité de cet article ne nous permet pas d'explorer les nombreux domaines intertextuels dans ce roman.

g) *Al-Rawsha* [La Grotte aux pigeons] : lieu de salut

Deux visions différentes, voire contradictoires, marquent l'approche de Rawsha dans ce roman. La première est la mystification de ce lieu magique qui intrigue le narrateur, l'excite et suscite toute sa motivation. Plus on avance dans le roman, plus il devient le centre de la sphère du narrateur vers lequel convergent toutes ses intentions. Il l'observe de tous les côtés, le prend en photo sous tous les angles possibles et, comme s'il s'agissait du centre de l'univers, il dessine le plan du quartier sur lequel il le place distinctement (156). Toute la vie de Ralph, toutes les photos pri-

11 *Alice*, 153, 165.
12 Ibid., 151

ses de lui dans ce quartier et analysées minutieusement par le narrateur ne semblent être qu'un prélude à son dernier voyage à travers ce port énigmatique.

La deuxième vision semble s'opposer à la première. Parallèlement à cette vénération de Rawsha observée dans la démarche du narrateur, on constate, malgré tout, une certaine tendance à démystifier, voire même à banaliser, ce lieu emblématique et majestueux. Car, il est présenté aussi comme proche, familier et facile à y accéder. Parlant de la Grotte aux pigeons l'auteur écrit : « « non, elle n'est pas très loin » je me dis, nous avons besoin [pour y accéder] seulement d'un peu de déception, un peu de solitude et un peu de migraine » (152). Or, les trois conditions sont réunies chez le narrateur. La migraine *al-ṣudā*ᶜ dont il souffre est un état persistant dans la fiction. Elle est également présente dans d'autres romans, *Shāy aswad* [Thé noir], par exemple. Ce malaise symbolique en plus des deux autres facteurs soulignés suffisent pour aller chercher remède à 30 mètres de la côte, à Rawsha. La conciliation de ces deux visions s'effectue dans l'esprit compréhensif du narrateur et la fiction serait, dans ce cas, un magnifique hymne à la mort.

V. Savoir et mémoire

Si l'on admet que l'intertextualité fait appel à un « lecteur complice qui sera le partenaire d'un jeu qu'elle instaure avec son savoir et sa mémoire »,[13] il serait légitime de s'interroger sur le profil du lecteur éventuel de ce roman. Le texte de Rabīᶜ Jābir fait appel au savoir du lecteur et le sollicite sans répit à participer activement à l'élaboration du sens. « L'allusion littéraire, écrit N. Piégay-Gros, suppose en effet que le lecteur va comprendre à mots couverts ce que l'auteur veut lui faire entendre sans le lui dire directement ».[14]

Dans le chapitre où le narrateur décrit sa rencontre fictive avec R.R. à laquelle nous avons fait allusion plus haut, l'échange entre les deux personnages suit de près celui qui s'est déroulé entre Alice et Humpty Dumpty. Le texte de Rabīᶜ Jābir évolue dans le sillon du texte d'origine.

13 Piégay-Gros (1996), 111.
14 Ibid., 52.

Avant de se séparer, Alice et Humpty Dumpty avaient eu l'échange suivant :

> Au revoir dit-elle...jusqu'à notre prochaine rencontre !
> — Je ne vous reconnaîtrai pas si nous venions à nous rencontrer de nouveau, répondit Humpty Dumpty...vous êtes tellement faite comme tout le monde !
> — On reconnaît les gens à leur figure, dit Alice d'un ton pensif.
> — C'est bien ce que je dis, fit Humpty Dumpty, votre figure est celle de tout le monde...si, par exemple, vous aviez les deux yeux du même côté du nez...ou la bouche à la place du front, cela pourrait m'aider.[15]

Dans *R.R. fī al-mir'āt,* R.R. était aussi incapable de changer son physique qui est fait comme tout le monde : « Il [R.R.] m'a dit : durant toute ma vie je n'avais pas réussi à mettre ma bouche entre mes yeux. Ceci est très difficile, en plus à quoi ça sert ? » (97). À la même rencontre, les rôles s'inversent : R.R. devient Humpty Dumpty et le narrateur Alice: « Son rire est devenu plus large, comme s'il était lui Humpty Dumpty, s'il continue à sourire, les deux coins de sa bouches se rencontreront par derrière » (97).

On lit dans *De l'autre côté du miroir* : « Et sa bouche se fendit jusqu'aux oreilles quand il s'inclina et tendit une main à Alice. Elle le regarda avec une certaine inquiétude en la prenant : 's'il sourit encore un peu, les coins de sa bouche vont se rencontrer par derrière, pensa-t-elle, et alors, je me demande ce qu'il adviendra de sa tête ! Je crains qu'elle se détache !' ».[16] C'est aussi dans la description de cette rencontre que l'auteur, sans aucun signe explicite, fait le rapprochement entre l'existence de R.R. dans le rêve du narrateur et l'existence d'Alice dans le rêve du Roi Rouge.

Ceci étant, il me semble qu'une lecture spontanée de ce roman est quasiment impossible. En effet, la lecture de *R.R. dans le miroir* ne peut s'effectuer qu'avec une lecture simultanée et approfondie des deux œuvres mentionnées de Lewis Carroll. La philosophie de ces deux œuvres est une clef indispensable pour pénétrer dans l'univers du roman étudié. Le lecteur, en même temps comparatiste et interprète, met en œuvre tout son savoir pour aboutir à un sens qui ne sera en aucun cas univoque.

15 *Alice*, 207–208.
16 Ibid., 197.

VI. R.R. fī al-mir'āt *et mémoires : personnelle et collective*

Il est certain que les deux ouvrages *Alice au pays des merveilles* et *De l'autre côté du miroir* font partie du patrimoine universel et se réservent une place plus ou moins grande dans la mémoire de l'humanité. Mais l'usage dont l'auteur en fait dépasse de loin, à notre avis, la mémoire d'un lecteur libanais ou arabe en général. Prenant à titre d'exemple les deux paragraphes où le narrateur introduit en anglais l'intertexte suivant : « *Humpty Dumpty sat on a wall...* » (24 et 51).

Nous pouvons aisément supposer que cet intertexte relève de la mémoire personnelle de l'auteur / narrateur qui a reçu probablement une culture anglaise, mais il ne peut l'être de la mémoire collective. Ce texte souvent chanté n'appartient pas à la mémoire populaire et ne s'inscrit pas, par conséquent, dans une tradition nationale capable de le charger de sens. Mais une question de taille concernant ce roman se pose. Est-ce que l'auteur vise vraiment à solliciter la mémoire collective ? Nous pensons que non. Nous avons tendance à aller encore plus loin et affirmer que c'est plutôt la « non-mémoire » collective, par opposition à une mémoire personnelle sélective, qui donne à cet intertexte sa vraie signification. En effet, cet énoncé est exploité dans deux contextes narratifs différents voire opposés. Dans le premier, il est investi pour consolider un lien entre R.R. et Rabīᶜ Jābir, car il appartient à la mémoire commune des deux héros.[17] Dans le deuxième, le même intertexte, à savoir le même chant, est, au contraire, investi dans l'objectif de suggérer une rupture, de se démarquer de la collectivité. Dans le bus qui assurait le transport sur la ligne al-Ḥamrā — Antélias,[18] le narrateur nous décrit la mésentente entre lui et le passager assis à côté de lui ; il dit : « Il se mit à me fixer … à contempler le short gris que je portais, la chemise blanche à manches courtes, le verre cassé de ma montre, mes sandales noires en cuir. Qu'a-t-il donc à me fixer comme ça ? Est-ce la vue de mes pieds nus l'a gêné ? Je le regardai et à haute voix je me mis à chanter : « Humpty Dumpty sat on a wall… » À ce moment là, il se détourna complètement de moi » (51). L'écart entre les deux situations est éloquent : le même énoncé est un élément d'entente dans l'un, de mésentente dans l'autre.

17 Voir *supra*. n. 5.

18 al-Ḥamrā est un quartier à l'ouest de Beyrouth et Antélias est une ville à 7 km au nord de la capitale.

Cela dit, il me semble que l'absence d'une intersection entre une mémoire singulière et une mémoire collective est l'une des caractéristiques de l'intertextualité dans l'écriture romanesque de Rabīᶜ Jābir. L'écriture dans ce roman emprunte à la littérature européenne des fils pour tisser une chrysalide ou, soyons peut-être moins excessif, elle y emprunte les outils pour construire un foyer à l'intérieur duquel l'auteur établit son empire intime. Et c'est précisément autour de cet univers ambigu que l'auteur édifie sa fiction, d'où la tendance philosophique de ce roman.

Tous ces éléments aideront le critique à tenter une définition du profil du lecteur auquel s'adresse Rabīᶜ Jābir : il nous paraît, suite à cette analyse, qu'une telle écriture écarte *de facto* le grand public, non pas parce qu'elle se passe d'une structure classique respectant un schéma événementiel allant de l'état initial vers un état final passant par une intrigue, mais plutôt parce qu'elle est particulièrement exigeante à l'égard du lecteur. Ce dernier ne jouera pas son rôle actif s'il n'est pas armé d'un savoir confirmé lui permettant d'aplanir la voie sinueuse de l'interprétation. L'intertextualité, exploitée avec beaucoup de talent, enrichit fortement le texte dérivé mais sélectionne minutieusement ses destinataires en se réservant à une élite.

Transformations of the *Thousand and One Nights*: Zakariyyā Tāmir's 'Shahriyār wa-Shahrazād' and Muḥammad Jibrīl's *Zahrat al-Ṣabāḥ*

Ulrike Stehli-Werbeck
University of Münster

The year 2004 saw numerous celebrations of the three-hundredth anniversary[1] since the French Orientalist Antoine Galland (1648–1715) published the first European translation of *Alf layla wa-layla* in 1704 in Paris. This translation initiated a period of 'shared ownership' of the *Thousand and One Nights* between the Orient and the Occident and had far-reaching influence on the European arts. Some lament that the seedling of the reception of modern Arabic literature in Europe has so far failed to flourish in the shadow of the dominating *Arabian Nights*,[2] while others have pointed out that the famous story collection has had such a great influence on every aspect of the arts, that 'it is easier to name those who have not been influenced than those who have'.[3] The situation in the Arab world is very different, as the *Alf layla wa-layla* for many years suffered from its reputation as an example of popular literature, even though Arab dramatists had begun to use it as a source of inspiration from the middle of the nineteenth century.[4] From the 1930s the productive reception of charac-

1 A few results of symposia, lectures and exhibitions held in this context include: Aboubakr Chraibi (ed.), *Les Mille et Une Nuits en partage* [Actes du colloque « Mille et une nuits en partage », Paris, 25–29 mai 2004] (Paris : Ed. Actes Sud, Sindbad, 2004) ; a special number 'Ideological Variations and Narrative Horizons : new perspectives on the *Arabian Nights'*, *Middle Eastern Literatures* 7:2 (July 2004); *Dreihundert Jahre '1001 Nacht' in geteiltem Besitz von Europa. Ein Begleitheft zur Ausstellung in Münster, Tübingen und Gotha*, Anke Osigus (ed.), in cooperation with Heinz Grotzfeld (Münster: LIT, 2005).

2 Hartmut Fähndrich, 'Viewing "the Orient" and Translating its Literature in the Shadow of *The Arabian Nights*', *Yearbook of Comparative and General Literature* 48 (2000), 95–106.

3 Robert Irwin, *The Arabian Nights: a companion* (London: Lane/Penguin, 1994), quoted from Wen-chin Ouyang, 'Genres, Ideologies, Genre Ideologies and Narrative Transformation', *Middle Eastern Literatures* 7 (2004), 125–31 (125).

4 *Abū al-Ḥasan al-Mughaffal* (1849/50) by Mārūn al-Naqqāsh was the first drama to utilise the work in this way.

ters, themes, motifs, and structural elements started anew,[5] and during the last few decades there has been a conspicuous increase in the number of texts which in one way or another display manifold and complex references to the *Arabian Nights*.[6]

In this essay I present two remarkable examples of such narrative transformations, both published in the 1990s: Zakariyyā Tāmir's short story 'Shahriyār wa-Shahrazād' (1994) and Muḥammad Jibrīl's *Zahrat al-Ṣabāḥ* (1995). To analyse the system of references to *Alf layla wa-layla* (and other texts) I rely on the typology of transtextual relations developed by Gérard Genette, which is still valuable when dealing with relations between texts.

Genette's typology

For the phenomenon for which the term *intertextuality* has been adopted, Genette in his study *Palimpsestes. La littérature au second degré*[7] used the generic term *transtextuality.* As I employ his subcategories, I have decided to retain this terminology for the sake of consistency. *Transtextuality* or *textual transcendence*, as introductorily defined by Genette, is everything that puts a text into a manifest or secret relation with other texts: 'tout ce qui le met en relation, manifeste ou secrète, avec d'autres textes'.[8] Genette identified five types of such transtextual relations.

First, based on Julia Kristeva's research and the notion of 'intertextuality' coined in her *Sèméiôtikè* (1969),[9] Genette understood this category in a very narrow sense as the 'relation of co-presence of two or more texts' ('relation de coprésence entre deux ou plusieurs textes'), or in other words: the effective presence of a text in another text ('la présence effective d'un texte dans un autre').[10] This can be presented as (a) quotation, i.e. a literal borrowing, with quotation marks, and with or without source; (b) plagia-

5 With Tawfīq al-Ḥakīm's drama *Shahrazād* (1934).

6 For an overview that lists numerous examples of this productive reception, see Wiebke Walther, 'Modern Arabic Literature and the *Arabian Nights*', in: U. Marzolph, R. van Leeuwen (eds), *The Arabian Nights Encyclopaedia.* 2 vols (Santa Barbara, Ca.: ABC–Clio, 2004), I, 54–61.

7 G. Genette, *Palimpsestes. La littérature au second degré* (Paris: Seuil, 1982).

8 Ibid., 7.

9 Sèméiôtikè: recherches pour une sémanalyse (Paris: Seuil, 1969).

10 Genette, *Palimpsestes* (1993), 10.

rism, if the text has been borrowed literally without indication; (c) allusion, that is a statement, the full understanding of which presupposes the recognition of a relation between itself and another statement to which it refers ('un énoncé dont la pleine intelligence suppose la perception d'un rapport entre lui et un autre auquel renvoie nécessairement telle ou telle de ses inflexions, autrement non recevable').[11]

The second category of text relations, which encompasses the surroundings of the text in the widest sense, Genette called 'paratextuality': this concerns titles, subtitles, title links; prefaces, epilogues, notes for the reader, introductions; marginalia, footnotes; mottoes; illustrations; blurbs, covers etc. This category comprehends the pragmatic dimension of a text, as all elements mentioned serve to guide expectations and reading.[12]

Thirdly, 'metatextuality' means a relation between one text and another, which is usually referred to as 'commentary' and which deals with it without necessarily quoting it or mentioning it.[13] This commentary can be critical or scientific, but can also be indirect, a reflection of formal modes of presentation or of habits of perception.

Fourthly, the central category of 'hypertextuality' includes any relationship between a younger text ('hypertext') and an older text ('hypotext') that eclipses the younger one in a way other than that of the commentary.[14] This takes place by means of a transformation, be it parody, travesty, pastiche etc. Through this the hypotext becomes a counterfoil of the hypertext.[15]

Fifthly, the category 'archetextuality' investigates the relation between two texts with regard to their generic concepts. This relation mostly remains undeclared, except for paratextual references to a generic affiliation (for instance, by a subtitle like 'novel').[16]

11 Ibid.

12 Ibid., 9f.

13 'La relation, on dit plus couramment de « commentaire », qui unit un texte à un autre texte dont il parle, sans nécessairement le citer (le convoquer), voire, à la limite, sans le nommer', ibid., 10.

14 'Toute relation unissant un texte B [...] à un texte anterieur A [...] sur lequel il se greffe d'une manière qui n'est pas celle du commentaire', ibid., 11f.

15 Ibid., 16.

16 Ibid., 11.

As Genette conceded, these five types overlap to a certain degree.[17] One may be sceptical about the order of counting, which Genette explained by the order of increasing abstraction, implication and globalisation.[18] It also appears to me that the fourth category, hypertextuality, tends to encompass some of the others and in this case may come close to the main notion of transtextuality. Nevertheless, for a differentiating analysis of a net of references, his attempt to separate all the aspects listed above has proved remarkably fruitful, as may be seen in the following analysis.

Zakariyyā Tāmir, 'Shahriyār wa-Shahrazād' (1994)

A small but successful example of the rich possibilities for transtextual references is the short story 'Shahriyār wa-Shahrazād'[19] by the Syrian writer Zakariyyā Tāmir (b. 1931).[20] If we consult the *paratextual* elements first, we find that the title includes the names of the two principal characters of the frame-story of *Alf layla wa-layla*, thus simultaneously presenting an intertextual element, the citation of the two main characters — with which features, will be seen. The fact that Shahriyār precedes, may indicate political or patriarchal power — an assumption that is refuted by the first part of the short story, but, as far as the patriarchal aspect is concerned at least, supported by the second one.

17 Ibid., 14.

18 Ibid., 8.

19 In Zakariyyā Tāmir, *Nidā' Nūḥ* (London: Riad El-Rayyes, 1994), 231–5; a German translation is in Sakarija Tamer, *Die Hinrichtung des Todes. Unbekannte Geschichten von bekannten Figuren,* tr. from Arabic by Hartmut Fähndrich and Ulrike Stehli-Werbeck (Basel: Lenos, 2004), 31–35.

20 For introductory information about the author and further references see my recent article: 'Der Poet der arabischen Kurzgeschichte: Zakarīyā Tāmir', *Arabische Literatur, postmodern*, eds A. Neuwirth *et al.* (Munich: Edition Text + Kritik, 2004), 179–90, and: 'Nachwort' (together with Hartmut Fähndrich), in Tamer, *Hinrichtung*, 129–37; on earlier phases of Tāmir's writing, see also Sabry Hafez, 'The modern Arabic short story', in *Modern Arabic Literature* (Cambridge History of Arabic Literature), ed. M.M. Badawi (Cambridge: Cambridge University Press, 1992), 270–328 (318–24); E. Westney, 'Individuation and Literature: Zakariyyā Tāmir and his Café Man', in *Marginal Voices in Literature and Society: individual and society in the Mediterranean Muslim world*, ed. R. Ostle et al. (Strasbourg: European Science Foundation, 2001), 189–99.

The short story is divided into two parts, the first of which bears the subtitle 'al-Tazwīr' [The Forgery], which implicitly postulates the existence of an original. The subtitle of the second part 'al-Layla al-akhīra' [The Last Night] hints at the end of a series of nights; in combination with the main title of the short story, the keyword 'night' again presents an *intertextual* allusion to *The Arabian Nights*. As a clearly *intertextual* element the Arabic title *Ḥikāyāt alf layla wa-layla* of the famous story collection is quoted in the first part of Tāmir's short story.

Regarding the aspect of *hypertextuality*, both parts are parodies of the frame-story of *Alf layla wa-layla*, that is, satiric transformations of the content, while preserving most characteristic features.[21] As is well known, in *Alf layla wa-layla* the wise Shahrazād saves her life by telling stories every night and thus cures King Shahriyār of his thirst for revenge on women after having been cheated by his first wife. The first part of Tāmir's short story, which bears the subtitle 'The Forgery', presents the same *story* with changed roles and alienation effects: when the Queen Shahrazād asks her husband Shahriyār in the 1001st night to entertain her with exciting stories as usual, he refuses, arguing that, after working for a thousand nights, he deserves a rest. In view of his defiance she has him beheaded like her former husbands and during the following days invites 'reliable men of letters'[22] to rewrite *The Nights*. So the authenticity of the discourse of the frame-story handed down by tradition is questioned — an indirect (*metatextual*) commentary. Forgery of (hi)stories and despotism are the topics — indicating parallels to censorship and political oppression of the present.

In the second part, 'The last night', the action shifts to another stratum of society and to the present: Shahrazād, the daughter of a shoemaker, suggests telling stories to her newly-wed husband, the bootblack Shahriyār, on their wedding night, as tradition in future would relate about the two of them. But Shahriyār prefers the television broadcast of a football match, a soap opera and the film *Superman*, and he threatens to kill Shahrazād, if she does not keep silent. 'So Shahrazād was frightened and fell silent like every Arab man and Arab woman.'[23] Two reasons are given for the decline of the culture of story-telling: first, the replacement of the word by the modern media

21 *Metzler Literatur Lexikon. Begriffe und Definitionen*, eds Günther and Irmgard Schweikle (Stuttgart: Metzler, 1990), 342 ; Genette, *Palimpsestes* (1993), 33f.

22 Tāmir, 'Shahriyār', 234.

23 Ibid., 235.

of film and television and, second, the suppression of freedom of speech, which befalls both sexes at long last. Both parts deal with the end of narration. While Shahrazād in the *Arabian Nights* saved her life by narrating, in Tāmir's story the refusal to narrate leads to death and the ban on narrating to silence respectively: after 'the last night' no story-telling will take place.

So far as *archetextuality* is concerned (references to the genre conventions of the hypotext), which is here closely connected with *metatextuality*, the message as to contents is supported by form. It is true that there is a division into nights, but the short story only deals with the end in a series, the 1001st and the 'last night' respectively. In contrast to the extensive cycle of narration of the *hypotext*, with its sophisticated frame-within-frame structure, we here have only the sequence of two disparate stories, the smallest possible variant of a cycle of narration, so to say, reduced to a minimum before Shahrazād falls silent. So, by the inversion of the *hypotext*, both as to contents and formally, Tāmir parodistically combines the affirmation of the heritage — in this case the heritage of the highly developed, many-centuries-old Arabic *oral tradition* — with criticism of the cultural development and the political situation of the present.[24]

Muḥammad Jibrīl, Zahrat al-Ṣabāḥ *(1995)*

The second text to be analysed here is *Zahrat al-Ṣabāḥ*,[25] by the Egyptian writer Muḥammad Jibrīl,[26] which shows an extraordinarily high degree of

24 For further aspects of intertextuality in Tāmir's texts see Peter Dové, 'Probleme der Intertextualität im Werk von Zakarīyā Tāmir', *Asiatische Studien/Etudes Asiatiques* 55 (2001), 961–9, and Peter Dové, *Erzählte Tradition. Historische und literarische Figuren im Werk Zakarīyā Tāmirs. Eine narratologische Analyse* (Wiesbaden: Reichert, forthcoming 2006).

25 Muḥammad Jibrīl, *Zahrat al-Ṣabāḥ* (Cairo: al-Hay'a al-Miṣriyya al-ᶜĀmma lil-Kitāb, 1995).

26 Muḥammad Jibrīl, born 1938 in Alexandria, author of more than 25 novels to date, as well as nine short-story collections, an autobiography and several studies in literary criticism; he started publishing in 1970; 1975 awarded State Encouragement Prize in Literature; worked as a journalist from 1960 (for nine years editor-in-chief of the Omani newspaper *al-Waṭan* and for many years editor-in-chief of the feature section of the Egyptian newspaper *al-Masā'*) (information based on Shawqī Badr Yūsuf, Bibliyūjrāfiyā al-riwāya fī gharb wa-wasṭ al-diltā (Cairo: al-Hay'a al-ᶜāmma li-quṣūr al-thaqāfa, 1994), 328–349 (330) and

transtextuality, both explicit and clearly marked on the one hand, and implicit on the other hand.

Paratextuality

The title, which can be read *Zahrat al-Ṣabāḥ* [Blossom/Beauty of the Morning] or *Zuhrat al-Ṣabāḥ* [Light / Brilliancy / Beauty of the Morning], suggests a flourishing, a turn to the positive: a success in the morning. While this alone does not take the reader very far, the headings of the chapters immediately give a clear signal: 'The Second Night', 'The First Night', 'The Third Night', and so on. All the chapters have as a heading a numbered night, ending with the 1090th. These headings express a strongly marked reference to the most famous Arabic work dealing with nights both as a topic and as a structural principle, the *Arabian Nights*.

The cover of *Zahrat al-Ṣabāḥ* shows a picture of a young lady with white skin, only lightly dressed, decorated with long chains of jewellery, her hair covered by a coloured scarf, probably of noble descent. Behind her stands a second female with dark skin, possibly a servant. Neither cover nor first page bears a subtitle.

If one consults another element of *paratext*, the back cover, one can read:

> Zahrat al-Ṣabāḥ is the girl who expects her role in the nights of the *Thousand Nights*.[27] Does Shahrazād fail to continue narrating, or does Shahriyār become bored? How could Zahrat al-Ṣabāḥ live in the shadow of fear all these nights? That is what Muḥammad Jibrīl deals with in these nights, in parallel with the nights of the *Thousand Nights*, which he intertwines with texts of our popular heritage: the legend (*usṭūra*), the heroic epic (*sīra*), the tale (*ḥikāya*) and the fable (*ḥaddūta*), thus presenting a pioneering, unprecedented work.

Story and narrative structure

Before turning to other categories of references to the *Arabian Nights* a short overview of the basic structure and the *story* is indispensable. The text contains 106 parts or episodes of widely varying lengths, each of them under the headline of a numbered night. After the third night, there are repeated gaps in the sequence of numbering, ranging from one to 86 nights. At first glance some parts appear to be more or less unconnected

interviews with the author 18 March 1990 and 21 November 1997).

27 Shortened title of *Alf layla wa-layla* often used by Arabic speakers.

and independent, but the majority of them are linked by a *story*. While the young Zahrat al-Ṣabāḥ, chosen for the night after Shahrazād, lives in fearful expectation of marriage to King Shahriyār and subsequent death, she is saved from day to day — or rather from night to night — by Shahrazād's strategy of saving her own life by storytelling. Not only Zahra's parents and Shahrazād's father, the *wazīr* Dandān, but also all the inhabitants of Cairo, especially those who have daughters, are scared by the series of marriages and subsequent murders initiated by the king's wrath at the betrayal of his first wife. During the change of the ideal ruler and the decline of order, political riots and uprisings take place, which are suppressed by force, with the use of torture. Zahrat al-Ṣabāḥ is gradually relieved of the dominating fear, when she falls in love with the merchant Sa^c^d al-Dākhilī, whom she marries secretly. And Shahrazād finally succeeds, as in *Alf layla wa-layla*, in curing the king of his vindictiveness towards women and saving her life and that of al-Ṣabāḥ, whereupon the King repents and the just rule of former times is restored.

Intertextuality

Not only have several names or characters — including those of Shahrazād, Shahriyār, his brother Shāhzamān, Shahrazād's sister Dunyāzād, and her father, the *wazīr* Dandān — been borrowed from the frame-story of *Alf layla wa-layla*, but an extraordinary number of quotations have also been thoroughly integrated into the text. Several quotations are marked by a preceding colon;[28] others by quotation marks;[29] some only by contrast with the grammatical person of the surrounding passages,[30] which signals that a literal quotation from *Alf layla wa-layla* has been included in the narrative discourse of *Zahrat al-Ṣabāḥ*. We are now, however, in the area of plagiarism, the category to which the considerably more numerous unmarked literal quotations belong.[31] The introduction to Shahrazād's narration every night in *Alf layla wa-layla* ('*balaghanī ayyuhā l-malik al-sa^c^īd*'[32]) and the formulation ending every night's narration ('*wa-ayna hādhā mimmā sa-uḥaddithukum bihi al-layla al-muqbila in ^c^ishtu wa-*

28 For example, ibid., 43, 44, 63, 260, 270, 271, 282.
29 For example, ibid., 206, 208, 219, 226, 229, 244.
30 Ibid., 36f.
31 For example, ibid., 36, 37, 273, 240.
32 'It came to my ears, O happy King'.

abqānī al-malik'),[33] both functioning as formulas because of their regular repetition, appear in an episode of Jibrīl's text in which Zahra imagines the rites of the evening session of Shahrazād, Shahriyār and Dunyāzād.[34]

Numerous stories included in *Alf layla wa-layla* are quoted by their name,[35] some being paraphrased in one to four sentences[36] — especially as long as Shahrazād's narrating is still unfamiliar to the court members — or else being referred to in dialogue[37] or narrative.[38] In the 1001st episode, in which the Shahrazād of Jibrīl's *opus* also presents her three sons and asks to be exempted from death because of them, Shahriyār delays his answer and frightens her once more. The reader's expectation of what the king should say from one's knowledge of *Alf layla wa-layla*, which corresponds with Shahrazād's expectation in Jibrīl's text, is anticipated by the unmarked quotation 'yā Shahrazād, wa-llāh, innī ᶜafawtu ᶜanki qabla majī' hā'ulā'i al-awlād' ('O Shahrazād, by God, I had acquitted you before these children came')[39] which seems to originate from Shahrazād's thoughts or consciousness and thus functions as a *stream of consciousness* in this context. Only then does Shahriyār fulfil all expectations by uttering / repeating this most decisive sentence.

Hypertextuality

These examples lead us to the central category of *hypertextuality*. In this respect, several aspects deserve attention: first, the picturing and continuation of the frame story with regard to action, setting and time. The radius of the action is widened considerably by the introduction of numerous secondary characters to illustrate the atmosphere of fear and violence.[40] Events are located in an historic Mamluk Cairo, as can be deduced from the

33 'What is this compared to what I shall tell you tomorrow if the King spares me and lets me live?'
34 Jibrīl, *Zahra*, 43f.; the first formula also 240.
35 For example, ibid., 7, 35, 39, 45, 55, 59, 63, 94, 97, 123, 139, 176, 202, 204, 206, 270.
36 For example, ibid., 35, 94, 100, 139, 204f., 260.
37 For example, ibid., 35, 46, 59, 94, 97, 111, 167, 204f., 239f., 262.
38 For example, ibid., 156.
39 Ibid., 273.
40 Aḥmad Darwīsh, *Taqniyyāt al-fann al-qaṣaṣī ᶜabra al-rāwī wa-al-ḥākī* (Cairo: Longman, 1998) in his chapter 'Muḥammad Jibrīl. ᶜindamā yamtazij al-ḥākī wa-al-rāwī fī « Zahrat al-Ṣabāḥ »', 255–67 (263).

depictions of the society and of the court life, in which many details of professions, tasks, ranks, rites and customs are reported.[41] The temporal prolongation until the 1090th night, as well as *Zahrat al-Ṣabāh*'s personal story, present a utopian element: though threatened by a deadly fate, her secret marriage and ensuing pregnancy indicate the beginning of a new age of self-determination, also supported by her name 'Blossom of the Morning'.

Events in *Zahrat al-Ṣabāḥ* are juxtaposed with stories of *Alf layla wa-layla* either by paralleling or mirroring on the one hand, or by contrasting on the other hand. To give a few examples: the king's recall of the betrayal by his first wife is mirrored by the *Tale of the Third Shaykh* (*Ḥikāyat al-shaykh ṣāḥib al-baghla*) of the second night of *Alf layla wa-layla*, a story that also deals with the betrayal by a wife. In *Zahrat al-Ṣabāḥ* this story is also told on the second night, as the reader comes to know on the seventh night.[42] Thanks to Muḥammad Jibrīl's very careful composition the temporal distribution of stories and nights corresponds well.[43]

The technique of mirroring, however, is countered by the technique of contrasting. A parallel to the *Tale of the Merchant and The Demon* of *Alf layla wa-layla* is apparently constructed: like the merchant there, in *Zahrat al-Ṣabāḥ* a gardener is condemned to death, but when he asks for a period of temporary leave to solve pending matters at home this is denied to him.[44] While in *Alf layla wa-layla* the merchant can save his life a third at a time, thanks to the odd tales of the three *shuyūkh*, in *Zahrat al-Ṣabāḥ* — in addition to the gardener — three *shuyūkh* are tortured and killed: one of them for writing a petition of protest, another for citing a *qaṣīda* of Ibn al-Rūmī criticising the state of society, and the third one for participating in allegedly conspiratorial evening gatherings in a mosque.[45] Thus, on the one hand, *hy-*

41 Ibid., 3f., 11-20, passim. Jibrīl also dealt with topics and figures of Arab-Islamic history and tradition in earlier and more recent novels, e.g. in his historical novel *Qalʿat al-Jabal.* See Abier Bushnaq, *Der historische Roman Ägyptens. Eine literaturwissenschaftliche Untersuchung am Beispiel der Mamlukenromane* (Berlin: Klaus Schwarz, 2002), 411f.; Abd Allah Abu Hasha, 'Literatur und Identität. Überlegungen zu den Romanen *Henri Quatre* von Heinrich Mann und *qaʿlatu al-gabal* (Die Zitadelle auf dem Berge) von Muhammd Gibril', *Kairoer Germanistische Studien* 6 (1991), 483–502.

42 Ibid., 35.

43 Aḥmad Darwīsh comes to the same conclusion; see *Taqniyyāt*, 266.

44 Jibrīl, *Zahra*, 49f.

45 Ibid., 51–53, 61f., 65–68.

pertextuality here functions to picture the life of the society of *The Arabian Nights* in great detail, and, on the other hand, to criticise suppression and the abuse of power. By inversion of contents, in the given example by the inversion of the motif of storytelling as ransom, and in combination with effects of alienation,[46] light is shed on political circumstances of the present.

Archetextuality

Like *Alf layla wa-layla* also, *Zahrat al-Ṣabāḥ* is a cycle, that is, a sequence of literary texts of different length, structured by a system of nights-division.[47] But while *Alf layla wa-layla* has been transmitted in different versions and combinations, Jibrīl's text is of course fixed. The aspect of incompleteness of the old story-collections is imitated by omitting a different number of nights, the aspect of variation of the order of arrangement and of genres on the other hand by including quotations, paraphrases, or imitations of other genres of *popular literature*, like the heroic epic (*sīra*), the legend (*usṭūra*), also of Christian origin, and colloquial poems (*mawwāl, zajal*).[48] The insertion of more or less disparate 'oral' texts is made possible by the structural principle of the nights-division, in this corresponding with the *Arabian Nights,* which also drew on 'a large narrative repertoire'.[49] Thus, Muḥammad Jibrīl partially took up the artistry of the *Nights* which 'lay not in the invention of original fiction *ex nihilo* but in the creative arrangement of conventional material and traditional narrative motifs'[50] and creatively developed this further. All insertions echo, comment on, or satirise topics of the major narrative action — be it love, rebellion or suppression; they are partially integrated into the action, as Zahra's father, while controlling the markets as the *muḥtasib*, has the opportunity to listen

46 People collect stones for an uprising (263); the gardener is accused of having cut the words 'Shahriyār is a murderer' in the sweet basil (49).

47 This is regarded as paradigmatic for *Alf layla wa-layla*, but was not included in all transmitted collections.

48 Most of the famous heroes are present here: ᶜAntara ibn Shaddād (157, 168, 216, 282f.), Sayf ibn Dhī Yazan (186, 219, 229, 255), Dhāt al-Himma (139, 208, 251), al-Ẓāhir Baybars (95), Abū Zayd al-Hilālī (96, 259), Mār Jirjis (126).

49 Legends, chronicles, stories from independent 'analogue' traditions, poetic anthologies, formulaic systems, formulaic prose-rhyme clusters. David Pinault, 'Alf layla wa-layla' in *Encyclopedia of Arabic Literature*, ed. by J.S. Meisami and P. Starkey (London/New York: Routledge 1998), Vol. 1, 69–77 (74).

50 Ibid.

to several reciting or singing story-tellers and poets (*rāwī, qāṣṣ, shāʿir*); and they are usually introduced by a formula (usually *'qāla al-rāwī'*, 'the storyteller said'),[51] which also in *Alf layla wa-layla* serves as a marker for the oral performance or simply occurs at transition points.[52]

Viewed from a (post)modern perspective, however, Jibrīl has created a novel which partially employs the device of collage. By equipping the main persons with different characters and — though concealed — modern ideas and using common modernist narrative techniques (episodic structure, point of view technique, stream of consciousness, allegory) he has composed a novel in this respect comparable to Najīb Maḥfūẓ's novel *Layālī alf layla.*[53]

The division into nights in *Zahrat al-Ṣabāḥ* does not merely have the function of temporal division and providing a chronology to the narrative, but creates an additional level of meaning. For to survive night after night is vital for the two female protagonists, for their families, and, beyond their families, for the population of Cairo in general.

That the second night, which is planned to be fateful for Zahrat al-Ṣabāḥ by her marriage to Shahriyār and her consequent death, is uprooted from the chronological order and placed at the beginning,[54] demonstrates its specific significance for Zahrat al-Ṣabāḥ personally, as well as for one topic of the novel — fear and abuse of power — on a larger scale. During this second night her fate takes a different turn from the one expected, like Shahrazād's fate one night before. The focus of interest thus shifts to Zahrat al-Ṣabāḥ whose fate nonetheless remains closely connected with that of Shahrazād, as is also clear from the fact that the counting of the nights starts from Shahrazād's viewpoint.

51 Jibrīl, *Zahra,* 96, 126, 179, 208, 211, 216, 219, 226, 229, 231–3, 243–4, 251, 255, 284.

52 Pinault, 'Alf layla', 72.

53 Najīb Maḥfūẓ, *Layālī alf layla* (Cairo: Maktabat Miṣr, 1982) presents a highlight of a narrative transformation of *Alf layla wa-layla* with a rich net of references. See also Rasheed El-Enany, *Naguib Mahfouz: The Pursuit of Meaning* (London / New York: Routledge, 1993), 159–68; Ferial J. Ghazoul, *Nocturnal Poetics.* The Arabian Nights *in Comparative Context* (Cairo: AUC Press, 1996), 134–49.

54 The author considered it necessary to help the reader by adding a footnote (another *paratextual* element) to the headline 'The first night' above the second chapter: 'With respect to the narration an exchange of the first and the second chapter took place' (8).

Metatexuality

Narrating is not only vital for Shahrazād and Zahrat al-Ṣabāḥ, it is also the second central topic of the whole text. The course of events takes an unexpected turn with Shahrazād's narration of '*a* story of *a* merchant with *a* demon',[55] as is reported full of amazement. Shahrazād's tales arouse astonishment and fascination, not only on the part of Shahriyār, but also on the part of several other listeners. Thanks to the housekeeper (*qahrawāna*) Najwā, who is allowed to listen behind a curtain in the harem, Shahrazād's stories are transmitted to the secretary, that is, Zahra's father, who tells the stories sometimes to his wife, but always to his daughter, who relates them to her beloved later husband.[56] Thus a chain of transmitters, a sort of *isnād*, is developed. The Arabic *oral tradition* of story-telling and of transmission is celebrated in an entertaining way.

With that, we arrive at the last of Genette's categories of references which has been deferred until now: *metatextuality*, which in this case involves numerous comments on the modes of presentation and perception. Time and again, narration and the act of narrating are topics of conversation and of the narrative in *Zahrat al-Ṣabāḥ*. The act of narrating is questioned, when the persons worry about their technique of narration: whether they have narrated well,[57] or not chosen well;[58] how to achieve interest and suspense, be it by embellishment,[59] frame-within-frame technique,[60] or interruption.[61]

Another point of discussion is the play with parallelisms between reality and imagination, that is, between the fictitious reality of the novel and the invention of fiction in it, and between the narrated world of the text and present day reality, thus doubling or rather multiplying the layers of meaning. Several times, Shahrazād has to calm Shahriyār down with a reply like 'this is an invention from fantasy',[62] when he time and again threatens to equate the behaviour of fictitious persons with that of his subjects, or on the other

55 Ibid., 7 [my italics].
56 Ibid., 43–45, 54, 206f.
57 Ibid., 39.
58 Ibid., 207.
59 Ibid., 45.
60 Ibid., 44, 271.
61 Ibid., 7, 36, 45. The tale of Ṣalāḥ al-Dīn is reported to take more than 16 nights (97). On the art of interruption, see R. van Leeuwen, 'The Art of Interruption: the *Thousand and One Nights* and Jan Potócki', *MEL* 7 (2004), 183–98.
62 Ibid., 40; also 59, 111,124, 140.

hand, gradually learns his lesson.[63] Blurring of the diegetic levels[64] sometimes further teases the reader's expectations.

Conclusion

Muḥammad Jibrīl employs the transformation of different *hypotexts,* parody and political allegory for criticism of political and gender conditions past and present. But in contrast to Zakariyyā Tāmir's parody 'Shahriyār wa-Shahrazād' this happens only partially by inversion and irony. Moreover, in *Zahrat al-Ṣabāḥ* the affirmation of the cultural heritage redounds to a celebration of narration and transmission, a homage to the Arabic *oral tradition,* including several other popular genres in addition to its most famous *opus*, *Alf layla wa-layla*,[65]. The increased *transtextual* reference to older texts, the parodistic play with elements of the tradition, the combination of different types of texts and discourses, the metafictional discussion of the act of narration, the replacement of unambiguity by ambiguity and consequently the questioning of the single, generally accepted discourse by presenting different versions of the same *story* — all these are aspects of postmodern narration. Both Tāmir's short story and Jibrīl's novel show distinctive features of hybridity — another common phenomenon of postmodern literature — and thus present significant generic variations.[66]

63 Ibid., 90, 124.

64 Zahrat al-Ṣabāḥ meets Hārūn al-Rashīd, his *wazīr* Ja^{c}far al-Barmakī and his servant Masrūr in the streets of Baghdad (107–9); the events of the prologue in which both Shahriyār and his brother Shāhzamān recognise being betrayed by their wives are presented partly as if Shahriyār recollects his own memories, partly as if he has a vision of another King Shahriyār and his brother (36–38).

65 In this *transtextual* process of re-writing the *Nights*, not all authors are aware of the extent to which the shape of the collections, and of those available nowadays, has been influenced by European 'Orientalists'. See Grotzfeld, 'Dreihundert Jahre *1001 Nacht* in Europa: *1001 Nacht* in geteiltem Besitz von Orient und Okzident' in: *Dreihundert Jahre* (n. 1), 9–30 and Ouyang: *Genres* (n. 3), 125.

66 On this topic see Ouyang, *Genres* and *eadem*, 'Whose Story is It? Sindbad the Sailor in literature and film', *MEL* 7 (2004), 133–147.

Intertextual and Intratextual Processes in *al-Malik huwa al-malik* by Sa^c^d Allāh Wannūs

Rosella Dorigo
Università Ca' Foscari, Venice

I. Introduction

The text of *al-Malik huwa al-malik* (1978),[1] by the late Syrian dramatist Sa^c^d Allāh Wannūs (1941–1997),[2] will be examined here with the aim of analysing its intertextual features and, at the same time, studying the process of textual interfaces produced by two previous literary works sharing some elements with it. I am referring to the play *Abū al-Ḥasan al-Mughaffal aw Hārūn al-Rashīd* (1848),[3] by the Lebanese dramatist Mārūn al-Naqqāsh (1817–1855),[4] and to the tale *Ḥikāyat al-Nā'im wa-al-yaqẓān*, included in the Catholic Beirut collection of *Alf layla wa-layla*, edited in 1889.[5] With regard to the two plays, a single literary analysis will be offered here, taking into account the theatrical elements only when explicitly referred to in the written text and only when necessary for my analysis. So, the paradigmatic process of the written theatrical text will be expressly separated from the act of staging: in other words, the interpretation of the two plays will not differ from that of any other literary written text.[6]

Mārūn al-Naqqāsh, one of the pioneers of the Arabic theatre, began writing in the middle of the nineteenth century, after travelling on

1 Sa^c^d Allāh Wannūs, *al-Malik huwa al-malik* (Damascus: Dār Ibn Rushd, 1978; repr. Dār al-Ādāb). See Muḥammad al-^c^Azzām, *Masraḥ Sa^c^d Allāh Wannūs* (Damascus: Dār al-^c^Alā' al-Dīn, 2003), 253.
2 The author, born in 1941, died in 1997. For his life and works see al-^c^Azzām (2003).
3 Yūsuf Najm, *al-Masraḥiyya fī al-adab al-^c^arabī al-ḥadīth* (Beirut: Dār al-thaqāfa, 1956), 367–81.
4 Ibid., 31–40.
5 *Alf layla wa-layla* (Beirut: al-Maṭba^c^a al-Kāthūlikiyya, 1889), pp. 153 *et seq.*
6 For a critical comparison between literary semiotics and theatrical semiotics, see Marcello Pagnini, *Pragmatica della letteratura* (Palermo: Sellerio, 1988).

business to Egypt and Italy, where he went to acquaint himself with Italian opera and European theatre. After *al-Bakhīl* [The Miser], in 1847, inspired by Molière, the writer created and staged, between the end of 1849 and the beginning of 1850, the play *Abū al-Ḥasan al-Mughaffal aw Hārūn al-Rashīd*, turning to a tale of the *Arabian Nights*,[7] and, in 1853, he composed a third play, *al-Ḥasūd al-salīṭ* [The Envious Insolent], again inspired by Molière. He used different sources of inspiration, both from the Western dramatic literature and from Arabic traditional fiction. As far as I know, he never expressed critical theories on Arab drama, except some generic observations about the great difficulty, for a writer of that epoch, to compose and stage texts belonging to a literary *genre* which was considered absolutely new.

On the contrary, some theoretical declarations on the functions of modern Arabic theatre and on its bonds between the traditional heritage and the modern public were published by Sa^c^d Allāh Wannūs from the very beginning of his career as a dramatist.[8] On the basis of his theories about theatre, he aimed to strengthen the political conscience in his audience. With this aim, he composed some clearly symbolic plays, such as *Ḥaflat samar min ajl al-khāmis min Ḥazīrān* (1968), where he faced the themes of the consequences of the 1967 defeat and put in evidence the collective Arab responsibility towards it. In his subsequent works, *Mughāmarat ra's al-mamlūk Jābir* (1971) and *Sahra ma^c^a Abī Khalīl al-Qabbānī* (1972), he showed an increasing interest in the fabric of local culture and in historical events. With the play *al-Malik huwa al-malik* (1978), a little later, he concentrated on the use of 'words' as a completely autonomous means of expression, loading this work with a relevant amount of abstraction, even maintaining his attention to the local cultural heritage.[9]

The literary critic ^c^Abd Allāh Abū Hayf[10] pointed out that Wannūs took the theme of his play *al-Malik huwa al-malik* from a tale of the *Arabian Nights* to explain the real nature of the system of laws governing modern

7 See Rachid Bencheneb, 'Les Mille et une nuits et les origines du théâtre arabe', *Studia Islamica* 40 (1974), 133–60.

8 Sa^c^d Allāh Wannūs, 'Bayānāt li-masraḥ ^c^arabī jadīd', *al-Ma^c^rifa* 104 (1970), 5–32, special issue on theatre.

9 Ismā^c^īl Fahd Ismā^c^īl, *al-Kalima; al-Fi^c^l* (Beirut: Dār al-Ādāb, 1981).

10 ^c^Abd Allāh Abū Hayf, *al-Ta'sīs: maqālāt fī al-masraḥ al-sūrī* (Beirut, 1977; Damascus: Ittiḥād al-Kuttāb al-^c^Arab, 1979), 171–2.

countries, because he was convinced that the choice of this literary loan from so well-known a work could act effectively on the minds and consciences of his public. All this is clear, reading the text, and it is both evident in its connection with the *Arabian Nights*. Nevertheless, looking for an eventual hypotext relating to *al-Malik huwa al-malik*, I should like to refer to a chronologically more recent text, the play by Naqqāsh, *Abū al-Ḥasan al-Mughaffal*, which was equally inspired, as I have already mentioned, by the tale *al-Nā'im wa-al-yaqẓān*, included in one of the editions of the *Nights* which was evidently known to the dramatist.[11] As regards the relationship between *Abū al-Ḥasan al-Mughaffal* by Naqqāsh and *al-Malik huwa al-malik* by Wannūs, it is possible to affirm that both took their inspiration from the same earlier tale, following the practice, common in that period, of turning to themes and motives of local tradition in addition to Western literature.[12] An intertextual analysis between the two plays and the tale of the *Nights* could lead us to assign the role of progenitor to the tale, in common with the two plays: from this point of view the tale could be considered an archetext, which generated a second, more recent, hypotext, comparable to the modern hypertext.

II. Plot and structure of the three texts

A structural analysis reveals some elements shared by the three texts. Let us call the oldest text 'A', that from the nineteenth century 'B', and the contemporary text 'C'.

Plot

Text A deals with an episode connected with the life of the ᶜAbbasid caliph, Hārūn al-Rashīd, who was said to have a habit of disguising

11 It is presented as the 153rd 'Night'. See the Catholic edition of Beirut. The tale does not appear in the Calcutta edition (1839–1842), nor in the Cairo edition (Bulaq, 1835).

12 Among the works on the subject, see Jacob M. Landau, *Études sur le théâtre et le cinéma arabes* (Paris: Maisonneuve et Larose, 1965); Atia Abul Naga, *Les Sources françaises du théâtre égyptien, 1870–1939* (Algers: Société Nationale et de Diffusion, 1972); M.M. Badawi, *Early Arabic Drama* (Cambridge: Cambridge University Press, 1988).

himself as a commoner and walking in the streets of Baghdad by night. Once, during these wanderings with his execution Masrūr, he met the merchant Abū al-Ḥasan, who had a dream of being a caliph one day, just to take revenge on his previous friends who had ruined him, reducing him to misery, by making him spend all his money on drinks and feasts. Hārūn al-Rashīd, unrecognised, was invited by the man to have dinner with him, and during the night devised a trick against him. With Masrūr, he drugged the merchant and took him to the palace, making the merchant awake the following morning in place of the caliph. Reality and dream were confused in the mind of the poor man when he woke up, because everybody in the court treated him as a caliph, to the point that he began acting as if he really was one. The trick was concluded at the end of the day, when the merchant was drugged again and taken back to his house and his bed. Although his mind was again terribly confused when he awoke, finally everything was clarified and a great sum of money was given to him, as recompense for his suffering.

A subtle irony permeates the tale, with some amusing and even paradoxical elements in the situations described, created by the transformation of one person into another. At the same time, the return to normality and to original roles averts the danger of any attack on royalty and power; the sleeper is awoken; reality takes its usual aspect again: the whim of the caliph is compensated through a sum of money given to the object of the trick.

Text B: The plot is very similar. There is also a merchant who was ruined and abandoned by people who were his friends only for his wealth. His dream to be a caliph came from his wish to take revenge against them and from his yearning to enjoy good food and splendid women. Hārūn al-Rashīd and his minister, Jaᶜfar, were informed about this man and his desires, so they decided to take the opportunity of amusing themselves. Helped by ᶜArqūb, the servant of Abū al-Ḥasan, they drugged the silly merchant and took him to the palace. Here they convinced him to be the caliph and for twenty-four hours he believed that he was Hārūn al-Rashīd. Of course, when he was taken back to his house again, he was so confused that he was thought to be mad by his relatives. The explanation of the caliph and a great sum given to everybody concludes the play and puts events back on the right track.

Text C shows some affinities with A and B: first of all, the idea of disguising and substituting the king by a commoner. The plot here is based on the story of a monarch who, oppressed by his boredom and conditioned by his royal role, decides to prepare a trick to get free from the annoyance of governing: a joke against people and country. The point of the joke is to give his throne and his mantle to the commoner Abū ᶜIzza and to dupe people by making them believe that the man on the throne is the real king. The trick is carried out, but Abū ᶜIzza, even if he is a stupid merchant ruined by bad friends, takes on his new role as if it has always been his. He assumes the personality of the real king and begins acting in his place. At the same time, the king's mind feels confused and he gradually looses his own personality: with his royal mantle, his crown and his throne he is no longer the king of the country. The conclusion of the story shows that when royalty is based only on exterior or superficial elements, its essence is like an empty pot, which could be filled up by anybody.

Structure

In the structure of the three texts some analogies are evident, at least from a formal point of view. The following four sequences form the structure of the story in all three: 1. Premise; 2. Dream; 3. Accomplishment; and 4. Consequences. Nevertheless, the content of each segment is slightly different in the third text, as shown in the following scheme:

Text A

1. *Premise*: the story of the merchant Abū al-Ḥasan and of his failure.
2. *Dream*: the merchant dreams of being a caliph.
3. *Accomplishment*: disguising and substitution of personality.
4. *Consequences*: temporary, with a final return to the previous situation.

Text B

1. *Premise*: the story of the merchant Abū al-Ḥasan and of his failure.
2. *Dream*: the merchant dreams of being a caliph.
3. *Accomplishment*: disguising and substitution of personality.
4. *Consequences*: temporary, with a final return to the previous situation.

Text C

1. *Premise*: the story of the king and of his boredom.
2. *Dream*: the king dreams of being a commoner.

3. *Accomplishment*: disguising and substitution of personality.
4. *Consequences*: the roles are inverted for ever.

As we can clearly see, the premise is based on a situation of inconvenience and unhappiness, a dream is the compensation to this pain, the realisation of the dream seems to meet the dreamer's requirements, and the consequences of the change of the roles are connected with the realisation of the dream itself. But actually, the first and the fourth sequences in texts A and B are not the same as text C. As an example, let us consider the first sequence, in order to compare the three texts, and let us analyse the reasons which gave birth to the trick.

Text A: In the tale structure, the premise to the main nucleus is constituted by the events which had happened to the merchant in the past. It recounts that Abū al-Ḥasan, after having squandered half of his patrimony in a pleasure-seeking life with false friends, had sworn that he would spend the remaining heritage of his father only with occasional companions and only for a night.[13] His dream of taking revenge on his false friends, who had first taken advantage of him and then abandoned him, is presented in the tale as a mere utopia, in which he indulged. He casually met the caliph and invited him to have dinner in his house, without recognising his majesty: in fact, the caliph was wandering in Baghdad with his executioner Masrūr, both disguised with the dresses of dervishes *ka-ᶜādatihimā* [as was their habit]. The caliph accepted the invitation of the poor man only because of his insistence: *mā zāla yalajju ᶜalayhi ḥattā ajābahu ilā suwālihi* [the man did not stop insisting with him until he complied with his request].[14] It is evident that the cruel trick was prepared by chance, without any previous intention on the part of the caliph.

Text B: The premise in the text is based on a sequence of dialogues, from which the story of the foolish merchant Abū al-Ḥasan emerges. The role of ᶜArqūb, the cunning servant who takes advantage of everything and everybody, is prevalent. The joke of drugging Abū al-Ḥasan, disguising him and making him think he could be the caliph himself, derives from the dream of the merchant, who should have wished to be powerful for one day, to take revenge against his enemies. There is no

13 *Alf layla wa-layla*, 153.
14 Ibid., 154.

previous declaration on the part of the caliph about wishing to prepare a cruel trick against anybody. The atmosphere is amusing; the situations are clearly those that one could have expected from a *riwāya muḍḥika* [comic play] at the time of Naqqāsh.[15]

Text C: The deep boredom of the king is explicitly put at the basis of the trick. In the premise he is the dreamer, not the merchant. And his dream is exactly the opposite of Abū al-Ḥasan's. His desire emerges from a dialogue between him and his prime minister, dialogue which introduces the process of disguise. In the text he says: *Mā ashadda ḍajarī wa-iᶜtilāl mizājī ayyuhā al-wazīr!*[16] [How heavy is my boredom and how bad is my humour, dear minister!] […] *Urīdu an alhuwa, urīdu an alᶜaba luᶜba sharisa*[17] [I want to amuse myself, I want to play a cruel joke] […] *Ladayya mayl shadīd ilā al-sukhriyya. Bi-al-ḍabṭ, hādhā huwa mā aḥtājuhu: an askhara bi-ᶜunf wa-qaswa!* [I have a great wish for joking; this is just what I need. / To joke against somebody with cruelty and violence!][18] […] *Urīdu an uᶜābitha bi-al-bilād wa-al-nās!* [I want to amuse myself with people and country!].[19] The trick against the merchant Abū ᶜIzza was used by the king in order to satisfy his desires.

III. Some examples of language comparison

If we make an intertextual analysis of the language, we can see that a certain number of affinities exist among the three texts, but at the same time some divergences are evident. The following paragraphs will show some examples.

Chronology and localisation

Places and times, when quoted, lead to an almost complete coincidence between A and B. In fact, in both texts, it is clearly explained that the events of the story happened at the time of Hārūn al-Rashīd, in the city of

15 Mārūn al-Naqqāsh, 'Abū al-Ḥasan al-Mughaffal', in Yūsuf Najm, *al-Masraḥ al-ᶜarabī. Dirāsāt wa-nuṣūṣ* (Beirut: Dār al-thaqāfa, 1961), 1.

16 Saᶜd Allāh Wannūs, *al-Malik huwa al-malik* (Beirut: Dār al-Ādāb, 2002), 17.

17 Ibid., 18.

18 Ibid.

19 Ibid.

Baghdad. This explanation is completely missing in C, where the author seems to have tried to make his play free from any precise feature bound to a previously defined place or time. The following examples may be useful.

Text A: At the very beginning one can read: *Kāna rajul tājir fī khilāfat Hārūn al-Rashīd*[20] [There was a merchant, during the caliphate of Hārūn al-Rashīd]. There is also a similar clear declaration that the events of the tale happened *fī madīnat Baghdād*[21] [in the city of Baghdad].

Text B: Among the main characters, who are listed at the beginning of the play, there is the name of the above-mentioned caliph, al-Khalīfa Hārūn al-Rashīd.[22] When the hero Abū al-Ḥasan enters the stage, he is described as a man wearing the clothes of a middle-class inhabitant of Baghdad. *Abū al-Ḥasan al-Mughaffal yaẓhur lābisan athwāb mutawassiṭat al-hāl ka-ahl Baghdād* and Salma is also described as wearing clothes typical of the girls of Baghdad: *Salmā, fī thiyāb banāt Baghdād.*[23]

Text C: The main characters are introduced without any name: simply as *al-malik* [the king], *al-wazīr* [the minister], *al-sayyāf* [the executioner], and so on.[24] Their clothes have no references to exact places, as can be read in the text: *al-jamīᶜ yartadūna malābis shakhṣiyyātihim*[25] [all are dressed with the typical clothes of their roles]. The place where the plot is developing might be found anywhere, because it is simply called *al-bilād* [the country], and the time might be yesterday, or today, or tomorrow, without any specification.

Characters

Texts A and B show several affinities, reflected indirectly in C, although sometimes the latter departs from them. It is also possible to find some examples in which text B departs from A and text C joins text B. For instance:—

20 *Alf layla wa-layla*, 153.
21 Ibid., 158.
22 al-Naqqāsh, 'Abū al-Ḥasan al-Mughaffal', in Najm, *al-Masraḥ al-ᶜarabī*, 71.
23 Ibid.
24 Wannūs, 5.
25 Ibid.

Text A: The main characters are the merchant Abū al-Ḥasan, his mother, the caliph Hārūn al-Rashīd, the executioner Masrūr, the minister Ja^{c}far.

Text B: The main characters are the same and have the same names as in Text A. Nevertheless, some figures which were not present in A can be found here, including the servant ^{c}Arqūb, whose cunning and arrogant behaviour resembles that of some of Goldoni's characters, or the two couples of lovers, Da^{c}d / Sa^{c}īd and Salmā / ^{c}Uthmān, recalling the heroes of some love intrigues created by Molière. The presence of those new characters, added to the others, was probably due to the wish of Naqqāsh to produce a play which could amuse the public, through the presentation on the stage of realistic situations and lively figures, well-known to everybody.[26]

Text C: Names and functions of some main characters show small changes. In fact, the merchant Abū al-Ḥasan of texts A and B becomes Abū ^{c}Izza here. Abū al-Ḥasan's mother, present in A and B, is here substituted by Abū ^{c}Izza's wife; the caliph al-Rashīd becomes simply *al-malik*; the executioner Masrūr, companion of al-Rashīd in his wanderings, becomes here a simple *sayyāf* and his place is taken by the prime minister Barbīr, present in A and B with the name Ja^{c}far and playing a less important role there. It is also interesting to notice that text C gives great importance to the figure of ^{c}Arqūb, present in B but totally missing in A.

IV. Intratextual elements in al-Malik huwa al-malik

It is possible to discover a relationship between the micro-structures constituted by some parts of the text and the general macro-structure constituted by the work in its whole complex. It is an example of intertexuality on which it is perhaps convenient to focus one's attention, in order to understand the text in its entirety. One can notice that, besides evident repetitions of words and concepts, there is a subtly different use of tenses and moods in verbs, combined with the introduction of new elements added to previous dialogues, giving them a new meaning. First of all I shall examine the *madkhal* [prologue] and the *khātima* [epilogue]

26 Bencheneb, *Les Milles et une nuits*, 139–40.

of *al-Malik huwa al-malik*, comparing them in their reciprocal action, on the basis of some examples which I consider significant.

Stage directions

At the beginning of both the prologue and the epilogue, some stage directions are given by the author between parentheses, to direct producers. These instructions show clear signs of an artificial correlation between the two parts, as one can see from the following few examples:—

Prologue: The opening scene is meticulously described, giving instructions for the actors of the play, their method of entering on the stage, their exact position in the scene, their role in the events. The word *ḥayawiyya* [liveliness] characterises their movements, that Wannūs wants to be forced and unnatural like those of acrobats in a circus. As noted above, their clothes should be suited to their roles in the play: *al-jamīᶜ yartadūna malābis shakhṣiyyātihim.*[27] Two characters, named ᶜUbayd and Zāhid, have the role of commenting on and coordinating people and events on the stage. As stated by the author, they *yaqūdāni al-luᶜba* [direct the play].

Epilogue: Again, one finds some instructions by the author between parentheses. In them there is a clear reference to the prologue, the intents and the dialogues of which are constantly repeated. For example, the word *ḥayawiyya* introducing the group of actors to the scene is the same as the prologue. And even the description of their clothes is the same. Wannūs explicitly declares that everything must be *kamā fī al-bidāya* [like at the beginning].[28]

Dialogues

Dialogues also show very similar features, between prologue and epilogue. First of all, both the term *luᶜba* and its derivations assumes particular relevance, although in the epilogue it shows that some changes have already happened.

27 Wannūs, 5.
28 Ibid., 108.

Prologue: The opening part is characterised by the words *Hiya luᶜba!* [It's a joke!], repeated by ᶜUbayd and Abū ᶜIzza.[29] A similar sentence, containing the same root [*lām–ᶜayn–bā*] is later uttered by the king, when he says *Naḥnu nalᶜab* [we are joking]. The term *luᶜba* is passed on from mouth to mouth in the scene. The same term completes the last lines of this part: *Sanabqā munzawīn fī hādhihī al-ḥikāya kamā huwa ḥālunā fī al-ḥayā. Marratan naẓharu hunā wa-marratan naẓharu hunāk, walākin fī fawāṣil ṣaghīra wa-khārija siyāq al-luᶜba.*[30] [We shall remain apart in this tale, just as we are in our life. Once we appear here and once there, but for short interludes and outside the context of the joke.]

Epilogue: The first words which are pronounced are again *Hiya luᶜba!* Some following sentences increase their effectiveness and, at the same time, join the epilogue to the events which had happened before. For instance, the man who had previously been the king of the country affirms: *Lā budda annahā luᶜba!* [Surely it is a joke!],[31] using the present tense, to deny any real change in the situation. Later the verb *laᶜiba*, which was used by the original king in the prologue in the present tense in the sentence *Naḥnu naᶜlab!* [We are joking!],[32] is used by the same king in the past tense: *laᶜibnā* [we joked] to mean that the action on the stage has already been concluded;[33] and some lines later, he says *Qālū kānat luᶜba* [They said it was a joke], underlining the presence of a doubt in his mind.[34] His words appear in clear contrast with those — only apparently very similar — of the new king: *Rubbamā kānat luᶜba!* [Maybe it was a joke!],[35] where the dubitative adverb *rubbamā* implies the monarch's refusal to admit that it had only been a joke, a simple fiction without concrete consequences.

29 Ibid., 5.
30 Ibid., 13.
31 Ibid., 108
32 Ibid., 5.
33 Ibid., 108.
34 Ibid., 109.
35 Ibid.

Concepts

Another relevant aspect of interference between the prologue and the epilogue in the text is constituted by the concepts of actions forbidden or allowed in the country, before and after the change of the king.

Prologue: In the dialogue between ᶜArqūb and Mansrūr the two terms *masmūḥ* [allowed] and *mamnūᶜ* [forbidden] are opposed to one another with obvious relevance to the actions that are considered dangerous by the government. Among the elements allowed one can find *al-khayāl* [illusion], *al-wahm* [fantasy], *al-ḥulm* [dream]; the same are forbidden when they become collective actions, reality, or revolts.[36]

Epilogue: Exactly the same sentences are used, to underline again what is allowed and what is forbidden in the country; but one can notice that there are two subtle changes here. First of all it is the new king himself who declares what is and what is not forbidden. Secondly, he adds *al-luᶜab* among the things forbidden, to underline that joking could be very dangerous for the caliph (as it was for the previous king).[37]

Tales

One can find a whole story, told both in the second act and in the epilogue, in exactly the same words. Its importance is evident, because it contains the key message of Wannūs about power.[38] In the second act ᶜUbyad tells ᶜIzza the story of a group of people who lived in the past. They were governed by an oppressive and unjust king and, after a long period of misery, decided to get free of the tyrant: they killed him, cut him into pieces and finally ate him. In this way they gained their freedom and, at the same time, 'became' the king, incorporating him in their bodies as food. One can read the following dialogue:

> *ᶜUbayd: 'Tarwī kutub al-tārīkh ᶜan jamāᶜa ḍāqa sawāduhā bi-al-ẓulm wa-al-majāᶜa wa-al-shaqā'. Fa-ishtaᶜala ghaḍabuhā wa-dhabaḥat malikahā. Thumma akalathā.'*
> *ᶜIzza (murtaᶜida): 'Akalū al-malik?'*
> *ᶜUbayd: 'Hākadhā yarwī al-tārīkh.'*

36 Ibid., 6–8.
37 Ibid., 109.
38 See R. Dorigo, 'Il teatro contemporaneo in Siria. L'impegno di Saᶜd Allāh Wannūs', *Quaderni di Studi Arabi* 1 (1983), 53–66.

ᶜIzza: 'A lam yatasammamū?'
ᶜUbayd: 'Bi-al-bidāya shaᶜarū bi-al-maghṣ. Wa-baᶜḍuhum taqayya'a. Walākin baᶜda fitra ṣaḥḥat jusūmuhum. Tasāwā al-nās wa-rāqat al-ḥayā. Thumma lam yabqa tanakkur wa-lā mutanakkirūn.'[39]
[ᶜUbayd: 'The history books record a community, a group of people, most of whom became angry against tyranny, starvation and suffering. Their fury broke out and they killed their king. Then they ate him.'
ᶜIzza (trembling): 'Did they eat the king?'
ᶜUbayd: 'The history books tell us so.'
ᶜIzza: 'Were they not poisoned?'
ᶜUbyad: 'At the beginning they had colic and some of them vomited. But after a short time their bodies recovered. People all became equal and life became attractive. No disguise was left, nor anyone disguised.']

Epilogue: The same story is repeated word by word by the characters in the final scene, after they have abandoned their roles and removed their clothes. Sentence by sentence, the story passes from mouth to mouth, in a slow voice; it is then repeated by the whole group together, as in a chorus. With the repetition of the story, told by the group, the play finishes.

V. Conclusion

When we examine the relationship between the above-mentioned tale from the *Nights* named *al-Nā'im wa-al-yaqẓān* (Text A), the play *Abū al-Ḥasan al-mughaffal* by Mārūn al-Naqqāsh (Text B), and *al-Malik huwa al-malik* by Saᶜd Allāh Wannūs (Text C), it is evident that the modern Syrian dramatist made extensive use of the two previous works to compose his text, but it is equally clear that he made use of them only for those elements that allowed him to achieve his aims as a politically and socially committed writer. To confirm his interest in the Arabic literature of the past and his conviction about its utility even now, in an interview in 1978, about *al-iqtibās* [literary adaptation] and *al-iᶜdād* [drafting] he declared:

39 Ibid., 54.

*Innanā naqtabisu aw nu*ᶜ*iddu li-annanā nabḥathu* ᶜ*an ru'yatinā al-*ᶜ*arabiyya al-mutajāwiba ma*ᶜ*a wāqi*ᶜ*inā. Aw li-annanā nuḥāwilu an yakūna fi*ᶜ*lunā al-masraḥī rāhinan, ay fa*ᶜᶜ*ālan hunā wa-al-ān.*[40]
[We adapt or compose because we are studying our Arab viewing, corresponding with our reality. Or because we are trying to make our theatrical action be up-to-date, that is efficacious here and now.]

Actually, evidence was given in my short analysis of the fact that Wannūs sometimes referred to the two previous texts exactly, maintaining their main elements and implicitly accepting the process of interrelationship between his work and the two others. An example of interaction [*tafā*ᶜ*ul*] between the older tale *al-Nā'im wa-al-yaqẓān*, Naqqāsh's play *Abū al-Ḥasan al-Mughaffal*, and the drama of Wannūs *al-Malik huwa al-malik* can be found in the dialectical link between royalty and disguise — an element that is present in all three works and which is the central pin for the substitution of the king with a common man, through the action of dressing up.

Sometimes, however, a process of rejection or transforming some characters or actions that were present in the two previous texts, was noted in the play by Wannūs. This behaviour confirms the idea that he wanted to liberate himself from several intellectual constraints implicit in the older literary heritage; or, at least, that he wanted to use them only as much as he desired. That is the reason why, in his play *al-Malik huwa al-malik*, he made his king anonymous, and similarly for time and place, just to be allowed to distinguish his king's behaviour and ideas from that which common people would have expected from a monarch. In this way, the author was certainly freed to pursue his dramatic and political aims. It is evident, in fact, that by creating a long section of his text as an explicit declaration of the king's need to harm somebody, Wannūs wanted to remove the features of the caliph Hārūn al-Rashīd from his king, offering his public the sight of a different character — cruel, arrogant, bored and silly enough to give his mantel and his crown to a common merchant and to threaten his royal power for a whim. At the same time, the dramatist carried out a kind of historical and literary *déplacement*, borrowing the figure of the caliph from the two previous texts, but using it in his texts

40 Saᶜd Allāh Wannūs, 'Mulāḥaẓa ḥawla al-iqtibās aw al-iᶜdād al-masraḥī', *Al-Ḥayā al-masraḥiyya* 6 (1978), 112. Quoted by Abū Hayf, *al-Ta'sīs*, 178. Also quoted by Ismāᶜīl, *al-Kalima; al-Fiᶜl*, 196.

only for its basic and symbolic value: the unspecific royalty represented by Hārūn al-Rashīd, his fame, his relevant position in the collective imagery. Although Wannūs removed his name, the city where he governed, and the time of his caliphate, his image would surely have remained in the mind of readers or audience.

Another example of rejection or transformation is offered by Wannūs when he concludes his play in a way differing from Texts A and B, and even diverging from the modern public's expectation. As a matter of fact he seems to infringe the rules of the logical conclusion of his text, as far as one could imagine it in conformity with the local literary tradition, and he seems to use the shock provoked in his audience as a means of obliging people to pay attention to the ending of the play, to think about its implications and to search their own conscience on the matter.

As regards the functions of the text itself, it is clear that Wannūs, with *al-Malik huwa al-malik*, wanted to create a very complex and elaborate play, in which every element has a precise function in the whole, and each part has a predetermined interior construction. The abundance of repetitions, correspondences and analogues between different parts of the text confirms this opinion. Moreover, it is possible to note the author's use of dialogue to increase the dramatic tension in his play, by repeating the same sentences, the same pronouns or the same verbs. For instance, at the end of the drama, when the concept of disguising is substituted by those of splitting and reflecting in a mirror, and, later, by that of a complete fusion of two different personalities in one, he utilises few essential sentences, some of which I shall quote as examples in what follows.

The deep doubt, which is a burden on the original king's mind, preventing him from realising the distinction between fiction and reality, between dream and joke, is expressed by his question *Man anā?* [Who am I?],[41] where the personal pronoun of the first person is the main object of attention. This question is followed by an attempt to reassure himself, by saying: *Anā al-malik, innī al-malik*[42] [I am the king, I am surely the king], although he is in terrible doubt at the sight of another man sitting on his throne. As if he was looking at himself in a mirror, he asks: *Anā*

41 Wannūs, *al-Malik*, 108.
42 Ibid.

huwa aw huwa anā?[43] [Am I him or is he me?]. This question shows his total loss of personality and draws the attention of the public to the second entity, different from that of the speaking person, superimposed on him but at the same time separated from him, for a curious trick of destiny which the man who was the king does not succeed in understanding or accepting.

To conclude, the meticulous construction of *al-Malik huwa al-malik*, the extremely attentive choice of words, structure and dialogues, their collocation and re-collocation in the text itself, offer a concrete example of intertextuality in which it is clear that the author wishes to be absolutely free in his composition, free to use or not use previous texts, free to borrow some elements from the literary Arab heritage but also free to modify his borrowings as far as he desires, free to create a deep relationship within the text itself at the level of language, symbols and political messages, even if this last action might limit the natural or spontaneous artistic value of his play.

43 Ibid.

From Intertext to Mixed Media: the case of Edwār al-Kharrāṭ

Robin C. Ostle
Oriental Institute, University of Oxford

This study takes as its starting point the work of scholars such as Magda al-Nowaihi (1994), Emma Westney (2000) and Anna Zambelli Sessona (2001) who have worked on intertext, memory and narration, both in general terms and with specific reference to Edwār al-Kharrāṭ and his Alexandrian Duet: *Turābuhā za^{c}farān* (1986), and *Yā banāt Iskandariyya* (1990). It then seeks to develop some of their conclusions in order to demonstrate that the peculiar nature of al-Kharrāṭ's intertextual strategies has the effect of pushing his writing to the very limits of the medium, to the extent that the writer comes close to a deliberate confusion of the arts. Of course, it not particularly surprising to point out that the *œuvre* of Edwār al-Kharrāṭ is more or less synonymous with intertext, or more precisely, it is possible to think of the majority of his work as one vast and continuous intertextual exercise. This is so to some extent in the traditional sense of the term 'intertext', in that al-Kharrāṭ's writings are replete with references and allusions to texts of all types and from all periods of the literatures which have shaped the life since childhood of someone whom few can match in the breadth of his reading across a wide range of literatures and cultures. But on reading Edwar al-Kharrāṭ, it soon becomes obvious that intertext is much more than a transformation or a re-creation of literary antecedents. Here the author engages in a constant process of the re-iterating and re-visiting of the texts which he himself has created. Mīkhā'īl is the author's *alter ego* in the present, in the past, and in the often frightening premonition-laden future; he appears and re-appears from text to text, in different places and times, accompanied and re-visited by Rāma, by the dragon, or by friends and members of his family. While this strategy is particularly clear in three of his three major novels which effectively form a trilogy — *Rāma wa-al-tinnīn* (1979), *al-Zaman al-ākhar* (1985), *Yaqīn al-^{c}aṭash* (1996) — it is the case that throughout his creative writing the same scenes and contexts re-appear from text to text and are re-played and re-iterated, as of course does

Alexandria which is his fundamental text, the city which is timeless and also time-fixed, usually in the 1930s and 1940s of the author's childhood and adolescence.

It has long been clear that the works of any creative writer are anything but a series of isolated or self-contained statements. Thus Albert Camus, in *Le Mythe de Sisyphe*,[1] asserts:

> De même, la création unique d'un homme se fortifie dans ses visages successifs et multiples que sont les œuvres. Les uns complètent les autres, les corrigent ou les rattrapent, les contredisent aussi.

Roland Barthes has noticed the pleasure authors may take in the re-writing and re-working of their texts, in spite of the danger of becoming imprisoned in one continuous and infinite text of lustreless repetition.[2] It has to be said that this is a prospect which al-Kharrāṭ not only does not shrink from, but generally welcomes. For him, Barthes's concept of the search for the infinite self within an infinite text is a constant and a positive feature of his creative endeavour:

> Yes ... I am writing a single book, but I think it is a book which by its nature doesn't conclude because it is intermingled with life itself. And although the experience of life is essentially one, it also has infinite variety in its different manifestations. I imagine then that my writing is one writing, but it is also extremely varied, or so I hope.[3]

Here he is echoing the words of William Faulkner who once remarked of his own work:[4] 'I am telling the same story over and over, which is, myself and the world.' The working and re-working of the same or similar motifs has been much more obvious in the plastic arts than in literature, but in literature as in the plastic arts, it would be wrong to think of such

1 Albert Camus, *Le Mythe de Sisyphe* (Paris: Gallimard, 1942).
2 Roland Barthes, *Roland Barthes par Roland Barthes* (Paris: Éditions du Seuil, 1975).
3 Edwār al-Kharrāṭ, *Akhbār al-Ādāb* (Cairo, 28th November 2004), 16.
4 A.W. Friedman, *William Faulkner* (New York: Frederick Ungar, 1984), 13, quoted in A. Zambelli Sessona, 'Intertextual Strategies and the Poetics of Identity in Imil Habibi's Literary Works', unpublished D. Phil. Thesis, University of Oxford (2001), 19.

exercises as examples of sterile repetition: after all, one would not take this view of Monet's succession of canvases of the façade of Rouen cathedral, nor of the numerous still-life studies of bottles by the Italian painter Giorgio Morandi (1890–1964). As for al-Kharrāṭ, he has always been very deliberate in his own literary re-iterations and re-incarnations, adopting this strategy as an essential feature of his creative work.

It becomes clear that when faced with this conscious and deliberate technique on the part of al-Kharrāṭ, the usual term 'intertextuality' is less than adequate. Much more appropriate to his case is 'Auto-intertextuality', a term used by Anna Zambelli Sessona which she encountered in the work of Edward W. Hood on the fiction of Gabriel García Márquez, and which she used as a critical category to good effect in her own excellent study of Imīl Ḥabībī.[5] The texts of Edwar al-Kharrāṭ are clearly the story of his 'self and the world', to coin Faulkner's phrase, and he tells the story in a very self-reflexive way. One need no longer wonder whether texts such as his Alexandrian Duet, *Turābuhā za^cfarān* and *Yā banāt Iskandariyya*, are short stories, novels or autobiographies: what they certainly are, along with many if not the majority of his texts, are creations of auto-intertextuality. One might parody the title of a previous EMTAR[6] publication and describe the work of al-Kharrāṭ as *Re-Writing the Self.*

It is clear that al-Kharrāṭ's major preoccupation in much of his work, and especially in the Alexandrian Duet, is memory, a subject which has already caught the attention of some of his finer critics:[7] this is not the remembering of characters, episodes and places in the past, but it is the actual working of memory. One could say that narrative for al-Kharrāṭ is an account of the act of recollection rather than of what is recollected, it is a recording of the way in which memory works.[8] The one fixed point in

5 Zambelli Sessona (2001), 16–20.

6 EMTAR = European Meeting of Teachers of Arabic Literature (since 2005 renamed EURAMAL = European Association for Modern Arabic Literature).

7 M. al-Nowaihi, 'Memory and Imagination in Edwār al-Kharrāṭ's *Turābuhā za^cfarān*', *Journal of Arabic Literature* 25 (1994), 34–57; Emma Westney, 'Arabic Literary Modernism: the short-story cycles and episodic novels of Imīl Ḥabībī and Idwār al-Kharrāṭ', unpublished D. Phil. Thesis, University of Oxford (2000), 183ff, 194ff.

8 See S. Wild, 'Searching for Beginnings in Modern Arabic Literature', in: R.C. Ostle, E. de Moor and S. Wild (eds), *Writing the Self: autobiographical writing*

these often disjointed waves of recollecting and imagining is Mīkhā'īl who is both narrator and main character: he is an old man and a child and an adolescent; he is both the first person and the third person as a narrative voice; he embodies both past and present as he tries to make sense of the unsolved puzzles and the loose threads that have marked his life; and true to the way in which memory works, Mīkhā'īl continues to re-visit and to re-consider these events, these people and these places as he re-writes his self. One of the most obvious effects of narrating the act of memory is that in traditional modernist fashion, linear mimetic narrative is completely de-constructed: it fluctuates from one time level to another; stories begin and have no conclusions. They are simply left hanging in the air, and on occasion they will re-appear or even be completed in another text. The overall effect is one of fragmentation and a complete lack of continuity. At times there are passages of lyrical and often mystical language that can be described as incomprehensible in their lack of apparent relation to other components in the texts in which they occur; they almost have the force of independent prose poems embedded within the text.[9]

To record the fact of the destruction of linear time and the dissolution of mimetic narrative in modernist writing is banal, whether in modern Arabic or in any other literature with which we are familiar. But when these common traits of the modernist style are combined with al-Kharrāṭ's auto-intertextual technique, this creates the following typical features of his writing:

(i) As al-Kharrāṭ writes the act of memory, it is clear that for him the timeless is much more significant than the time fixed and the contingent. He has made this clear in his own words:

> The absolute is incarnate in man, in the relative, transient and contingent … the category of 'time' is challenged and refuted, the problematic of temporality and eternity ceases to be posed, the relationship itself is negated

in modern Arabic literature (London: Saqi Books, 1998), 96.

9 See for example the hymn of *nūn* and the hymn of *mīm*, Edwār al-Kharrāṭ, *Turābuhā zaʿfarān* (2nd edn; Beirut: Dār al-Ādāb, 1991); English tr. Frances Liardet, *City of Saffron* (London: Quartet Books, 1989), 48–9, 166–7.

> ... Timelessness is the key conception of my fiction; or so I believe, as it is the key trait of Alexandria.[10]

Thus, just as the author has not ceased to walk the streets of Gheit el-Enab as a child and as an old man, there is some part of his soul and his love's passions that have grown from the God-preserved harbour, golden haven, vision of Alexander and work of Sostrates the mighty engineer, pearl of Cleopatra the eternal beauty.[11]

(ii) Because of this constant mingling of different temporal levels, the linkages between the different periods of time are often created by focusing on a particular theme, a particular motif, a particular place, or a particular male or female character type.

(iii) Because of this insistence on the perennial and the eternal, or on the divine that is incarnate in the human, character types are created which in the final analysis become removed from their specific spatial and temporal contexts. Consequently in their representation a process of de-personalisation and de-individualisation takes place.

The work of Emma Westney on the Alexandrian Duet has highlighted numerous practical examples of these traits of al-Kharrāṭ's writing, especially the manner in which the constantly shifting temporal levels move around certain themes or motifs, and this then drives the theme or the motif to provide the common thread of the fragmented narrative. This technique has been referred to as 'thematic clustering'.[12] For example the disjointed narrative episodes in the story 'al-Sayf al-brūnzī al-akhḍar' all revolve around the theme of loss.[13] There is the loss of his childhood and his childhood dwelling:

10 Ostle, Moor and Wild (1998), 17.

11 See Edwār al-Kharrāṭ, *Yā banāt Iskandariyya* (Beirut: Dār al-Ādāb, 1990); English tr. Francis Liardet, *Girls of Alexandria* (London: Quartet Books, 1993), 73.

12 See Sabry Hafez, 'The modern Arabic short story', *The Cambridge History of Arabic Literature: modern Arabic literature*, ed. M.M. Badawi (Cambridge: Cambridge University Press, 1992), 326; Westney (2000), 198ff.

13 al-Kharrāṭ (1989), 107–29, Liardet (tr.).

> These ruins, these remnants of babyhood and childhood and youth! Shattered and strewn as they are, they are still discernible, and not yet effaced. His heart is a heap of ruins, wrecked by the glories of past passions; but the columns are still standing steadfast against disintegration, against collapse.[14]

There is the loss of people that he loves, symbolised by the scream as he is in the grip of a nightmare:

> That scream! It is the same one which still moans on the edge of his sleep in his old age, beware it, try to skirt its menace as he might.
>
> The faint light is empty after the clamour of his scream, empty and silent. He smokes a cigarette, reclining against the headboard of his bed. Those whom he loves have gone to sleep. His affection for them, his gratitude pulses like a vein in the darkness of the night.[15]

This harping on the theme of loss is recurrent throughout the story: the loss of the precious silver half-franc which had been the benediction from the hands of the old Patriarch; the loss of the wooden inkstand carved in the shape of a camel which had come from Jerusalem and which was one of his most prized magic-charged possessions as a child; the loss of his beloved cousin Wiṭwāṭ.[16] Death is another variation on the theme of loss, which for example, permeates the story 'al-Nawāris bayḍā' al-jināḥ'[17] through different characters at different times: Mīkhā'īl as a child when he floated between life and death and heard the beating of the wings of angels and smelt their heavenly incense; the ghostly image of the dead prawns floating in phosphorescent light in the darkness of the kitchen from which emanates the slow music of death, a probably imaginary sound which is re-iterated at a later time from the portrait of St Simeon who can finally depart now that he has seen his salvation, a destiny that is also longed for by the ill and exhausted father of Mīkhā'īl.[18]

On occasion in al-Kharrāṭ's text a particular locality or detail of a locality will be revisited at different times, and the locality or the motif

14 Ibid., 107, Liardet (tr.).
15 Ibid., 114, Liardet (tr.).
16 Westney (2000), 199–201.
17 al-Kharrāṭ (1989), 85–106, Liardet (tr.).
18 Westney (2000), 201–204.

within it will take on different characteristics according to the temporal context: so the vine which grew on the wall enclosing the villa at the top of the stone stairway leading down to the edge of Stanley Beach changes according to the different phases of the narrator's life:[19] when he was a youthful poet he sees the spreading of branches as a form of orthography inscribing the beauty of creation, as the soft tendrils surround and respond to the pulsing emotions of his heart; when he was a revolutionary the convolutions of the creeping vine seemed to be charged with the power of his own ardour and frustration at the lack of social justice and truth; when he was yet again in the agony and ecstasy of a love affair, almost longing for his dragon with the gaping maw and the tongue of fire to bring a consuming finality to his suffering, the vine on the wall is hot and thick and heavy as it binds and couples in unquenchable lust. Finally, in his older age, in an older time, the wall itself is 'disfigured by black pocks and abrasions. It has suffered injuries and nobody cared'.[20] As for the vine itself, it has dried up and fallen away.

These then are some of the techniques through which al-Kharrāṭ conquers time as he narrates the act of memory, thereby creating his own omni-temporality. But we shall now focus in more detail on the effects that al-Kharrāṭ's auto-intertextual meanderings have on the nature of narrative, and in particular on the representation of characters. As the characters, especially the female characters, appear and re-appear from text to text, it is as though they start to meld into each other, to lose their individual characteristics, to become various manifestations of the *one man* or the *one woman*. One can see that this is partly al-Kharrāṭ's insistence on the absolute being incarnate in man, his insistence on the inextricable nature of the divine and the human, and his ultimate belief in timelessness. There is also surely here a constant sub-text based on the neo-Platonic philosophy which was associated with Alexandria, the city which is his ultimate symbol of the time-fixed and the timeless. The effects of his auto-intertextual narrative technique have been commented on by other critics, including Frances Liardet, a brilliant translator of al-Kharrāṭ's work:

19 al-Kharrāṭ (1993), 67–91, Liardet (tr.),
20 Ibid., 73, Liardet (tr.).

> The girls of Alexandria inhabit every corner of his beloved city ... They are not so much streams of consciousness as torrents of the subconscious; and they are saturated with the presence, not of any particular one of these Alexandrian girls, but of the one woman who is all of them. 'However many she is, she is one: however fleeting, she is eternal.'[21]

> Many women pass through the story of this city. They are all different: fair and dark and golden-brown, smiling, quiet, inscrutable, secret, humiliated, wounded, killed, gone. They are all essentially the same, for they are each a reflection of *nun,* the symbol of femaleness.[22]

Magda al-Nowaihi has made the same point: 'Essentially Mikha'il is in love with woman, of whom all these individual women are manifestations. Perhaps that is why the identity, even reality, of the beloved often remains vague.'[23]

Likewise Emma Westney has produced excellent and detailed analyses of the manner in which al-Kharrāṭ's individual characters merge into one. The opening story of *Yā banāt Iskandariyya* chronicles the youthful passion of Mīkhā'īl for Mona, but the character of Mona soon dissolves into a web of auto-intertextual references, back and forth in the Alexandrian Duet, involving Mona's sister Gamalat, involving the woman with whom Mīkhā'īl swims on Chatby Beach, and also Iskandara with whom he somehow merges into the vine trellis.[24] On occasion, all reference to individuality in the text ceases when the second person or the third person you/she is used, particularly when the 'you' or the 'she' becomes the votive object of mystical outpourings of passion and ecstasy.[25] What we are witnessing in these narratives of the act of memory, which visit and re-visit the different characters from text to text, is a cumulative process of de-personalisation, a stripping away of individualities. And yet the texts of al-Kharrāṭ are replete with striking passages of mimetic representation, with traditional narrative imitation, but these usually function as the starting point for the disappearance of mimetic

21 al-Kharrāṭ (1993), viii–ix, Liardet (tr.).
22 al-Kharrāṭ (1989), viii, Liardet (tr.).
23 al-Nowaihi (1994), 52.
24 Westney (2000), 265–7.
25 See for example, al-Kharrāṭ (1989), 148–9, Liardet (tr.).

representation, to be replaced by images, symbols and language which are more and more abstract.

It is this cultivation of the abstract in al-Kharrāṭ's narrative that recalls some of the more recent theoretical contributions to the problems of narrative in literature and narrative in the fine arts. One of the earliest modern landmarks in this debate was the essays by Gotthold Lessing composed in 1766 under the title of *Laocoön or The Limits of Painting and Poetry,* in which he wrote in trenchant fashion of the superficial manner in which some contemporary critics had interpreted the assertion by the Greek lyric poet Simonides (*ca.* 467 BC) that poetry is a speaking picture and painting a mute poem. According to Lessing, the consequences of similar but cruder generalisations in his own time had been to engender in poetry 'a mania for description and in painting a mania for allegory, by attempting to make the former a speaking picture ... and the latter a silent poem'.[26] In spite of this irritated recognition of the dangers of superficial confusion of the arts, the possible correspondences between the different artistic media have intrigued critics and creative artists ever since the very beginnings of art criticism. One of the first attempts at separation and classification of the arts was undertaken by Aristotle in the *Poetics,* but it was the Apulian poet Horace's lines on poetry and painting in the *Ars Poetica* which were often taken out of context by the ancient critics and taken to mean that poetry and painting were one and the same, apart from the obvious distinction that one employs colour and line and the other words and rhythm:

> Ut pictura poesis; erit, quae, si propius stes,
> Te capiat magis, et quaedam, si longius abstes.
> [Poetry is like painting: one work seizes your fancy if you stand close to it,
> Another if you stand at a distance.][27]

One of the most important recent contributions to the debate was by the American art critic Clement Greenberg who in a stream of remarkable writings between 1939 and 1949 established himself as one of the most important theoreticians of the *avant-garde*. Of particular relevance here is

26 G.E. Lessing, *Laocoön,* tr. E.A. McCormick (Indianapolis and New York: Bobbs-Merrill, 1962), 5.

27 Quoted in Lessing (1962), Introduction by E.A. McCormick, xii.

his reprise of Lessing in an article which he wrote in 1940 entitled 'Towards a Newer Laocoön'.[28] To cut short his sophisticated account, Greenberg maintains that in the seventeenth and eighteenth centuries, painting and sculpture were very much subservient to the dominant art form of literature as they strove to reproduce the effects of literature with their own versions of mimetic narrative: painting and sculpture became the ghosts or the stooges of literature. All emphasis is taken away from the medium and transferred to subject matter, story and the imitation of reality. Everything depends on the anecdote or the message. But in the nineteenth century, crucial changes occur: for Greenberg, the story of the fine arts from Courbet (1819–1877) onwards is the story of the reassertion of the medium over the significance of subject matter: impressionism, expressionism, cubism, and all the successor movements and styles of modern art see the increasing destruction of realistic pictorial space, and art generally becomes more and more abstract. The fact that something is abstract does not mean that it is non-representational. It is just that what it represents has nothing to do with realistic or mimetic illusion. The abstract may be concerned with the psychological or the sub- or supra-logical, or the surreal. It may aim at the consciousness of the reader or the spectator, rather than their intelligence.[29]

What makes these ideas of Greenberg relevant to this study of certain of al-Kharrāṭ's narrative techniques is that so much of what he says about the fine arts is completely applicable to literature. Indeed much of his early formation as a critic was moulded in literary criticism. He has a great deal to say about how poetry began to reach out to painting and sculpture in the nineteenth century through the work of Verhaeren, Gautier, the Parnassians and the Imagists, all of it designed to explore the possibilities of the word as a medium going far beyond the traditional functions of narrative. Of Mallarmé's practice of poetry, he says:

> To deliver poetry from the subject and to give full play to its true affective power it is necessary to free words from logic. The medium of poetry is isolated in the power of the word to evoke associations and to connote. Poetry subsists no longer in the relations between words as meanings, but in the

28 Clement Greenberg, *The Collected Essays and Criticism* (Chicago and London: University of Chicago Press, 1986), Jonathan O'Brian (ed.), Vol. I, *Perceptions and Judgments, 1939–1944*, 23–38.

29 Ibid., I, 33.

> relations between words as personalities composed of sound, history and possibilities of meaning... The poem still offers possibilities of meaning — but only possibilities. Should any of them be too precisely realized, the poem would lose the greater part of its efficacy, which is to agitate the consciousness with infinite possibilities by approaching the brink of meaning and yet never falling over it. The poet writes, not so much to express, as to create a thing which will operate upon the reader's consciousness to produce the emotion of poetry.[30]

Another highly relevant source in this context is Greenberg's famous essay 'Avant-Garde and Kitsch'[31] in which he argues with great panache that many of the greatest modern artists and writers have derived their chief inspiration from the mediums in which they work, rather than the narratives which they were relating:

> It is significant that Gide's most ambitious book is a novel about the writing of a novel, and that Joyce's *Ulysses* and *Finnegan's Wake* seem to be above all ... the reduction of experience to expression, for the sake of expression, the expression mattering more than what is being expressed.[32]

It seems not unreasonable to suggest that much of Greenberg's theory of the abstract in the fine arts and in literature has relevance to the auto-intertextual creations of Edwar al-Kharrāṭ who himself was and is such an important influence on the *avant-garde* in modern Arabic.[33] It would be wrong to suggest that al-Kharrāṭ's writing is all about art for art's sake or that his preoccupation with the medium of the word marginalises the significance of subject matter and content, if one wishes to push Greenberg's views to the extreme. The fact that literature or art is abstract in no sense implies that it is divorced from social or political contexts, as a close reading of most of al-Kharrāṭ's work makes clear, and none more so than the trilogy of novels *Rāma wa-al-tinnīn, al-Zaman al-ākhar*, and *Yaqīn*

30 Ibid., I, 29–34.
31 Ibid., I, 5–22.
32 Ibid., I, 10.
33 See Elisabeth Kendall, 'Literature, Journalism and the *avant-garde* in Egypt: from *al-Hilāl* to *Gallery 68*', unpublished D. Phil Thesis, University of Oxford (1997), 112–17.

al-ᶜaṭash. And yet as we have seen above, it is clear that al-Kharrāṭ's literary recordings of the working of memory have the following effects:

(i) The sharply focused, often brilliantly written, passages of mimetic narrative are usually the introductions to the complete dissolution of traditional imitation and representation, and the destruction of traditional narrative.

(ii) Individual characters as they are re-visited and re-created lose their individual characteristics. They become more abstract and removed from specific time, location and personality. This does not of course mean that as representations they are any less powerful, but simply that they are more abstract.

(iii) Undoubtedly, time and again the word asserts itself and leaps away into its own worlds of sounds and associations, far removed from any narrative or logical meaning. Two notable examples of this already quoted above are the prose poems of *nūn* and *mīm* in *Turābuhā zaᶜfarān* with their remarkable alliterative cadences. These are only two of the best known examples of a recurrent feature of al-Kharrāṭ's work: embedded prose poems which may be incomprehensible in relation to the surrounding text. To use Greenberg's phrases, these are cases of the writer, through the medium of words, working on the consciousness of the reader, rather than the intelligence.

This obsession with the medium of the word, which on numerous occasions in the Kharrāṭian text becomes 'the reduction of experience to expression, for the sake of expression, the expression mattering more than what is being expressed', to repeat Greenberg on James Joyce, probably explains the constant trans-generic nature of al-Kharrāṭ's writing that has been analysed in detail by al-Kharrāṭ himself[34] and other scholars who have worked on him.[35] His texts are an amalgam of short stories, novels,

34 Edwār al-Kharrāṭ, *al-Kitāba ᶜabr al-nawᶜiyya* (Cairo: Dār al-sharqiyyāt, 1994a).

35 Westney (2000), 7ff; B. Hallaq, 'Autobiography and Polyphony' in R.C. Ostle, E. de Moor and S. Wild (eds), *Writing the Self: autobiographical writing in modern Arabic literature* (London: Saqi Books, 1998), 205.

autobiography and collages of prose poems. But it is not just the genres of literature that are transgressed: time and again he seems to aspire to go beyond the medium of the word itself. His character images, predominantly of women, are de-personalised and even de-humanised, but the occasions on which they then become extensions of buildings and sculpture are too frequent to be coincidental. They are an integral part of the fabric of the female city of the memory and imagination that is Alexandria, the eternal site of his love's passions. Again and again his figures are invested with monumental and architectural qualities:

> Silent madonna of Ghobrial
> Her body is an altar, her legs two strong smooth draped columns with one secret and treasured capital. Baptismal font and source of the water of life from which I drink and never thirst.[36]

On occasion it is the stones themselves that are invested with human qualities, rather than vice versa:

> Fluid marble pulsing with the carnal clamour of the flesh, columns swayed by rocks, cushioned by the darkness of the obdurate heart, the thickness of bodily juices oozing from the ancient fissure of love and the marmoreal capitals crowned by stony sprays of vine, watered by grape wine laid down for ever and never broached; turning their face in silence to the horizon, questioning it in silence, edifices defying the years, the ages, the aeons and the earthquake of denial does not submit to them.[37]

Sometimes the monuments, which are the transmuted female figures, are vegetable rather than mineral in their substance:

> Imperial palm soaring smooth-limbed, clear-skinned brown, long leaf-tresses pinnate green, something vicious in the spikes of those soft buds ... Short palm trees line the Mahmudiya Canal as if it leads to an individual private Serapeum or to a personal Alexandrian Karnak whose palatial pillars stand unrelentingly firm, tumble constantly down.[38]

36 al-Kharrāṭ (1993), 56, Liardet (tr.).
37 Ibid., 124, Liardet (tr.).
38 Ibid., 104, Liardet (tr.).

These monumental abstract characters and images created and re-created by al-Kharrāṭ seem to reach out beyond the medium of the word. It is not coincidental that al-Kharrāṭ himself has long been engaged with painting and sculpture, both as a critic and in his practical collaborations with artists such as Aḥmad Mursī or ᶜAdlī Rizqallāh. In much of what he has written as a critic, he loses few opportunities to establish the links and the commonalities between the medium of the word and the image. In 1991, Aḥmad Mursī exhibited a series of lithographs entitled 'The Cavafis Suite' of which al-Kharrāṭ writes:

> It's as though his words and passages [here referring to Cavafis' poetry] are decisive in their direction if not in their belief, that is they are a graphic lithograph in language, as far as we can judge from the English translation especially, and the French one after that. You will not find in his work any sort of ornate frippery, scarcely a simile, metaphor or allusion, no dense or splashy colouring …
>
> These are precisely the features of Ahmad Mursi's lithographs.
>
> The figure of the severed horse's head in 'The Cavafis Suite' is not a metaphor but a visual value, it is not an idea laden with connotations, but it is line and figuration. Is it in the end a severed horse's head, or an ambiguous bird-figure, a stone statue or a heart muscle, the muscle of a physical love? All interpretations are possible.[39]

Significantly, the title of this study is *The Painter Ahmad Mursi: a figurative poet*. Aḥmad Mursī and ᶜAdlī Rizqallāh are the two artists with whom al-Kharrāṭ has long been associated both personally and profess-ionally. For example, the cover design of the novel *Makhlūqāt al-ashwāq al-ṭā'ira*[40] is by ᶜAdlī Rizqallāh while each of the nine parts contains drawings by Aḥmad Mursī. In addition to the detailed studies which he has produced on ᶜAdlī Rizqallāh,[41] he has also written commentaries in the form of prose poems on individual paintings.[42] The following extract

39 Edwār al-Kharrāṭ, *al-Fannān Aḥmad Mursī, shāᶜir tashkīlī* (Cairo: al-Hay'a al-ᶜāmma li-quṣūr al-thaqāfa, 1997), 13.

40 Edwār al-Kharrāṭ, *Makhlūqāt al-ashwāq al-ṭā'ira* (Cairo: al-Hay'a al-miṣriyya al-ᶜāmma lil-kitāb, 1992).

41 See for example, Edwār al-Kharrāṭ, *Ma'iyyāt 86*, catalogue with study on ᶜAdlī Rizqallāh (Cairo, 1986a).

42 Edwār al-Kharrāṭ, *Ta'wīl*. Prose poem on the painting by ᶜAdlī Rizqallāh,

from the prose poem 'Second Interpretation to Adly Rizkallah, Once Again' is a direct extension of the style of most of his narratives and a clear illustration of how close he feels as a writer to the painting of Rizqallāh:

> Marmoreal and tender planes, rounded sinuosities, topaz yellow, red as clay: and the topaz a pure, a longing yellow, clear and sullied
> Love's seductions speak to the woman-world in colours: they are without end
> Falcon-phoenix-colossal thigh, sundered and welded column of the world: a hidden blue, an iron, terra-cotta blue: or else flesh transparent, flourishing, ferocious, suppressed
> Hymn of the cosmos to Rama the monumental, the woman in perfection, priestess
> Of carnal mystical desire
> Hymn of colour and form to A'isha the butterfly, hovering on solid wings
> Hymn to colour and cosmos, a music a tempest incarnate: a spirit in gnosis consumed by fire: a song lifted to the woman beloved: the feverish incense of a rite of the body:
> savage colouration, dough in ferment, bathed in deliberation's light:
> conception architectural: coming to be in no Place. In no Time.[43]

The many responses in painting by ^{c}Adlī Rizqallāh to the writing of al-Kharrāṭ take the form of the numerous book covers that the artist has illustrated, especially for those works by the writer published by the Dār al-Ādāb in Beirut. The female figures that adorn the covers of the Beirut editions of *Turābuhā za^{c}farān* (1991), *Yā banāt Iskandariyya* (1990), *Rāma wa-all-tinnīn* (1992) or *al-Zaman al-ākhar* (1992) are massive, monumental and seductive at the same time. They are also abstract and de-personalised and the perfect visual complements to his writing.

In 1994 al-Kharrāṭ published *Iskandariyyatī* which he himself categorises as a 'novelistic collage'. It consists of a continuous stream of narrative, descriptive and lyrical fragments drawn from a wide variety of his own creative writing on the City of Saffron. He sees this verbal collage as being very close to the same technique known to the fine arts, for it puts together images and various fragments which may be from

'Testimony of Anger'. Printed pamphlet (Cairo, 1986b).

43 Quoted in A. Rizkallāh (1995), *Ma'iyyāt naḥtiyya: sculptural water colours. Kullu hādhā al-shi^{c}r* (Cairo, 1995), 18, Liardet (tr.).

different materials and various sources, thus producing a new picture.[44] In December 2004 al-Kharrāṭ actually put on his own art exhibition at the El-Hanager Art Centre in Cairo, consisting, perhaps not surprisingly, of some forty collages. Echoing much of his writing, the female form and the author's *persona* are dominant presences, amidst fragments of the different monuments, cultures and religions of Egypt's past and present (see cover illustrations). In this most creative of Egyptian artists, the desire for confusion of the arts, which was always a motive force behind his texts, has been taken a stage further.

44 Edwār al-Kharrāṭ, *Iskandariyyatī* (Cairo and Alexandria: Dār wa-maṭābiᶜ al-mustaqbal, 1994b), 5.

Intertextuality and the Arabic Literary Tradition in Edwār al-Kharrāṭ's *Stones of Bobello*

Paul Starkey
Durham University

This chapter will discuss some aspects of intertextuality and the Arabic literary tradition in Edwār al-Kharrāṭ's *Ḥijārat Bobello*. I have a particular interest in this book, having recently completed an English translation of it,[1] and I shall allude to the subject of translation later in this paper. I shall begin, however, with a very brief description of the work itself.

Ḥijārat Bobello [The Stones of Bobello] was first published in Arabic in 1992.[2] Cast in nine short chapters, it comprises a series of autobiographical reminiscences, centring largely on the narrator's (al-Kharrāṭ)'s childhood experiences of family and friends in the Egyptian Delta in the 1930s and 1940s, with some later material as al-Kharrāṭ indulges in 'flash-forwards' of various kinds — 'anachronies', to use Genette's terminology.[3] Despite the shift in the main location from Alexandria to the countryside, some parts of the social context — and indeed, some of the characters themselves — will already be familiar to readers of al-Kharrāṭ's earlier works, particularly *Yā banāt Iskandariyya* (1990) and *Turābuhā zaᶜfarān* (1986), either in the original Arabic or in one of the translations into several European languages: the English translations of those two works by Frances Liardet, published under the titles *Girls of Alexandria* and *City of Saffron* respectively, are indeed particularly fine examples of translation from modern Arabic literature

1 *Stones of Bobello*, tr. Paul Starkey (London: Saqi Books, 2005; Cairo, American University in Cairo Press, 2006).
2 Edwār al-Kharrāṭ, *Ḥijārat Bobello* (Beirut: Dār al-Ādāb, 1992).
3 On anachronies, see Gérard Genette, *Narrative Discourse*, tr. Jane E. Lewin (Ithaca, NY: Cornell Univrsity Press, 1980), 35–85; *idem*, *Narrative Discourse Revisited*, tr. Jane E. Lewin (Ithaca, NY: Cornell University Press, 1988), 21–32; also Shlomit Rimmon-Kenan, *Narrative Fiction: contemporary poetics* (London and New York: Methuen, 1983), 46–51.

into English.[4] In addition to the reappearance, or perhaps we should say, reworking, of these characters and locations from previous works, *Bobello* is also characterised by a strong and distinctive Coptic ambiance, with priests, deacons and indeed the church building itself, playing a prominent part in the narrative.

A number of intertextual features of al-Kharrāṭ's work are discussed elsewhere in this volume by Robin Ostle, who suggests, indeed, that it is possible to view the majority of his work as 'one vast and continuous intertextual exercise'.[5] I do not propose to go again over the ground covered by Ostle, except to note that, in terms of its relationships with al-Kharrāṭ's earlier writings, *Ḥijārat Bobello* conforms almost exactly to the patterns described in Ostle's earlier chapter. My concern in this chapter is rather to explore some of the ways in which intertextual dimensions intrude into this work, in terms of the way that the author orientates his text, either explicitly or implicitly, through its relationship with other texts in the Arabic and other literary traditions, and of the role that 'literature' in its widest sense plays in shaping the recalled environment of the narrator and the way in which he describes it. In so doing, we shall use the work of Genette and others as a theoretical background to the discussion, though I do not propose to make a detailed analysis on the basis of Genette's categories.

We begin with the title itself, together with those other items of the 'paratext' (to use Genette's term)[6] that precede, surround and inevitably to some extent influence the reader's reaction to the actual text itself. Immediately, the uninitiated potential reader — and we may almost certainly include even most well-educated Egyptians among the 'uninitiated' for this purpose — are confronted with a linguistic and cultural challenge: who, or what, is Bobello? Although it will be immediately obvious to all that the word is not Arabic, or even 'Arab', most readers are likely to be grateful for al-Kharrāṭ's explanation (in his

4 Edwār al-Kharrāṭ, *Yā banāt Iskandariyya* (Beirut: Dār al-Ādāb, 1990); English tr. Frances Liardet, *Girls of Alexandria* (London: Quartet Books, 1993) and Edwār al-Kharrāṭ, *Turābuhā zaᶜfarān* (2nd edn; Beirut: Dār al-Ādāb, 1991); English tr. Frances Liardet, *City of Saffron* (London: Quartet Books, 1989).

5 See above, p. 133.

6 On this, see Gérard Genette, *Paratexts: thresholds of interpretation*, tr. Jane E. Lewin (Cambridge: Cambridge University Press, 1997).

note preceding the text itself)[7] of this reference to an archaeological site near the town of Ṭarrāna in the Egyptian Delta: as the note explains, 'Bobello' is a corruption of 'Apollo', the Greek God of music, light and knowledge, whose followers had a centre of worship there. The implied cultural transformation is immediately picked up by al-Kharrāṭ on the first page of the narrative proper, where he refers to 'Apollo, the singer, the liberator, player of the lyre in ancient times — Apollo, who had now become the Beheira peasant Bobello ...'[8]

The title of the work, then, immediately situates it, or, at least, situates its location, in a culture that is neither Arab nor Islamic, nor indeed even Coptic. Things, however, are not so simple, for, almost as if to compensate for this pre-Islamic, pre-Christian cultural environment, the author at once introduces a further twist to the work's cultural setting by quoting from a work by the Islamic mystical poet al-Imām al-Shaᶜrānī, *al-Anwār al-qudsiyya*:[9]

لا يدري المحبّ فيمن حبّه / لا يتعيّن له محبوب

[The lover knows not who his love might be /
He has no destined lover.]

Before concluding these observations on paratexts, it is also worth noting at this point that, despite the strongly autobiographical nature of the work (to which we shall shortly return), it is described on the cover as a *riwāya* rather than a *sīra dhātiyya*, emphasising, perhaps, the imaginative qualities of the work over the autobiographical elements. In practice, however, like much of al-Kharrāṭ's writing, it defies classification, since the nine chapters are each effectively self-contained, the links between them being at times scarcely stronger than those between the present work and previous examples of al-Kharrāt's œuvre; parts of the work, moreover, read more like prose poetry than a reminiscence. In this respect, Roger Allen's remarks elsewhere in this volume on the

7 *Ḥijārat Bobello*, 5, *Stones of Bobello*, [5]. Subsequent references to the Arabic text and English translation will be given in abbreviated form, e.g. '5 / [5]'.

8 *Bobello*, 9 / 13.

9 Ibid., 7 / [6].

'pedantries of generic designation'[10] seem indeed particularly applicable to al-Kharrāṭ.

Let us, however, now turn to the text itself, in an attempt to uncover the sort of prior texts, the 'hypotexts'[11] (implicit or explicit), that underlie not only al-Kharrāṭ's text itself, but also, more importantly perhaps, the youthful experiences that provide the material for the text — for despite the description of the book as a *riwāya*, the autobiographical nature of the work, with its first-person narrator and its profusion of characters clearly drawn from life, will be clear to most readers even after a single page of text. The extent to which prior texts, both oral and written, 'literary' and commonplace, inform and shape the memory of the narrator, is also quickly apparent. Indeed, the very first words of the first chapter consist not of the narrator's words, but of the words of Uncle Selwanes, as he sits calmly on the bench at the side of the ferry, softly crooning a popular song:

يا اللي ظلمت الوداد / ورضيت بنار البعاد / أفديك بروحي
[*You who abused our passion / Accepting the fire of separation / For you I sacrifice my soul*][12]

On one level, the words represent a 'double recycling' of an oral text, for the popular song is first recalled and recited by Uncle Selwanes — whose own recitation is then recalled, and recorded, by the narrator several decades later. On another level, the words, with their implicit lament for lost love, seem to echo the quotation from the quite different 'register' of al-Imām al-Shaᶜrānī's poetry that preceded the text itself. Snippets from oral literature, popular songs and the like recur at intervals through the text, for al-Kharrāṭ's concern for the 'word' (spoken or written) is mercifully unrestrained by the normal 'canons' of Arabic literature. The youthful al-Kharrāṭ (or so we may suppose him to be), stranded in the midst of the Egyptian delta, eagerly awaits the daily delivery of *al-Ahrām*

10 See above, page 6.

11 For this term, see Genette, Gérard, *Palimpsestes: la littérature au second degré* (Paris: Seuil, 1982); English tr. Channa Newman and Claude Doubinsky, *Palimpsests: literature in the second degree* (Paris: Seuil, 1982; University of Nebraska Press, 1997).

12 *Bobello*, 9 / 13.

by express train, or (even more eagerly) the occasional arrival of the magazine *al-Ithnayn wa-al-Dunyā*, 'a copy of which reached us once in a blue moon, sent by my father from Alexandria when he could.'[13] The words of this publication, directly quoted, evoke a vanished world:

> The queen of the music-hall revue, Badi'a Masabni, would be at the Opera Casino in Ibrahim Square (tel: 44814) from Saturday 30 November 1940 presenting a second musical revue, *Two Lucky Hours* — seven scenes packed with novelties and surprises by the famous maestro Abu al-Sa'ud al-Ibyari, set to music by the composer Farid Ghuṣn ... and the participation of world-famous dancer Tahiyya Carioca and popular comic actor Isma'il Yasin, with first-class restaurant, American bar and music hall.[14]

This same publication, *al-Ithnayn wa-al-Dunyā*, played another role in the life of the young narrator, for a picture of one Su^{c}ād Fahmī, 'wearing a dress with a wide slash under the armpits, through which could be seen part of her breast',[15] was responsible, he recalls, for his first pleasures of sexual awareness, As for al-*Ahrām*, not only did the old copies of the paper provide the young author with a support for his writing paper, but some of the villagers found other uses for it too:

> Karima would collect old pages from the out-of-date copies of *al-Ahram* that her father read ... [She] would cut out with scissors the name 'Muhammad', in small or large point sizes equally, and choose clippings from an illustrated book called *New Love Letters* by Salim ʿAbd al-Ahad, which she would smooth and stick with glue ... on Ministry of Education-style exercise book paper, then send them ... as love letters to Muhammad, the son of the *Sheikh al-balad*. She would slip them into old, coverless copies of pocket stories or stories from Ilyas Antun Ilyas's *Modern Library*, translated by the late Tanyus ʿAbduh.[16]

It would be difficult, perhaps, to find a more physical manifestation than this of the concept of 'text recycling' that underlies some at least of the discussion of intertextuality!

13 Ibid., 16 / 18.
14 Ibid.
15 Ibid., 17 / 19.
16 Ibid., 57 / 48.

The examples quoted so far have involved comparatively little direct quotation from a written hypotext. *Ḥijārat Bobello*, however, also contains several passages in which al-Kharrāṭ advances his narrative by including within his text what appears to be, in some sense, a 'historical document' — a technique that has become commonplace among writers of a later generation.[17] On 22 November 1943, for example, Fanus Arsanius writes to Abu Amin, the narrator's father, to report that when his son had stayed with them he had behaved 'in exemplary fashion'.[18] A few months before, on 17 August 1943, Fanus had written to Abu Amin consoling him on the death of his son Émile from typhoid. This letter too is reproduced in full — recycled, as it were, to serve a purpose slightly different from, though clearly related to, that for which it was originally composed.[19] Other examples where information is conveyed through, or attributed to, prior texts include the news of the death of Khadra Mahmud, reported by *al-Balāgh*,[20] and an advertisement that appears in *al-Ahrām* on the very day that the Second World War has been declared.[21]

Thus far, we have been talking about rather mundane documents, which have led us some way, perhaps, from the 'Arabic literary heritage' that forms part of the title of this essay. The narrator's childhood, however, was also full of texts that reflected not merely one but two distinct, if intermingled, cultural traditions. Under a wide ledge in Aunt Rosa's house, for example, 'one might find a book of chants, Coptic language teaching books, the *Thousand and One Nights* in four parts with its covers missing, and one part of a lithographed version of the *Kitāb al-Aghānī* on yellow, dried-up paper, so fragile it was on the point of disintegrating.'[22] These items were not merely family heirlooms but were actually used. The narrator reads Aunt Rosa some pages of the *Alf Layla wa-Layla*, while in turn his sister Aida, who later died from typhoid, recites from the same book, though delicately leaving out some passages

17 Prominent examples by Egyptian authors include Jamāl al-Ghīṭānī's *al-Zaynī Barakāt*, Ṣunᶜallāh Ibrāhīm's *Dhāt* and Yūsuf al-Qaᶜīd's *Akhbār ᶜizbat al-Manīsī*. This list could of course be multiplied several times over without difficulty.

18 *Bobello*, 165–6 / 129–30.

19 Ibid., 142 / 111.

20 Ibid., 41–42 / 37.

21 Ibid., 176 / 108–9.

22 Ibid., 24 / 24.

that are considered too sexually explicit — though the narrator himself, who knows the *Alf Layla wa-Layla* more or less off by heart, is the only person to notice.[23]

Of particular interest, perhaps, if our concern is to locate the text in its cultural heritage, is the intermingling of the Christian and Islamic traditions at the level of folk belief. What to do, for example, to escape from a donkey possessed by the *jinn*? Here, the two religious traditions appear effortlessly to merge into one. The only escape was to plant a knife 'in the name of the Father and of the Son and of the Holy Spirit, One God, Amen, in the name of God, the Merciful, the Compassionate, and through the power of the Throne Verse, or the Sura of Ya Sin' — to plant a knife between the wicked *jinn*-donkey's flanks while you recited either 'Our Father, Who …' or else the *Fatiha*'.[24]

Despite the narrator's claim that he himself never bothered to learn the Lord's Prayer, the words of the Christian liturgy in fact figure rather prominently in certain sections of his account, most notably in the account of Fānūs and Wadīda's wedding, where al-Kharrāṭ constructs an elaborate interplay between the words of the priest, grounded in a solemn and unchanging tradition, and the narrator's recollection of the event. The effect is an almost musical one, somewhat akin to counterpoint — like a solemn chorale melody over which a new tune has been written.

> We stood on the open *mastaba* behind Father Andrawus, who began, *In the name of our Lord Jesus Christ, the Redeemer, we are here to celebrate the betrothal of the blessed Wadida, daughter of Sawiris and Amalia, to her fiancé, the blessed Fanus, son of Arsanius and Victoria. Let us pray and say together: 'Our Father ..'*
>
> When he raised his head and right arm to say the Lord's Prayer, so quiet, quick and garbled that hardly anyone could hear it, the sleeve of his wide black cloak fell from his arm, and a large, green, veined tattoo of the cross could be seen on his right wrist. We were following him and responding to him, *Oh true Lord, the Word of the One Eternal God, Oh you who gave human kind in betrothal to eternal joy*, when he quickly, almost mechanically, mumbled, *In His sublime and glorious incarnation ...*[25]

23 Ibid., 176 / 137–8.
24 Ibid., 170 / 133.
25 Ibid., 156 / 122.

It is worth mentioning here that the use of this technique — the interplay of two texts involving two different 'registers' — is not confined to this passage; we find it elsewhere, for example, where snatches of popular songs from time to time interrupt the flow of the main narrative. This passage, however, seems to me to be a pivotal passage, not only because of the very obvious contrast it implies between the words of the divine eternal and the rather trivial recollections of the narrator as a young boy, but also through the ending of the episode:

> ... and he sprinkled the blessed water with the drops of oil from the sacred chrism on the head of Aunt Wadida, on the head of Uncle Fanus, on the door of the house and on the ancient marble threshold engraved with hollow, sunken figures and writing in hieroglyphics now worn away by the march of footsteps over them, and the rubbing of the wide wooden door.[26]

Here, yet another, even more ancient, dimension is added to the solemnity of the liturgy, for the words and rituals of the Church lead us back to a yet older civilisation whose ancient texts, readable at best only by a few, are now lost to all.

Al-Kharrāṭ's sentiment here, which seems to combine a strong awareness of the eternal with an equally strong sense of the fragility and transitory nature of human life, would of course not be foreign to the pre-Islamic poet, for whom the passage of time was also evidenced by the faded inscriptions on the rocks:

فمدافع الريّان عرّي رسمها   خلقاً كما ضمن الوحيّ سلامها

[And the flood channels of Ar-Raiyan, their traces are stripped away
Worn smooth, just like writings on rocks][27]

There is no way, of course, of telling whether such an echo of a pre-Islamic Arabic literary tradition is a conscious or unconscious one on the part of the writer — and indeed, the question is probably of little or no importance. What does seem clear, however, is that such echoes do indeed exist, and that they form an integral part of the cultural

26 Ibid., 156 / 123.

27 Labīd, *Muᶜallaqa*, 2. English translation taken from Labid ibn Rabiah, *The Golden Ode*, tr. by William R. Polk (Cairo: AUC Press, 1977), 5.

contextualisation of the work, an example of intertextuality in its wider sense of 'participation in the discursive space of a culture'.[28]

This connection, or re-connection, with the Arabic literary tradition is to my mind particularly evident, almost explicit, in the Chapter entitled 'Farah al-ᶜArabawi',[29] a passage set this time not in a Coptic church but in the open sands of the Egyptian desert. I shall quote this passage at some length, because it seems to me to exemplify a certain sort of 'intertextuality' that is characteristic not only of the particular work under discussion, but indeed of much of al-Kharrāṭ's work — in the present instance manifesting itself in a distinctive combination of explicit references to a classical literary tradition, combined with an implicit equation between the recollected circumstances of the narrator as a young boy and the environment of his literary 'heroes'.

> Sometimes I would spend hours wandering freely in the desert, closing the tent up after everyone had taken what they needed for the day, and wandering alone in the sand. I never let the tops of the telegraph poles disappear from my eyes, however. These were my way marks to safety, and I was constantly checking that they were there (every moment, it seemed!), for I had read a lot about, and been scared by, the trials and tribulations of wandering in the desert. For all that, I was unable to resist the magic of the solitude and silence in the depths of the sand, when the tent and the workmen had disappeared, with the ballast machine and the smell of molten pitch, the black heaps of soft-bodied asphalt and gravel, and the tiny pieces of crushed white stones. I was sunk in my daydreams and fantasies, returning to the company of 'Umar ibn Abu Rabi'a and Majnun, and Buthayna's Jamil and Imru' al-Qays, to their lovers and sweethearts, and their fat-bellied Bedouin women with wide red cloths tied round their soft round bodies, their noses pierced with jagged-edged gold rings, and chins tattooed with two parallel lines, and dark blue colouring on their full lower lips, promising pleasure that was both carnal and refined.
>
> I found a broad, highish hill, covered with pebbles of different colours, shapes and sizes, soft to the touch. There were conical ones, purely shaped ones, wavy, granulated ones, round and polished ones, long and thick ones, and thin eroded ones — delicate white lines like hairs bunched around a grey

28 On this, see Jonathan Culler, *The Pursuit of Signs: semiotics, literature, deconstruction* (1981; London / New York: Routledge, 2001), 110–31.

29 *Bobello*, 120–45 / 95–114, especially 120–33 / 95–105.

circle inclining to black, and sharp, thin edges — the shining brown giving the smooth edge a softness at odds with its biting sharpness, while the shining white was dotted with fine spots that seemed to sparkle under the transparent pebble. Small sunken lines split the disintegrating carved faces. I said: 'The sea was here a thousand thousand years ago, the sea is still here, and will remain for a thousand thousand years.' I gathered together what I could of these treasures, lost with time. Had not every treasure been lost? Including the treasure of love? Were they not lost? Quick, sweet, soft bursts of laughter, one after the other, from a neat and beautiful mouth; brief glances, honeyed but sharp-edged, one after the other, from eyes completely calm; a boundless freedom within the soul; blue-winged birds flapping their wings expansively — had they been lost?

Every light has its shadow, of course, isn't that so?

Pure she was, pure she is, dark and cunning also, sometimes full of desire, but more often shy and reticent, like a child with her trusting nature and undisguised duplicity; sophisticated, worldly wise in her body, her boldness and her knowledge were frightening. She was forward and petulant, meek, submissive, humble and obedient, but fickle when I doubted her and my soul and my fate were in her hand — was this her secret? Was she lost? Where had she gone?[30]

This passage seems to me to be particularly rich in cultural allusion, as in addition to the explicit references to pre-Islamic and early Islamic poets and their lovers, beginning with Imru' al-Qays, it is suffused with the spirit and the themes of the pre-Islamic poet, contrasting the transitoriness of human existence with the endurance of nature reflected in the sea and the stones, while at the same time echoing the poetic conventions of a later age in its allusions to the smiles and glances of the beloved. (These allusions, to revert briefly to the topic of translation, pose obvious dilemmas for the translator, who in 'transplanting' the work to a different cultural context, is inevitably faced with choices about whether, and to what extent, the allusions should be made explicit.) Much has been made of the affinity between al-Kharrāṭ's exploration of the workings of memory and that of Proust;[31] on another level, however, and using a different set of parameters for the process of 'cultural contextualisation', one might suggest that the essential theme of *Bobello* may be regarded as

30 Ibid., 129–30 / 102–3.

31 In his *À la recherche du temps perdu*, 7 vols (Paris, 1913–1927).

a lament for lost love, in which the *nasīb* of the pre-Islamic poet is rewritten using modern conventions, almost as it to emphasise the universality of the pre-Islamic poet's themes.

There is one more aspect of 'intertextuality' relevant to a discussion of *Bobello*, and that is the question of the relationship of the text to earlier works of the author. We have already alluded to this, with particular reference to *Yā banāt Iskandariyya* and *Turābuhā zaᶜfarān*.[32] So numerous, indeed, are the cross-references to the author's earlier publications, not only in *Bobello* but also elsewhere, that it has been suggested that his entire corpus consists essentially of a series of reworkings of his earlier works — in particular, the seminal *Rāma wa-al-tinnīn*, a work often regarded as ushering in a 'new sensibility' in Arabic literature, and which clearly forms a model for much that succeeded it. This view, as Robin Ostle notes elsewhere in this volume, al-Kharrāṭ himself appears not to dispute.[33]

A more detailed analysis of the links between *Bobello* and the two earlier works, *Yā banāt Iskandariyya* and *Turābuhā zaᶜfarān* would be of particular interest in view of the change of the principal setting from Alexandria to the Egyptian countryside. In the meantime, however, we may note that the intertextual references in *Hijārat Bobello* that pose such a challenge for the reader are by no means confined to the author's earlier works, but rather form part of a tapestry of explicit and implicit allusions and references that extend across the Islamic and Coptic traditions, as well as far beyond them.

32 See above, page 149.
33 See above, page 134.

The Past in the Present: aspects of intertextuality in modern literature in the Gulf

Gail Ramsay
University of Uppsala

Theoretical Concepts

In this article a number of novels and short stories from the United Arab Emirates (UAE), Oman, Bahrain and Qatar are presented with the aim of identifying some of the intertextual aspects of this literature. I intend to demonstrate that it is possible to speak of the existence of a modern Gulf literature constituting an intertextual mesh of traditional and modern literary strands, interwoven with its Arabic and Western predecessors and anchored in its societal context.

Intertextuality, in this article, refers to the various ways in which the present text, the hypertext, relates to and interacts with other texts, the hypotexts, and reactivates and remodels themes, motifs and scenes from these earlier texts.[1] It refers to presuppositions in the vein of Jonathan Culler's analysis of intertextuality and Gérard Genette's observations on peritext and paratext as important vehicles for intertextual connotations.[2] More specifically, intertextuality here entails 're-presenting', bringing up to the present and recycling archetypal characters, themes, imagery and literary techniques from the more than a thousand-year-old Arabic literary heritage, as well as modern Arabic literature from the 1900s and literature from the West. Central to the concept of intertextuality in this study is that the identification of an intertext 'need not depend upon conscious authorial intention', because we are aware that 'intertextuality may

1 Gérard Genette, *Palimpsests: literature in the second degree*, tr. Channa Newman and Claude Doubinsky (Paris: Seuil, 1982; University of Nebraska Press, 1997), 5–10, 51–52, 381.

2 Jonathan Culler, *The Pursuit of Signs: semiotics, literature, deconstruction* (Ithaca and London: Routledge and Kegan Paul, 1981), 115; Gérard Genette, *Paratexts: thresholds of interpretation*, tr. Jane E. Lewin (Cambridge: Cambridge University Press, 1997), 16–17, 117–36, esp. 134–5.

function either as trace or as representation'.[3] Anders Olsson has elaborated on this point, maintaining that a resemblance between two texts, x and y, does not necessarily mean that there exists 'a genetically imperative bond between x and y'. Rather, the similarities which we observe in these texts may spring from the fact that the representation of thought and art of the age(s) in question derive from mutual sources, all of which have influenced both x and y.[4]

In this chapter, 'traditional literature' refers to the popular Arabic chivalry romances of the pre-Islamic and early Islamic periods, such as those included in the narratives of the battles of Abū Zayd al-Hilālī, Dhāt al-Himma and al-Amīr Rizq and in the tales of *A Thousand and One Nights*. By 'early modern Arabic literature', we mean literature from the early to the mid-1900s, and by 'modern Arabic literature' we mean works created from approximately the 1960s and onward.[5]

Although a few short stories had been published in Bahrain by the 1940s and 1950s, short-story writing on a wider scale began in this country in the 1960s.[6] In the UAE, modern literature began to appear in the 1970s, and in Oman in the 1980s; in Qatar, works of modern fiction appeared in mature form in the 1990s.[7] These Gulf States illustrate how the mosaic of Arabic literature, both traditional and modern, is combining

3 Michael Worton and Judith Still (eds), *Intertexuality: theories and practices* (Manchester and New York: Manchester University Press, 1990), 46.

4 Anders Olsson, 'Intertextualitet, komparation och reception', ed. Staffan Bergsten, *Litteraturvetenskap: en inledning* (Lund: Lund studentlitterature, 1998), 51–69 (59). Genette's stance on this aspect of intertextuality is that 'there are works that we know or suspect to be hypertextual whose hypotext is missing, temporarily or not' (*Palimpsests* (1997), 381). Culler notes that 'Intertextuality thus becomes less a name for a work's relation to particular prior texts than a designation of its participation in the discursive space of a culture ... the various ... signifying practices of a culture and its relation to those texts which articulate for it the possibilities of that culture' (1981), 103.

5 In this article we follow the literary parameters, with minor adjustments, suggested by Roger Allen in his study *The Arabic Novel: an historical and critical introduction* (New York: Syracuse University Press, 1995), 11–137.

6 ᶜAbd Allāh Ibrāhīm Ghulūm, *al-Qiṣṣa al-qaṣīra fī al-Khalīj al-Arabī: al-Kuwayt wa-al-Baḥrayn* [The Short Story in the Arabian Gulf: Kuwait and Bahrain] (Beirut: al-Mu'assasa al-ᶜarabiyya lil-dirāsāt wa-al-nashr, 2000), 777–99.

7 Thābit Milkāwī, *al-Riwāya wa-al-qiṣṣa al-qaṣīra fī al-Imārāt, nash'a wa-taṭawwur* (Abu Dhabi: Cultural Foundation, n.d.), 17.

with Western influences and branching out into contemporary Gulf styles. This literature is taking form in a post-/neo-colonial society which is rapidly changing from a traditional Bedouin society to a modernised, urbanised and industrialised society in an increasingly globalised world.[8]

We will consider the social and cultural dimensions of the texts from the vantage point of Hisham Sharabi's theory on societies influenced by the processes of modernisation, simultaneously and to varying degrees regulated by norms and values of traditional society, entitled neo-patriarchy.[9] Neo-patriarchy entails, among other things, growing up and obtaining an education in a technologically advanced and modernised society which outwardly conforms to the standards and developments of the industrialised world. At the same time, people's lives are governed, to a lesser or higher degree, by the norms of traditional tribal and patriarchal society, a situation applicable to Gulf societies today.

Yūsuf al-Shārūnī's analysis of the role of the expatriate workers in the Gulf in his study *Fī al-adab al-ᶜUmānī* [On Omani Literature] (2000), and Alain Touraine's definition of subjectivisation versus fixation in the role of the subaltern in the domain of the text will guide us in our discussion of the stereotype of the Asian foreign worker in Gulf society.[10] Homi Bhaba's discussion of the ambivalence of the identity of the

8 Our theoretical vantage point regarding post- / neo-colonialism is offered by Gayatri Chakravorty Spivak and Ania Loomba and our understanding of globalisation is enhanced by Arjun Appadura's observations on 'The megarhetoric of developmental modernisation (economic growth, high technology, agribusiness, schooling, militarization)', a tangible reality of the Gulf region. Consult Arjun Appadurai, *Modernity at Large: cultural dimensions of globalization*, Vol. I, *Public Worlds* (Minneapolis: University of Minnesota Press, 1998), 10. See also G.C. Spivak, *A Critique of Postcolonial Reason* (Cambridge, Mass., London: Harvard University Press, 1999), 3, 190 and Ania Loomba, *Colonialism / Postcolonialism* (London: Routledge, 1998), 6–7, Peter Childs and R.J. Patrick Williams, *An Introduction to Post-Colonial Theory* (Hemel Hempstead: Prentice Hall, 1997), 7.

9 Hisham Sharabi, *Neopatriarchy: a theory of distorted change in Arab society* (New York and Oxford: Oxford University Press, 1988).

10 Alain Touraine, *Can We Live Together?* (Stanford, Ca.: Stanford University Press, 2000). I have analysed the situation of the expatriate guest-labourers as it is reflected in contemporary literature in the United Arab Emirates and Oman in an article entitled 'Confining the Guest Labourers to the Realm of the Subaltern in Modern Literature from the Gulf', *Orientalia Suecana* 53 (2004), 133–42.

stereotype in colonial discourse is also useful to our understanding of the emergence of the expatriate workers as the subaltern in the text.[11]

History and Romance

The existence of the 'pull' of the Arabic literary past and Western romantic tradition in translation in a modern Gulf novel is brought to our attention in the first novel by Rāshid ᶜAbd Allāh, *Shāhanda*, published in the UAE in 1974. The romantic theme has roots both in the Arabic translations of Western romantic writing of the eighteenth and nineteenth centuries and in the early modern Arabic historical romances, as well as the Arabic chivalry romances stemming from the early Islamic era.[12] *Shāhanda* is intended to offer a vista of days past; it is specifically geared towards informing the present generation about the 'old, unhappy far-off times' of slavery and poverty. In fact the novel's author explicitly says:

> My story springs from a reality in which we lived … I am writing it for this generation which is building a great country with its strong arm … I am writing it for coming generations so that it will be a window through which they can view the life of their fathers and grandfathers…[13]

قصتي هذه .. تنبع من واقع عشناه ..
... أكتبها لهذا الجيل الذي يبني بقوة سواعده بلدا عظيما ...
... أكتبها للأجيال القادمة لتكون لهم نافذة يطلون منها على حياة
آبائهم وأجدادهم ... (راشد عبد الله، 1998، الإهداء)

This kind of didactic, historical romantic writing is not new to the Arab world. In fact, historical romances represent the beginnings of modern

11 The 'major discursive strategy' of 'colonial discourse' was to incessantly let the identity of the colonial subject 'vacillate between what is always in place, already known, and something that must be anxiously repeated', says Homi K. Bhabha, *The Location of Culture* (London: Routledge, 1994), 66.

12 Gail Ramsay, 'The Novels of an Egyptian Romanticist: Yūsuf al-Sibāᶜī', doctoral dissertation, Stockholm University, University of Oriental Languages, Department of Arabic (Stockholm, 1996), 14–17, 47–48.

13 My translation. Rāshid ᶜAbd Allāh, *Shāhanda* (3rd ed.; Sharjah: Emirates Writers' and Literates' Union, 1998), 'Ihdā'' [Dedication].

prose fiction in the Arab world and the first generation of historical romanticists includes Jurjī Zaydān, Salīm al-Bustānī, Faraḥ Anṭūn and Ya^cqūb Ṣarrūf. Most notable of these writers is Jurjī Zaydān (1861–1914), who in his romances emulated the historical romances of Sir Walter Scott and whose novels about the early Islamic conquests and victories inspired a whole generation of Arab novelists. Sabry Hafez has notably remarked about Zaydān that this resort to history was not 'a sheer love for antiquity ... but an endeavour to awaken the readers' sense of national pride ... and to provide them, by recalling past glories, with an inspiration and model in their search for a national identity.'[14]

The intertextual value of Rāshid ᶜAbd Allāh's dedication in the paratext of *Shāhanda* supports this tradition in no unclear terms.[15] It sets the tone of the novel, inspiring our memory of textual material, themes, characters and techniques gathered from the early modern Arabic historical romances, which in turn are patterned on the Western historical romances that they emulate.

Shāhanda is the story of how the female protagonist, Shāhanda, and her poor family from the Persian coast of the Gulf, become slaves in a village on the Arabian coast of the Gulf after a shipwreck. Her life is a struggle for survival in a society that looks down on her both in her capacity as a slave and as a woman. She eventually gets her revenge on her former lover and enemy, Maḥmūd, who on her command is brought to the court of the ruler, whose powerful consort she has become. There he is made one of the castle's *aga*s (eunuchs).

The date of this novel's appearance is significant, for it is during the 1970s that the decisive economic steps gained momentum which pulled society out of the age of poverty, placing it in the age of material abundance and technical advancements.[16] A generation of men and women were then embarking on their educational careers, learning to read and write. They were confronted with a massive volume of impressions from other parts of the world, Western and Arab alike, through the various

14 As quoted by Allen (1995), 25–26.

15 Genette, *Paratexts* (1997), 135–6.

16 ᶜAbd al-Ḥamīd Aḥmad, 'Tawṣīfāt ᶜāmma ḥawla al-qiṣṣa wa-al-riwāya fī dawlat al-Imārāt', *al-Multaqā al-awwal lil-kitābāt al-qaṣaṣiyya wa-al-riwā'iyya fī dawlat al-Imārāt al-ᶜarabiyya al-muttaḥida*, 27 February–1 March 1985 (Sharjah: Dā'irat al-thaqāfa wa-al-iᶜlām in co-operation with Emirates Writers' and Literates' Union, 1989), 9–22 (16).

expressions of mass-communication, newly formed literary and cultural clubs and establishments, and travels abroad. It was in the face of these rapid and overwhelming changes that it became of vital importance to the sense of national awareness in these newly established Gulf States to register the cultural heritage of bygone days which was so quickly fading away. As was the case with the early Arabic novels that had appeared more than half a century earlier in Egypt and Lebanon, *Shāhanda*'s dominant features are those of romantic tales of love, chivalry, deception and vengeance, and of moralising and didacticism.

A salient characteristic of *Shāhanda* is the perspective it places on the heroine. She is poised to struggle for her cause, to gain respect and take revenge in a society that has no mercy for persons like her and in a situation with little hope of rising in the societal echelons. Popular romances sprung out of tales and legends from the days of Muslim wars, and victories over the unfaithful are well stocked with powerful female warriors and commanders.[17] Princess Dhāt al-Himma, or Dalhama as she is also called, was a master equestrian and lancer, who according to the story, commanded the Muslim warriors in their campaigns against the unfaithful. Queen Qannāṣa was another indomitable female character who, so the story goes, fought lions with her bare hands.[18] Powerful and valiant women often appear in the tales of *A Thousand and One Nights*; Princess Ibrīza is Prince Sharkān's superior both in chess and combat — a statement which we may take the liberty of interpreting as meaning that she is his superior in both intellect and physique.[19] As for al-Datmā', who

17 Consult Remke Kruk, 'Warrior Women in Arabic Popular Romance: Qannāṣa bint Muzāḥim and other Valiant Ladies', *JAL* 1 and 2 (1993), 213–30 and *JAL* 25 (1994), 16–33. Kruk observes that: 'One of the misconceptions about medieval popular fiction one occasionally comes across is that the role of women in popular Arabic storytelling is almost exclusively confined to either that of the coquettish sensuous ... young beauty' (1993), 213.' See Marius Canard, 'Les principaux personnages du roman chevaleries Arabe Dhāt al-Himma wa-l-baṭṭāl', *Arabica* 8 (1961), 158–73.

18 While Qannāṣa belonged to the ranks of the infidels, Hārūn al-Rashīd found no other Muslim commander fit to subjugate her except Dalhama. This she also does in a terrific combat between the two of them. See Kruk (1994), 29–31.

19 References to *A Thousand and One Nights* in this article are to *Alf layla wa-layla* [Alf Layla wa Layla, A Thousand and One Nights, Mille et Une Nuits], introduction by Dr Afif Nayef Hatoum (Beirut: Dar Sader, 1999), I–VI.

was endowed with extraordinary skills in the martial arts, she would not marry a man who could not conquer her in combat. A final example is the army of the powerful *jinn* king who guarded Ḥasan's wife (Ḥasan being the adventure-loving goldsmith from Basra), while she was imprisoned on the Wāq islands. This army consisted of twenty-five thousand women and was under the command of the king's own daughters.[20]

Eight years after the publication of *Shāhanda*, in 1982, ᶜAlī Abū al-Rīsh from Abu Dhabi published his novel *al-Iᶜtirāf* [The Acknowledgment], a long and winding tale, constructed in instalments as if it were a serial for a magazine.[21] It is woven in a fabric similar to novels such as *Zaynab*, published nearly seven decades earlier in 1913 by the Egyptian writer Muḥammad Ḥusayn Haykal, and ᶜAbd al-Ḥalīm ᶜAbd Allāh's *Baᶜd al-ghurūb* [After Sunset] (1949), not to mention works by Yūsuf al-Sibāᶜī such as *Bayn al-aṭlāl* [Among the Ruins] (1952), *Rudda qalbī* [My Heart Returned] (1954), *Nādiya* (1960) and *Naḥnu lā nazraᶜ al-shawk* [We do not Sow Thorns] (1969). In all of these novels, as is also the case with *al-Iᶜtirāf*, the core of the story is the question of marriage and of being able to marry the partner of one's choice: relationships involving pathos are central.

ᶜAlī Abū al-Rīsh's novel is a sentimental story of a young man, Ṣārim, whose father, Suhayl, is murdered whilst visiting his date palm grove. The central theme is Ṣārim's quest to find the culprit in order to avenge his father and to marry his beloved, Riḥāb. The plot is complicated and melodramatic: Ṣārim's best friend, Muḥammad, who is engaged to his sister Rayḥāna, is the son of a murderer, Samḥān. In the end, both Ṣārim and Muḥammad are happily married to their respective fiancées. Most readers would probably agree with Yūsuf Khalīl, who notes that the writer makes extensive use of fate, chance, sentimentalism and sermonising. All of these traits are typical of the early attempts at writing fiction in Arabic and relate to works such as those mentioned above.[22]

20 For the adventures of 'Ḥasan the Goldsmith', see *Alf layla wa-layla* (1999), V, 321–93.

21 ᶜAlī Abū al-Rīsh, *al-Iᶜtirāf* (Abu Dhabi: Mu'assasat al-ittiḥād lil-ṣiḥāfa wa-al-nashr wa-al-tawzīᶜ, 1982).

22 Yūsuf Khalīl, 'Al-shakl wa-al-maḍmūn fī al-qiṣṣa al-qaṣīra wa-al-riwāya fī dawlat al-Imārāt al-ᶜarabiyya al-muttaḥida', *al-Multaqā al-awwal lil-kitābāt al-qaṣaṣiyya wa-al-riwā'iyya fī dawlat al-Imārāt al-ᶜarabiyya al-muttaḥida*, 27 February–1 March 1985 (Sharjah: Dā'irat al-thaqāfa wa-al-iᶜlām in cooperation

As the theoretical concept of neopatriarchy prescribes, traditional norms and values dominate the lives of the characters of *al-Iʿtirāf.* At the same time, features of modern, urban societal arrangements impinge on their lives and their affairs. The protagonist's friend, Muḥammad, is forced to leave his home by his stern and egoistic father because he refuses to marry the girl of his father's choice rather than the girl whom he loves, Rayḥāna. He struggles to acquire a respectable position at one of the offices of the Ministry of Labour and Social Affairs. Muḥammad finally acquires a position at the Ministry's Department of Social Affairs in Dubai, with the assistance of the father of his friend Fāhim, who wields his influence on his behalf. Hence, hints of the existence of a 'new', industrialised society are touchstones vital to the sense of the plot. Modern primary and secondary education, the possibility of acquiring higher education abroad, cars, telephones, mechanical watering equipment, governmental institutions such as ministries, police departments and monthly wages, are further examples of this. The scene has been far removed from the pre-oil days of illiteracy, pearl-diving and fishing. Yet many societal rules of these bygone times prevail.

ʿAlī Abū al-Rīsh's novel reflects the romantic themes and the intricate structure of early modern romantic novels such as *Rudda qalbī, Naḥnu lā nazraʿ al-shawk* and *Bayn al-aṭlāl. Rudda qalbī* records the events leading to the 1952 Revolution in Egypt and seeks to enhance the idea that the gap between the aristocracy and the common man was bridged so that Prince Ismāʿīl's daughter Injī could marry the son of his lowly gardener, the cavalry officer ʿAlī. In *Naḥnu lā nazraʿ al-shawk*, the working-class woman, Sayyida, falls in love with Ḥamdī, a man from the educated upper-middle class, but is never able to marry him due to her low social status. Both of these novels are long and intricate stories in which improbable events, fate and chance are called for in order to wind up their plots.

The most convoluted novel of the aforementioned is *Bayn al-aṭlāl*, in which two stories run parallel to each other. As is the case in ʿAlī Abū al-Rīsh's novel *al-Iʿtirāf*, numerous coincidences and serendipitous events guide the characters of the story. In *Bayn al-aṭlāl*, the principal story concerns the female protagonist, Sāmiya, who wants to marry her English professor, Kamāl. The secondary story concerns her stepmother and is

with Emirates Writers' and Literates' Union, 1989), 49–82 (70).

told through an unpublished manuscript which Sāmiya reads during the course of the novel's time span. In the end, it is revealed that Kamāl is Sāmiya's stepmother's son, whom she has been told nothing about and who has grown up with his father. Fate has it that out of all the people that Sāmiya and Kamāl are exposed to in Cairo (for this is where the story takes place), these two meet and fall in love with each other.

This *dénouement*, satisfactory to all the main characters, is just as improbable as that of ^{c}Alī Abū al-Rīsh's novel *al-I^{c}tirāf*. In this novel the protagonist's best friend, who is in love with the protagonist's sister, turns out to be the son of the murderer of the protagonist's father, all of which we noted above. In the end, everything turns out to the satisfaction of the main characters; both companions are married to their respective fiancées, Rayḥāna (the protagonist's sister) and Riḥāb, and the murdered protagonist's father is avenged.

The Mafia

One of less than a handful of writers of modern novels in Oman is Sa^{c}ūd bin Sa^{c}d al-Muẓaffar (Sa^{c}ūd al-Muẓaffar / Saud Al Mudhaffar), born in 1951, whose novel *Inna-hā tumṭiru fī Abrīl* [It Rains in April] (1992), is closely patterned on the Mafia-style novel with its archetype *The Godfather*, by Mario Puzo, from 1969. The title of Sa^{c}ūd al-Muẓaffar's novel constitutes the secret password for a major operation which entails killing the leading members of a rival Mafia family. This operation has been triggered by this afore-mentioned Mafia family's brutal killing of the only son of the region's leading Mafia family. While this title gives no hint as to which direction this novel will take us, the dedication text immediately sets us on a specific track. It reads: 'Oh, ignorant [ones], oh, informed [ones], oh anonymous [ones], I dedicate this novel to you, to the Mafia here!' (my translation).

أيها الغافلون ..
أيها العارفون ..
أيها المتسترون ..
إليكم أهدي الرواية!!؟ ...
إلى ...
مافيا ... هنا ...!! (سعود المظفر، 1992، الإهداء)

The scenes, characters and events of *Inna-hā tumṭiru fī Abrīl* resemble those we encounter in *The Godfather*. The clichés and stereotypes that we associate with this type of gangster novel have been adapted to a contemporary Omani setting. The novel opens with a scene in which a large car in the typical style of the genre drives up to an iron gate behind which stands a luxurious villa. This setting reflects both the textual, as well as the extra-textual, reality of the life-style which is usually associated with the living quarters of the renowned 'gangster' families in the United States of America. Next, an Asian driver opens the door of the car for a tall man dressed in black who is carrying a briefcase and wears glasses. No sooner does he reach the top of the marble staircase when another Asian servant in elegant attire greets him and shows him in to *al-raʾīs* — the 'Boss', the equivalent of the *Don* in Puzo's novel. During a brief but to-the-point meeting between these two men, the protagonist of the novel, ᶜAbd al-Rasūl, receives the message that he is to be the next *raʾīs* of this Mafia family.

In *The Godfather*, key positions are reserved for close family members, and Sicilian Italians outside the near family circle may be included as *caporegimes*, captains of semi-independent branches of the Family. The important role of *consiglieri* (Puzo's expression is *consigliori*), that is, advisors in legal matters, messengers and negotiators, is to be undertaken by close family members. In spite of this Mafia 'rule', as pronounced in *The Godfather*, the German-American Tom Hagen (who, the reader learns, is regarded in the USA by American, Sicilian Italians as 'Irish') succeeds the Corleone family's *consigliere*, Genco Abbandando, upon his demise from cancer. This, we learn, is a drastic break with the Sicilian tradition in the delicate matter of *consiglieri*. In Puzo's novel: 'The Don had broken a long-standing tradition. The *consigliori* (sic) was always a full-blooded Sicilian' (48). In comparison, in *Inna-hā tumṭiru fī Abrīl*, key positions are held by Omanis such as the aforementioned ᶜAbd al-Rasūl, who corresponds to Don Vito Corleone, while Mr Di Silva in the Omani novel is patterned on the prototype of Tom Hagen and is not an Omani national, but an Italian.

As in the Western Mafia novel, the subject matter of the various events and episodes may be divided into three main categories. These may be summarised as: first, creating a safe and economically stable situation for the family; secondly, seeing that justice is done according to what is seen as justice from the family's perspective, and thirdly, securing a suitable heir to lead the clan. Much of this is realised through working outside the established rules of law and order, and through outright crimes such as extortion and assassinations requested as 'repayments' for tasks performed for parties seeking assistance from the Don. The last-mentioned subject is the starting point of the story about the Sicilian Mafia in New York, *The Godfather*. Amerigo Bonasera, whose daughter has been cruelly hurt and injured by two young men, is deeply disappointed when they are sentenced only to three years' imprisonment by a New York judge. He is so overwhelmed by his rage and bitter feelings of revenge that he seeks out Don Corleone in order to receive help to punish the two culprits in a way that he sees just.

In *Inna-hā tumṭiru fī Abrīl*, this theme is reflected in the episode in which ᶜAbd al-Rasūl is approached by a woman whose husband not only abuses and batters her but who does not pay the alimony for their child either. Her problem is 'solved' by ᶜAbd al-Rasūl and his Mafia family. He advises his man to see to it that the woman's husband is thrown into jail and to extract the sum for the child's support from him. This type of operation, whether in the case of *The Godfather* or *Inna-hā tumṭiru fī Abrīl*, does not necessarily exact a price. It is not important that the person requesting help has no means with which to repay the Don — *al-Ra'īs*. What he requests is loyalty and he does not let anything stand in the way of a solution. Underlining this moral, is the fact that the woman who is assisted by ᶜAbd al-Rasūl and his Mafia clan is only requested to pay a token sum while Amerigo Bonasera does not pay a cent but is called upon later in the story, in his capacity as an undertaker, to dress the corpse of Santino Corleone.

The ubiquitous presence of Asian servants throughout *Inna-hā tumṭiru fī Abrīl* is a reflection of the stamp which has been embossed in the literature of the Gulf States due to the existence of a vast number of expatriate workers in these countries. As Yūsuf al-Shārūnī acutely remarks: 'This Asian element is that which distinguishes Omani literature — perhaps Gulf literature generally.'[23] The stereotypical character of the Asian servant is that of the obliging and voiceless driver, housekeeper, gardener, cook and so on. In *The Godfather*, Johnny Fontane, the godson of Don Corleone, has a black domestic servant, something which is a reflection of the state of affairs in American middle- and upper-class society of the early to mid-1900s. To these classes it was natural to have a black maid or manservant serving in the home. This is not to say that they

23 Yūsuf al-Shārūnī, *Fī al-adab al-ᶜUmānī* [On Omani Literature] (Cairo: Markaz al-ḥaḍāra al-ᶜarabiyya, 2000), 130, my translation.

were not treated well and paid fairly for their services. As is the case with contemporary Gulf society, they were needed in their capacity as servants but unwanted as equals to the people that they served. All of this is in keeping with Bhabha's observations on stereotypical fixation by which the colonised was kept in place as the subaltern in the domain of the text.[24]

As I have noted in my article 'Confining the Guest Labourers to the Realm of the Subaltern in Modern Literature from the Gulf',[25] Saᶜūd al-Muẓaffar's novel *Rimāl wa-jalīd* [Sand and Ice] (1988), reflects an important difference between the European colonisation under the Portuguese between 1507 and 1650, and the postcolonial situation in which society has been flooded with Asian expatriates. Al-Shārūnī's explanation for this situation is that the Portuguese never penetrated the Omani hinterlands but clung to the long coastline, where they dominated seafaring and trade. Consequently, they did not dig their roots deep into the soil of the Gulf region spiritually, culturally or geographically, and the marks of their existence on the exterior margins of the land were easily extricated, leaving few lasting cultural impressions. Foreign labourers today, al-Shārūnī underlines, are intricately woven into Gulf society. They are employed as servants, cooks, drivers, secretaries, accountants and blue-collar workers, and the women are nannies, nurses and wives, thus making up an indispensable base of society. 'Therefore, this party is more dangerous than the European party which never blended into the basic Omani fundament', concludes al-Shārūnī.[26]

This situation is emphasised in Saᶜūd al-Muẓaffar's novel, *Inna-hā tumṭiru fī Abrīl* (1992). The Asians in this novel reflect the status of the foreign workers as unable to construct themselves as subjects — Alain Touraine's definition of subjectivisation being 'the individual's right to live an individual life, to be different from others, and above all to be truly self-consistent' (65). This means that the Asian worker is held in place in his or her capacity as both essential to the running of daily affairs and a threat to what is thought to be indigenous Gulf culture. This ambivalent status has been described by Bhabha as stereotypisation and implies that at all times the expatriate is fixed in the role of the subaltern,

24 Bhabha (1994), 66–67.
25 Ramsay (2004).
26 al-Shārūnī (2000), 140–1, 171–2, my translation.

the non-subject, confronted with modern, globalised Gulf culture in the text.[27] In other words, the novel reinforces the solidity of the Gulf communities in which is embedded and positioned the stereotypical character of the Asian expatriate worker in the textual domain.[28]

As for the Europeans in *Inna-hā tumṭiru fī Abrīl*, in accordance with their 'lesser danger' to the indigenous culture of society, as explained by al-Shārūnī above, they are allowed to play the important role of *consiglieri*, advisors and negotiators, and are allowed to enjoy a higher status in Sa^cūd al-Muẓaffar's Mafia-novel, albeit only for a while. As is the case in *The Godfather*, where the 'Irish' Tom Hagen is removed from his office as *consigliere* by Michael Corleone, the Don's successor, ᶜAbd al-Rasūl's Italian advisor and middle-man, Di Silva, is in due course replaced by an Omani national, Shihāb. The effect of this is that Di Silva initiates the establishment of a rival Mafia family and has ᶜAbd al-Rasūl's wife and mother-in-law assassinated to take revenge on ᶜAbd al-Rasūl for his sacking. This triggers a vendetta in which first Di Silva himself, then ᶜAbd al-Rasūl's son ᶜUmar, are killed. *Inna-hā tumṭiru fī Abrīl* is the secret password for a planned operation in which all of the members of Di Silva's Mafia family will be killed in revenge for the death of ᶜUmar. This great war between the Mafia families in the Omani novel reflects the Corleone family's revenge for the assassination of Don Corleone's eldest son, Santino. In this major operation all the key persons of the other Mafia families are killed, Michael Corleone's power consolidated and the reputation of the Corleone family restored.

27 Bhabha (1994), 66; G.C. Spivak, 'Can the Subaltern Speak ?', *Marxism and the Interpretation of Culture*, eds Carl Nelson and Lawrence Grossberg (Urbana and Chicago: University of Illinois Press, 1988), 271–313 (272, 308); Touraine (2000), 59.

28 I am here thinking of Benedict Anderson's observations on the mechanisms of 'print-capitalism', the relationship between large-scale publishing, a sense of national solidarity and the conjuring up of 'imagined communities'. Benedict Anderson, *Imagined Communities* (1983; rev ed., London and New York: Verso, 1991), 26–27.

The Gothic

Su[c]ād Āl Khalīfa, who is from Bahrain, published her short-story collection *al-Ghurfa al-mughlaqa* [The Closed Room] in 2001. 'Al-[c]Ankabūt' [The Cobweb], in this collection, is the story about a young woman who has lost her modern and comfortable home through divorce and therefore persuades her brother Aḥmad to let her move in to the childhood home which has stood empty since the death of their parents.

This story follows the pattern of the mysterious folktale and gothic traditions inspired by Perrault's *Barbe-bleue* or *Bluebeard* and expressed in scenes like Miss Havisham's cobwebbed and rat-infested chamber in Charles Dickens' *Great Expectations*. Aḥmad instructs her that she has full use of all the rooms in the house save the room of their late father. 'Listen to me carefully,' he tells her, 'there is nothing of interest to you in this room … my only wish is that you stay away from that room.'[29]

"إسمعيني جيدا لا شيء يهمك في هذه الغرفة ... فإن رجائي الوحيد هو ألا تقتربي من تلك الغرفة .. " (سعاد آل خليفة، 2001، 26)

Naturally, after this instruction, the protagonist cannot keep her mind off this room and what her brother might keep hidden inside. In accordance with Culler's formula for intertextual presuppositions, the reader is able to carry on this story with a great deal of precision without even reading it.[30] Contemplations such as 'What is my brother Aḥmad hiding in that room? … great riches, private secrets, documents related to the dispute between my brothers about the inheritance' and 'her mother and sole comfort in life is dead … need she be afraid of this locked room which her brother has warned her from opening? What could he possibly do? And what could he be hiding in it?' all belong to this pattern.[31]

29 Su[c]ād Āl Khalīfa, 'al-[c]Ankabūt', *al-Ghurfa al-mughlaqa* (Beirut: al-Mu'assasa al-[c]arabiyya lil-dirāsāt wa-al-nashr, 2001), 25–38 (26), my translation.

30 Culler (1981), 111–12, 115. We here refer to Culler's example of pre-suppositional intertextuality pertaining to the folktale motif: 'Once upon a time there lived a king who had a daughter.' This sentence holds literary and pragmatic presuppositions and from the start informs the reader about the details that will organise and the moral that will govern the story (115).

31 Āl Khalīfa (2001), 32–33, my translation.

" ترى ما الذي يخفيه أخي أحمد في تلك الغرفة .. ثروة كبيرة .. أسرار خاصة .. وثائق تخص الخلاف بين إخوتي على الإرث .. ماذا يخفيك هناك .. "
(آل خليفة، 2001، 32)

" أمها رحمتها الوحيدة توفيت .. ليس لديها أخت أو صديقة ... ستخاف بعد ذلك من هذه الغرفة المغلقة التي حذرها أخوها كم أن تفتحها .. ماذا عساه سيفعل؟ ... وماذا عساه سيخبئ فيها؟؟ .. "

When she forcefully opens the door, she finds it full of thick, silky cobwebs hanging from the ceiling, clinging to seven firmly locked, heavy, black chests seeping with a yellowish fluid from which emanates the scent of sandalwood. In the end, the reader has the feeling that the protagonist is strangulated in her struggle to penetrate the cobwebs which only tighten their grip on her the more she tries to free herself from them. The outcome of this story is left for the individual reader to seek out.

Dr Kaltham Jabr from Qatar, in her short story *Waja^{c} imra'a ^{c}arabiyya* [The Pain of an Arab Woman], included in her short-story collection with the same title published in 1993, presents the reader with a split vision between Western past and present Gulf reality. It also holds a thematic parallel to an earlier Western work, namely *Wuthering Heights*, by Emily Brontë. The protagonist of Kaltham Jabr's story is a married woman from the Gulf who suffers from a psychological ailment which prevents her from remembering her own identity and recognising her loved ones. Before being sent for treatment in a Western country she recollects some impressions, and a conversation that her husband has tried to carry out with her: 'The dusty winds of my city rap at the doors and the window and the echo of my irritated husband's voice rumbles: Isn't it time for this wife to become reasonable?'[32]

رياح مدينتي المحملة بالتراب تقرع الأبواب والنافذة وصدى صوت زوجي المتأزم يتذمر ..
(أما آن لهذه الزوجة أن تعقل!) (جبر، 1993، 26)

Abroad, unaware that she is married and a mother of a child, she becomes acquainted with a stranger whom she falls in love with. Momentarily, she remembers details from her life such as her mother, father and tribal roots, but most of the time she is unaware of these facts. At one point she

32 Kaltham Jabr, *Waja^{c} imra'a ^{c}arabiyya* (Qatar: Wizārat al-i^{c}lām bi-al-minṭaqa al-sharqiyya, 1993), 26, my translation.

declines to take her medication and lies about her identity in order to impress upon her lover that she is a young woman of twenty who is abroad for studies.

We cannot but help wondering at times whether this protagonist indeed wishes to be cured. The split vision of her dilemma lies in the fact that her illness is positive and negative at the same time. Her illness makes it possible for her to stay with her lover, and it is also this illness that could be accepted as an excuse if it were ever by chance found out that she had had an extra-marital affair. Cure will bring her home to her family and society which she naturally misses, but also to a man whom she does not seem to care for. Whether healthy or unwell, should she persist with her life-style abroad, choosing to remain with her lover, it would result in her having to sever the ties with her family and society.

The physician who treats her does not inspire confidence. During a session in his office she is pronounced cured. 'He smiled scornfully as he said "cured"', the protagonist relates.[33] It is at this point in the story that she gazes through the window of the doctor's office at a black and naked branch of a tree while the rain hammers against the window, producing a thick mist. Three pieces of imagery are especially important to setting the atmosphere of the scene: heavy rain, a solitary, black tree and a clutched hand.

> The rain grew dense on the window with a remarkable viciousness and generated a thick steam on its inside. I shivered as I sat in the soft chair and through the other window I saw the branches of a naked tree, the drops of water streaming down its sides until they reached the ground or remained suspended. I clutched my hand placing it on my chest and kept quiet ...[34]

المطر يتكاثف فوق النافذة بشراسة عجيبة ويتوالد بخارا كثيفا بالداخل، ارتجفت في المقعد الوثير، وأنظر من النافذة الأخرى إلى أغصان الشجرة العارية، وقطرات الماء تنزلق فوقها حتى تصل اليابسة أو تبقى معلقة .. أضم كفي إلى صدري وأصمت ... (جبر، 1993، 28)

The narration of Lockwood's experience in *Wuthering Heights* with the then dead Catherine, who raps at the window in the middle of a stormy and cold winter night, does indeed emerge as a precursor to the

33 Ibid., 28, my translation,
34 Ibid., my translation.

contemplations of the protagonist in Kaltham Jabr's story. Consider the centrality of the heavy snow, the (imagined) bow of the tree and the knuckles of the hand against the window in the following quotations from the chapter in which Lockwood has his terrifying experience in the oak-closet. Lockwood has settled in his bed and has unsettling dreams which awaken him. He tries to calm himself by finding an explanation for the tapping that comes from the window. 'Merely the branch of a fir-tree that touched my lattice, as the blast wailed by, and rattled its dry cones against the panes!'[35] He continues:

> ...I heard distinctly the gusty wind, and the driving of the snow: I heard, also the fir-bough repeat its teasing sound ... I must stop it ... knocking my knuckles through the glass, and stretching an arm out to seize the importunate branch: instead of which, my fingers closed on the fingers of a little, ice-cold hand![36]

This hand, the reader learns, belongs to the troubled ghost of Catherine, longing for her beloved Heathcliffe.

It may seem unfair to either of the two works under discussion here to compare them with each other. Emily Brontë's novel is recognised as one of the classic masterpieces of the literary heritage of the West, first published in 1847, while Qatar ventured into the field of modern literature little more than a decade ago. However, both of the narratives seem to imply that the psychological problems of the protagonists of both of these works are in some way linked to the moral rules of their respective societies. Romantic passion was not the primary factor to be considered when choosing one's spouse in the world of Emily Brontë's protagonist. Had Catherine married the love of her life, Heathcliffe, she would have degraded herself socially. To avoid losing her high social standing, she marries Edgar Linton and after her marriage to him it is not possible for her to continue her relationship with Heathcliffe. When Heathcliffe returns to *Wuthering Heights* and begins visiting her at Thrushcross Grange, she is unable to face the tensions presenting themselves: her love for him, her inability to change her situation, and his pervasive presence

35 Emily Brontë, *Wuthering Heights*, World Classics (Oxford: Oxford University Press, 1983), 22.
36 Ibid., 23.

in her surroundings and memories. It is this situation that brings about her mental illness and Heathcliffe's misery and finally both her and his demise.

Like Catherine in *Wuthering Heights*, the protagonist of *Waja^c imra'a ^{c}arabiyya* is struck by an unspecified mental disorder which prevents her from recognising her husband and other family members. Like Catherine also, she is haunted by a love which cannot be realised without prodigious sacrifices. When at long last the physician utters the words: 'You are well,' she remembers that she has a husband and a child and is aware of her real identity. Her recuperation comes with a price; her lover realises that she is not abroad for studies and learns of her real identity and her husband. Broken-hearted, she sets out for the airport, leaving the man with whom she has shared her fantasy world during her treatment abroad. The last lines of her story further underline the ambivalent feelings which seem to battle inside the protagonist.

> He … recognised my husband and my son who now were waiting for me on the pavement of my city, so quiet on the outside and roaring on the inside with its blazing winds, opulence and ambivalence.[37]

... عرف وجه زوجي وطفلي، اللذين ينتظراني الآن فوق رصيف مدينتي الصامتة بالخارج الضاجة بالداخل، حيث الرياح اللاهبة والترف والازدواجية (جبر،و 1993، 32)

These final lines of the story shed some light on the 'doubleness' or ambivalent circumstances in which the nationals of the protagonist's country live. First, the statement 'he recognised my husband and my son', underlines the fact that Qatari society is tightly interwoven and that Qatari nationals, being few in number, are able to keep a keen eye on the behaviour of members of the respective family clans and circles of friends to which they belong.[38] Secondly, the ambivalence of neo-patriarchal

37 Jabr (1993), 32, my translation.

38 In an interview at the Sheraton, Doha (3 February 2002), Sa^{c}ūd A. Aziz Āl Ghānim, Acting Director of Culture and Arts, National Council for Culture, Arts and Heritage, Doha, informed me that the number of inhabitants residing in Qatar is approximately 600,000, of whom some 40% are foreigners. *Marhaba Magazine, Information Magazine of Qatar* 17 (March 2000), 7, states that the 1997 census gives a total of approximately 630,000 individuals residing in Qatar.

society is underlined when the country's climate and topography are mentioned in juxtaposition with its 'opulence'. 'Blazing winds' give rise to a barren and sterile desert environment, and 'opulence' points towards the extravagant and high-tech lifestyle of the country's nationals — both of which contradictory statements may be interpreted as the protagonist's shattered feelings in the face of her reality. Her life and ambitions must conform to traditional norms and expectations in her capacity as a woman, while simultaneously the newest and most modern in all forms of technology is at her disposal. This ambivalence has been observed and succinctly described by Fayad E. Kazan, who speaks about the political leaders in the Gulf and their efforts to modernise (and Westernise) society pointing out that

> Gulf political elites proclaim their commitment to development, but they do not seem to comprehend the concept of development. They are torn between their fascination with Western trappings and their commitment to rigid tradition. They import the outward forms of Western civilisation, such as the consumption aspects of it, but remain hesitant to pay the high price of attitudinal change that development requires. Gulf elites claim that they want to create a modern developed society without modernising the beliefs, attitudes and behavioral patterns upon which a modern and developed society is based.[39]

Just as in the case of Catherine's circumstances in *Wuthering Heights*, ruling societal norms weigh strongly in favour of her staying with her spouse, since she is dependent on her husband for support and it would be impossible for her to return should she elope with the other man. In other words, the question is left open whether her fate will be like that of Catherine in *Wuthering Heights*, who pined away in her longing after Heathcliffe, or if she will adjust to the demands of her neo-patriarchal society, resign and remain by the side of her husband in the Gulf.

39 Fayad E. Kazan, *Mass Media, Modernity and Development: Arab States of the Gulf* (Westport, Conn. and London: Praeger, 1993), 209.

The Little Red Riding Hood

One of Qatar's successful young woman writers is Hudā al-Naᶜīmī, whose professional field is medical biophysics, in which she holds a doctorate. Her short story 'Laylā wa-anā' [Laylā and Me], included in her collection *Abāṭīl* [False Talk] (2001), is a rewriting of the traditional folktale about the girl, clad in a red cloak with a hood, who is requested by her mother to deliver a basket of cake and wine to her ailing grandmother, living in the forest.

The protagonist in Hudā al-Naᶜīmī's story is Lumā, who is also the narrator of the story. Lumā is Laylā's cousin, *Laylā* being the Arabic name of Little Red Riding Hood in its Arabic version, 'Laylā wa-al-dhiʾb' [Laylā and the Wolf]. Lumā lives with her mother in the globalised environment of the modern metropolis which is saturated with the trappings of consumer society and the latest technological gadgets. She spends her time in front of the television watching the 'FUN-channel' while her mother sits in front of the mirror applying her makeup. The grandmother, who lives two stone-throws away in the 'neon-jungle', calls on the phone and the mother asks her daughter to go to the Kentucky Fried Chicken fast-food restaurant and bring a serving of crispy chicken to her grandmother. Handing her daughter a twenty-euro note, she instructs her to tell her grandmother that she herself has spent all day preparing the juicy drumsticks especially for grandmother.

In the traditional folktale, as related by the Grimm brothers, the grandmother would receive a home-made cake and a bottle of refreshing wine. During her walk through the forest, Little Red Riding Hood is diverted from her path when the wolf appears and entices her with reports of lovely flowers growing further on in the woods. Upon learning about this, she strays far away from the path, wandering for a long time in search of beautiful flowers for her grandmother. During this time, the wolf speeds to the grandmother's cottage.

In the Qatari story, Lumā is distracted by all the niceties that the big city has to offer. When she pays for the chicken, she gets three euros back in change. With these she plans to buy a chocolate bar for herself. When she reaches the candy store where she usually buys chocolate, she finds that it has been replaced by an internet café. For half a euro, she is provided with a place in front of a computer, and she promptly sits down and places an order for her favourite chocolate to be delivered to her grandmother. In this way she saves her change, because it will be her grandmother who pays for the chocolate, she reasons. Now she finds that she can use her remaining euros to buy pistachio ice-cream. When she passes a rubbish bin, a large creature with a big pouch, bushy eye-brows and a thick beard jumps out from behind it. When the wolf appears in the traditional story, Little Red Riding Hood is not frightened, for she knows nothing about this character and has not learned that he is wicked. Lumā is not frightened by this character's appearance either, and when he enquires about her name, she tells him. When Lumā learns that his name is Ḥasīb, she exclaims: 'You are Ḥasīb whom my mother detests and my grandmother prays will become an extinct species.'[40]

أنت "حسيب" الذي تكرهه أمي وتدعو عليه جدتي بالانقراض! (هدى النعيمي ، 2001، 46)

To this, Ḥasīb replies:

> No, my dear, extinction is not for the likes of me and it won't happen to me. I'm a global creature and I exist in order to quench the thirst of the children with water from the spring of the newborn, second millennium.[41]

لا يا حلوتي، فالانقراض ليس لأمثالي ولن يصيبني في مقتل، فأنا كائن عولمي، وجدت لأبقى وأسقي الصغار من ينبوع الألفية الوليدة ...(النعيمي، 2001، 47)

Ḥasīb now tries to tempt Lumā to accompany him to his cave at the top of the mountain by telling her about a special game that is waiting for her there. She hesitates but in the end gives in to his persistent invitation and finds that 'Ḥasīb owns a terrific game which I don't have and isn't to be found anywhere on the large internet web'.[42]

"حسيب" يملك لعبة خطيرة ولا تملكها شاشة الإنترنت الكبيرة ... (النعيمي، 2001، 48)

Eventually, Lumā enters her grandmother's house. She wishes to have her grandchild's company and begins telling her the stories that she usually tells her in order to persuade her to spend the night with her. But

40 Hudā al-Naʿīmī, 'Laylā wa-anā', *Abāṭīl* (Cairo: al-Dār al-Miṣrīyya al-Lubnāniyya, 2001), 43–50 (46), my translation.

41 Ibid., 47, my translation.

42 Ibid., 48, my translation.

these stories no longer interest Lumā. They cannot rub out her thoughts about Ḥasīb. She waves 'goodbye' to her grandmother, jumps out through the window and proceeds to the 'neon-forest', to Ḥasīb's abode beside the rubbish bin. Suddenly, she hears his voice accompanied by peals of laughter coming from her cousin, Laylā – *Little Red Riding Hood.*

> Her red dress was shining in the sun. Her braids had been let out and her locks where flowing over Ḥasīb's face which was covered with his beard. They were moving westward. I know how selfish Laylā is. She wants to monopolise the game. But I'll never let her.
>
> I ran after them.[43]

كان فستانها الأحمر يلمع تحت الشمس، وضفائرها قد فكت وطارت خصلاتها على وجه "حسيب" المكسو باللحية، كانا يتجهان غربا. أنانية "ليلى" أعرفها، تريد الاستئثار باللعبة، ولن أسمح.
جريت خلفهما .. (النعيمي، 2001، 47)

Comments and Conclusions

The intertextual lines which we have been made aware of in this study on modern Gulf literature can be pinpointed as themes, characters and literary techniques brought forth from both the Arabic and Western literary heritage, traditional as well as contemporary.

Both the historical novel *Shāhanda* (1974) by Rāshid ᶜAbd Allāh and the romantic and melodramatic novel *al-Iᶜtirāf* (1982) by ᶜAlī Abū al-Rīsh were, as we have seen, coloured by the early attempts at writing modern Arabic literature elsewhere in the Arab world. *Shāhanda* was also imbued with intertextual elements from the traditional folktales and chivalry romances of the early Islamic era.

The hypertext of *Shāhanda* constitutes a *multaqā* (meeting place) for traditional Arabic literary techniques and themes gathered from unspecified but recognisable archetypes or hypotexts of both the ancient and recent past. All of this conforms to Genette's observation that a hypertext may be a transformation and/or imitation of previous works, singular or multiple. It also exemplifies Culler's observation that intertextuality may be an expression of anonymous but mutual discursive practices and codes

43 Ibid., 50, my translation.

and Olsson's proposal that texts may be inspired by mutual historical and social circumstances. The novel is patterned on the early modern Arabic historical romance, which in turn was inspired by Western eighteenth- and nineteenth-century European romances, all of which make use of the romantic resources of chivalry, pathos, sentiment, and the glamour of an imagined past. That it was a question of enhancing these aspects, was underlined by the presuppositions brought to the fore in *Shāhanda*'s dedication.

Hence, this novel by Rāshid ^{c}Abd Allāh from the 1970s illuminates some themes and techniques of early modern Arabic literary expression. At the same time, it also fortifies and emboldens the character of the heroine by enabling her to gain inspiration from her thousand-year-old predecessors in the traditional Arabic literary repertoire, whose aspirations and actions she projects. *Shāhanda*'s heroine is set on overcoming the hardships that she encounters and the circle closes as she draws near to her ancient predecessors such as Dhāt al-Himma, al-Datmā' and the rest.

In *al-I^{c}tirāf*, by ^{c}Alī Abū al-Rīsh, the question is one of picking up the thread of the early developments of modern Arabic novelistic writing and inserting it in a contemporary Gulf mesh. The detailed and convoluted plot is held together by a romantic theme which calls for fate and serendipity in order to bring the story to its close. All of this calls to mind unspecified and multiple hypotexts; we highlighted some of the techniques and thematic strands linking us to a number of romantic novels by Yūsuf al-Sibā^{c}ī such as *Bayn al-aṭlāl*, *Rudda qalbī* and *Naḥnu lā nazra^{c} al-shawk*.

Al-I^{c}tirāf differs from *Shāhanda* inasmuch as the beginnings of neo-patriarchal societal arrangements impinge on the lives of its characters. At the time when this novel was being composed, a generation of UAE students had received higher education abroad, in the Arab world as well as in the West, during the 1970s. Upon their return, they were faced with a society that was undergoing change with an overwhelming speed. The result is that while a high-tech welfare society has taken form, pre-oil traditions and norms linger and shape the lives of UAE nationals. All of this is depicted in *al-I^{c}tirāf*, where marriage must be sanctioned by the family, blood revenge is a reality, but where salaries may be generated from white-collar work in a modern, government administration.

We found that Sa^{c}ūd al-Muẓaffar's novel *Inna-hā tumṭiru fī Abrīl* (1992) could be read as a hypertext to Mario Puzo's novel *The Godfather*.

Inna-hā tumṭiru fī Abrīl reflected modified themes and episodes as well as stereotypical Mafia characters adapted to an Omani setting. We applied Touraine's thesis on the subaltern and 'non-subject' to the state of the expatriate Asian workers in Oman. Supported by Bhabha's observations on stereotypisation we concluded that they were held in the place of the subaltern in their ambivalent capacity as essential and unwanted at the same time. This was seen to correspond to the situation of the black servants employed in Puzo's novel. In both cases, the servants, black or Asian, emerged as the subaltern in the textual domain.

Supported by Culler's analysis of intertextual presuppositions we distinguished intertextual threads from unspecified but nonetheless vivid hypotexts contained in the mysterious folktale and gothic traditions in the short story *al-ᶜAnkabūt*, by the Bahraini woman author, Suᶜād Āl Khalīfa. Specific utterances and scenes assisted in conjuring up some of the hypotexts of this story which we exemplified with *Bluebeard* and *Great Expectations*.

In Dr Kaltham Jabr's short story *Wajaᶜ imra'a ᶜarabiyya* (1993) we were made aware of how specific social and historical contexts may inspire the use of certain sets of themes, motifs and characters. We found that societal demands and economic pragmatism clashed with romantic emotions in two literary works separated from each other with respect to place and time. In Emily Brontë's novel *Wuthering Heights*, the two central motifs that we centred on in our discussion were Mr Lockwood's reference to what he believed to be the branch of a tree rattling outside his window in a snow-storm, and Catherine's melancholy and mental ailment due to her love for and separation from Heathcliffe. In Jabr's story, these motifs were matched with the protagonist's view of the naked tree outside the window, with rain pouring down its black trunk and branches, as she listened in fear to her intimidating physician's verdict on her mental disorder whilst placing her clutched hand on her chest. In the case of Catherine, it is her separation from her beloved that brings about her illness. In the case of Jabr's protagonist it is the opposite; her mental ailment makes it possible for her to be with her lover. Both protagonists choose separation from the men that they love. The fate of Catherine is known while the fate of the other can only be surmised. However, aware of her ambivalent feelings towards her neo-patriarchal society and husband, the reader is led to believe that the outcome of her return to her husband in the Gulf will be negative rather than positive.

The short story 'Laylā wa-anā', by the Qatari woman author Hudā al-Na^c^īmī, included in her collection *Abāṭīl*, was shown to pose as a hypertext to, and a contemporary Gulf rewriting of, the traditional folk-tale about the girl clad in a red cloak with a hood who is requested by her mother to deliver a basket of cake and wine to her ailing grandmother living in the forest, as related by the Grimm brothers. In other words, this story was read as a palimpsest projection of the hypotext of 'Little Red Riding Hood'. The main theme was, like the folktale, that of a girl delivering food to her grandmother. In the Qatari story, it is no longer a question of cake and wine but of Kentucky Fried Chicken. The thick forest of trees and its delightful flowers have been exchanged for a 'neon-forest' of the metropolis and its sundry temptations for the inhabitants of an industrialised, consumer-oriented society.

Hudā al-Na^c^īmī is not the first Arab female writer to draw inspiration from the story about the girl who sets out into the forest to assist her grandmother and who is led astray by a wicked wolf. The Lebanese woman writer, Emily Nasrallah (Imilī Naṣr Allāh), uses the same folktale as a backdrop to her short story 'Laylā wa-al-dhi'b' [Laylā and the Wolf] in her short story collection *al-Layālī al-ghajariyya* [Gypsy Nights] (1998). Emily Nasrallah's story keeps closer to the original than that of Hudā al-Na^c^īmī. Both stories go against the moral grain of the original folktale. In Emily Nasrallah's story about Laylā and the wolf, Laylā meets him in the forest while picking flowers and finds out that he is, in fact, a lovely companion who makes her feel safe and content. She finds that her mother has given him an unduly bad reputation. She has on no justifiable grounds made her afraid of him. Well aware that her mother and traditional views demand that she shun the company of the wolf, she throws away the flowers that she has picked for her grandmother, leaves the path leading to her house and sets out towards other goals, feeling happy in the company of the wolf.

Hudā al-Na^c^īmī's Laylā and her cousin Lumā are both attracted to her story's wolf, Ḥasīb, whom the reader is led to believe is a tramp and a social outcast. Ḥasīb, living in the margins of society, nonetheless, offers magical attractions to the girls passing his abode beside a large, steel, waste-bin. Like Emily Nasrallah, Hudā al-Na^c^īmī has chosen to transform the traditional character of the wolf, who in the folktale epitomises moral depravation and decadence. In the Qatari story he turns into an ambivalent character; he has the appearance of a bum, yet, he is att-ractive, he is inviting, but also threatening, he offers marvellous internet games, but in order to possess them, a visit to his distant cave is obligatory, and both Laylā and her cousin Lumā vie for his attention.

All three central female characters of the Arabic hypertexts, Emily Nasrallah's Laylā and Hudā al-Naᶜīmī's Lumā and Laylā, set out on their independent paths, breaking literary as well as societal traditions. They say their goodbyes to mothers and grandmothers and seek the company of the wolf.

The Mosaic of Quotations and the Labyrinth of Interpretations: the problem of intertextuality in the modern literature of the Gulf

Barbara Michalak-Pikulska
The Jagiellonian University, Kraków

> The word's status is thus defined horizontally (the word in the text belongs to both writing subject and addressee) as well as vertically (the word in the text is oriented towards an anterior or synchronic literary corpus) ... each word (text) is an intersection of words (texts) where at least one other word (text) can be read ... any text is constructed as a mosaic of quotations; any text is the absorption and transformation of another.[1]

There exists a view within modern literary criticism that texts are compiled from other texts: each text absorbs and processes other texts, and a work exists among other texts as a result of its relationship with them. The creation of texts is possible thanks to the pre-existing works to which they refer, with which they engage in controversial discussion, and which they reproduce or process The reader is able to understand a particular work only in the context of others to which it relates. Intertextuality notably widens the horizons for the possible interpretation of particular works, although it creates added difficulties too. The analysis of intertextual relations induces a considerable amount of controversy and discussion even among researchers of indigenous literature. However, students of Oriental literatures — researchers and interpreters of texts that originate from a foreign cultural zone — encounter additional problems, for in addition to intertextual relations that themselves may be hard to

1 Kristeva, influenced by the work of Bakhtin, charts a three-dimensional textual space whose three 'coordinates of dialogue' are the writing subject, the addressee (or ideal reader), and exterior texts; she describes this textual space as intersecting planes which have horizontal and vertical axes. Julia Kristeva, 'Word, dialogue, and the novel', in T. Moi (ed.), *The Kristeva Reader* (New York: Columbia University Press, 1986), 37.

grasp, it is necessary to tackle the thorny issues of text-genre and text-reality relationships.

At this point, it should be stressed that the first stage, as well as one of the crucial aspects, of research into intertextuality relations, is the reader's recognition of intertextual relations in the text. Although intertextuality researchers of the early period such as Riffaterre and Genette[2] did not raise the problem of the reader's understanding of intertextual relations, pre-assuming the existence of the so-called ideal reader, it is obvious that the entire process of a work's reception is a potential one, dependent to a great degree on the literary competence of the reader which is constituted by his or her knowledge of particular works.

An unquestionable hindrance for the average reader in the pursuit of intertexts is the fact that the subjects of reference (in the form of quotations, reminiscences, allusions, metaphors, etc.) are equally frequently works known and works unknown to him: thus, the probability of identifying them varies. The problem becomes more acute in the perception of foreign literature, although one should bear in mind the fact that intertextual relation recognition does not always exist as a condition indispensable for the understanding of the text in which the relations occur. The potentiality of intertextual relations gives them a fluid character — they may, in a certain type of reception, come forward in the text, while in another type of reading process they may appear to disappear (though of course still being present in the text). In some configurations, the real intertextuality becomes simply unrealistic.[3]

Modern writers willingly use intertextual relations in their texts, being conscious of the fact that they not only enrich the informative aspect of the work, but the artistic one too, adding to its interpretational dimension. Muḥammad ibn Sayf al-Raḥbī from Oman self-consciously plays a kind of intertextual game with the reader, referring to his knowledge of particular literary works, while at the same lime allowing for multiple possibilities for the reader's interpretation of the mosaic created. In the story entitled 'al-Ḥikāya' [The Tale], from the collection *Mā qālathu al-rīḥ* [What the Wind Has Told Him][4], the intertexts included refer to

2 Z. Mitosek, *Teorie badan literackich* (Warszawa: PWN, 1998), 333.

3 J. Culler, 'Presuppositions and Intertextuality', in his *The Pursuit of Signs: Semiotics, literature, deconstruction* (London: Routledge and Kegan Paul, 1981), 100–19.

4 Muḥammad ibn Sayf al-Raḥbī, 'al-Ḥikāya', in *Mā qālathu al-rīḥ* (Cairo, 1999),

various works that belong to the canon of Arabic literature. The names of the main characters of the story, Shahrazad and Shahriyar, as well as the quotations taken from *Ṭawq al-ḥamāma* [The Dove's Necklace][5] by Ibn Ḥazm are intertexts.

The action of the above-mentioned story by al-Raḥbī takes place in modern times. Shahrazad is a modern, beautiful woman surrounded by luxury, which is indicated by characteristic attributes such as her jewellery, the black Mercedes driven by an Indian chauffeur and a mobile phone. Shahrazad is also a public person (a model or an actress), as is suggested by the posters bearing her smiling image, omnipresent in the town. Waiting for Shahriyar to return home in the evenings, Shahrazad kills time in front of the television with a glass of vodka in her hand, flicking through the channels. She becomes slightly more animated only while watching fashion programmes, the CNN channel where Shahriyar is a presenter, and Larry King's talk-show in which Shahriyar is the guest that evening. For Shahriyar, like Shahrazad, is a well-known person, often featured on glossy magazines' covers and the topic of numerous articles.

The transfer of the characters of Shahrazad and Shahriyar into modern times, as well as the presentation of their life as a sequel to *The Thousand and One Nights*, is not a new idea. A similar literary manipulation had been applied among others by Najīb Maḥfūẓ in his book *Layālī alf layla* (1982), which was translated as *Arabian Nights and Days* in 1995, and by the Indian writer Githa Hariharan in *The Thousand Faces of Night* (1992). In the case of al-Raḥbī the idea of transferring the major characters of *The Thousand and One Nights* into present reality was not a goal in itself. The author shows, through the characters of Shahrazad and Shahriyar, an updated vision of everyday life in an Arab country — the representatives selected being perceived by the recipients as model ones for Arab society, even though it is known that the above names, like the entire story, are of Indian descent. And so Shahriyar is pursuing his television career while Shahrazad devotes herself to looking after her beauty, and in her free time she has other pleasures like watching television, reading women's magazines and relishing sophisticated foods and strong beverages. The reality pictured here does not differ too much from that of the contemporary

11–14.

5 Ibn Ḥazm, *Ṭawq al-ḥamāma* (Warszawa: PIW, 1976).

western world. What is striking, however, in the story 'al-Ḥikāya', is the clever manœuvre of the author, who having borrowed from *The Thousand and One Nights* seemingly just the main characters' names, has really borrowed the whole context of the *Entertainments.*

Al-Raḥbī realises the fact that his intertext, in relating to the literary canon, is a continuous, not a selective kind of reference, which means that the reader is not capable of totally separating the character from the plot and the whole of the literary context of the work known to him beforehand. Al-Raḥbī, not being able, but probably also not wanting, to devoid the characters of Shahrazad and Shahriyar of the references to *The Thousand and One Nights,* in whose context they are too deeply rooted, constructs them as if anew, in another reality. This does not, however, mean that they lose their features received from *The Thousand and One Nights*; what is more, they receive other, surprising attributes. Al-Raḥbī skilfully juggles the relations and even reverses certain dependencies between Shahrazad and Shahriyar. Rather than concentrating in particular on building the images of the main characters, as these are perfectly well-known to the reader, he takes his time to form a new reality in which the seemingly 'old' characters participate, undertaking a kind of intertextual game with the reader by surprising him with fresh situations and reversing the relations previously known from a totally different context. And so for instance, in the story 'al-Ḥikāya' it is Shahrazad who waits for Shahriyar to finish her story, and it is Shahriyar who has an affair with the servant.

Al-Raḥbī's reach for *The Thousand and One Nights* is an unusually significant step. For this 'tome' is not only one of the greatest, if not the greatest, collection of tales and stories, but the invaluable legacy of generations past and a source of wisdom for many nations. The tales in *The Thousand and One Nights* arose as a result of the meeting of many cultures and the mutual diffusion of numerous folklore elements characteristic of various territories and various epochs. The complexity and variety of this collection needs to be perceived just as much through the prism of the huge geographical area (stretching from the extremes of West Africa to India) from which the individual stories derive their origin, as through the chronological historical aspect (beginning with ancient, mythological motifs through to eighteenth-century short stories). Possibly, al-Raḥbī's intention was also to add to this treasure house of knowledge and customs a subsequent link — a vision of contemporary reality. Without interfering in the text already written, al-Raḥbī utilised the main characters of the collection, Shahriyar and Shahrazad being the most obvious and recognised conveyors of knowledge about the context of the *Nights,* to supplement the collection with new events forced by contemporary reality. By viewing al-Raḥbī's intention within this context, and the transfer of the main heroes of *Nights* into contemporary times, then the fact that the short story is entitled 'al-Ḥikāya' [The Tale] can be considered. For the tale possesses a startling strength in the context of the formation of man's outlook and the organisation of his systems of values. What is more, it constitutes its own form of magical mirror, in which the essence of mankind is reflected.

> The fairy tale arose as its own form of response to the life experience of many generations. It became especially the limpid projection of human fate, as its mythical and magical generalization, while at the same time the incantation for the victory of the just hero over the sinister.[6]

If, therefore, a fairy tale is a literary genre constituting its own form of projection of human experience, hopes, fears and desires, then the usage of such a name in relation to the title of a work which belongs completely to another literary genre, that of the short story, would result in the influence of genre features of the fairy tale on the actual text of the work. Going further along this route of enquiry, one may state that al-Raḥbī's short story is, on the one hand, a realistic work describing the contemporary reality of the inhabitants of an Arab country, while being on the other, a part of a larger entirety or a supplement to the collection of fairy tales *The Thousand and One Nights* which constitute both the achievement of past, and experience of contemporary generations. The interpretative possibilities of the work, utilising the intertext derived from the canon of literature, are, therefore, huge in this instance.

The intertext represented by two quotes from Ibn Ḥazm's *Ṭawq al-ḥamāma* [The Dove's Necklace] refers to a completely different work from *The Arabian Nights*. Finding the mentioned intertext (which belongs both to the canon of Arabic literature generally, and, to be more specific, that of Andalusia), to establish the source of its origin is, in this case, a simple matter, for al-Raḥbī uses quotation marks that make the

6 B. Gołębiowski, 'Przedmowa' [Foreword], in Vladimir Propp, *Morfologia bajk* (Warszawa, 1976).

localisation of the intertext that much easier, and besides, he even defines the source of the quote mentioned by Shahrazad and the servant. The first fragment read by Shahrazad comes from the twelfth chapter of the book, entitled 'On Keeping Secrets', and contains the anecdote about Abū Nuwās's bewitchment by the person of Ibn Zubayda, the son of Hārūn al-Rashīd, and the future caliph al-Amīn, together with his rejection of the poet's wooing. The second quote, addressed to Shahriyar by a servant, is however, a fragment of chapter XIV, entitled 'On Obedience' and concerns the story of a certain Muqaddam ibn al-Āṣfar and his fascination with a servant called ᶜAjīb. Both fragments relate to male-male fascination and consider the nature of homosexual love. The common element linking these stories is the decisive rejection of the wooing of potential lovers on the part of the objects of their desire, giving an undeniable negative note to the use of the two stories. The intention on the part of al-Raḥbī in utilising *The Dove's Necklace* could possibly show a desire to point to the topicality of social problems concerning homosexual love — which was clearly discussed openly even in the eleventh century.

Al-Raḥbī, in the short story 'al-Ḥikāya', attempts to present the current reality for the inhabitants of an Arab country — a reality that is at the same time grounded in Western culture. Shahrazad and Shahriyar do not only possess the weaknesses and faults of the representatives of Western societies, they also struggle with similar perplexities and problems, that is, alcoholism, betrayal or homosexuality. Al-Raḥbī, in equipping his short stones with intertextual links, achieves something more than the usual display of the similarity of life problems in Arab and Western culture. In making use of specific intertextual relations linking, for example, the work's plot with other figures and other texts, he conveys an additional dimension and depth to the problems under discussion to show that these problems have not lost their relevance over many centuries, as in the example of *The Dove's Necklace*, and are the lot of the most ordinary people as they are of those standing on a pedestal as, for example, in the characters of Shahrazad and Shahriyar.

A phenomenon which is much harder to interpret is the occurrence of intertextual relations of the type text / reality in 'realistic' literature. For this is a genre of literature in which intertextuality appears to be absent, but which can nonetheless appear sporadically as a reference to someone's literary or philosophical views. For the writer clearly declares the will to describe and present reality itself independently from any literary experience. A pronouncement on reality creates the effect of 'realness' not because it imitates reality but because it utilises speech which imitates the earlier set forms of linguistic experience. 'Realness' is an inseparable effect resulting from the text. Instead of a reflection of reality we have the reality of reflection, an image of the concept of reality defined in advance through a socio-cultural code, one saturated with platitudes, stereotypes and dead connotations. Intertext constitutes the total context of the linguistic experience that encompasses each individual. In this way, the understood concept of intertextuality gives us the possibility of examining the links between a literary text and reality as well as its social and cultural context.[7]

The short story 'al-Ru'ūs ilā asfal' [With Heads Downwards] from the collection *al-Ḥubb lahu ṣuwar* [Images of Love][8] by the Kuwaiti writer, Laylā al-ᶜUthmān, together with another short story by the earlier mentioned Omani writer, al-Raḥbī, entitled 'Dhākira lahā ṭaᶜm al-mawt' [Recollections of the Taste of Death] from the collection *Bawwābāt al-madīna* [The Town Gates][9] are realistic works. They present very similar stories in a similar way.

The heroes of both short stories are men betrayed by their wives. They feel humiliated, ridiculed and disgraced because of this. They decide to personally see justice done and to kill their unfaithful wives. They want to do this in defence of their own pride and in the name of honour. And so the man from Laylā al-ᶜUthmān's short story ends up in prison for murder, while the hero of al-Raḥbī's story is charged with attempted murder. After many years they are set free. Yet, ironically, they do not feel in the least free. Their thoughts are still demented by memories of betrayal and humiliation. There is still within them hatred towards their wives and dislike of other women. They do not regret what they did. What is worse, they consider that they were unjustly sentenced, for in actual fact they were the victims because they were betrayed and disgraced.

7 Z. Mitosek (1998), 327–33, and R. Nycz, 'Intertekstualność i jej zakresy: teksty, gatunki, światy', *Pamiętnik Literacki* 81 (2) (Wrocław, 1990), 106–14.

8 Laylā al-ᶜUthmān, 'al-Ru'ūs ilā asfal', in *al-Ḥubb lahu ṣuwar* (2nd ed., Beirut, 1983), 52–63.

9 Muḥammad ibn Sayf al-Raḥbī, 'Dhākira lahā ṭaᶜm al-mawt', in *Bawwābāt al-madīna* (Muscat, 1993), 7–14.

> 'Let her be damned. Despite the years I have not forgiven her... If she was only alive I would not hesitate but to commit the crime again! Even at this moment. I had to kill her... once, twice... and ten times. What a stupid woman. She was my wife. God will not even forgive her despite him being merciful and forgiving.'[10]
>
> 'Why did you try to kill her?'
>
> 'Because she was unfaithful.'
>
> 'Have you any proof?'
>
> 'Betrayal is the one thing that does not demand proof from us. [...]'
>
> 'Why did you try to kill her?'
>
> 'It's a question of honour...'
>
> 'Did honour order you to kill her?'
>
> 'Yes, when death is the one means to preserve something unique... '
>
> And the sentence was passed: ten years' imprisonment. [...] Those ten years nourished his insolence but did not allow him to forget about the betrayal. [...] What is more beautiful than prison when the punishment is proof of honour. ... Life is of less worth than betrayal. A loss of life is nothing in comparison to a loss of honour.[11]

The surrounding world horrifies the former inmates. They do not know what to do with themselves or where to go. For they have no homes, families or friends. They feel alien amongst people who do not understand them, they mock and ridicule them. The surrounding world turns out to be bad and dangerous.

> This huge world becomes cramped. It becomes so cramped that I feel how the rope tightens in a noose around my neck. I do not know anyone here. I have no family, or friends. I have no home where I could rest... Prison was my home. [...] For eighteen years I was distanced from real life in order to now return and find it turned upside down. [...] The world is cruel... in prison it is pleasanter. I have risen and run off in search of a new crime which will return me my freedom.[12]
>
> ... This road leads to people with dour faces distorted with disgust at his sight. They fear him for he is a criminal and they sneer because she betrayed him. [...] The world spins around him all the faster. The lines of the streets dance and laugh hysterically... they scorn... The letters on the shop signs wind

10 Laylā al-ᶜUthmān, 'al-Ru'ūs...' (1983), 53.

11 Muḥammad ibn Sayf al-Raḥbī, 'Dhākira...' (1993), 8.

12 Laylā al-ᶜUthmān, 'al-Ru'ūs...' (1983), 62–63.

> like snakes and form derisive words... sneering laughter in his head... [...] 'Prison is more charitable' came to mind and he was convinced that it was true... 'Prison is more charitable,' he whispered to himself, and the words span around his head until he found in them a ray of hope. He decided once more to embark upon that route... Let prison be redemption from a life devoid of taste. In prison there is somewhere to sleep and in the creaking of the bed one does not hear the notes of shame.[13]

The men discover that it is only safe in prison, that there is their home, a home they yearn to return to at any cost.

These short stories deal with only two matters, but these have been of extreme importance in the Arab world for centuries. The first is connected with the sense of male pride and honour, the second concerns the preservation of purity by a woman up until marriage, followed by faithfulness to her spouse until death. They are not merely a passive account of events portraying the social life of the countries of the Gulf. They also examine the problems of their citizens, the problems of the individual and his or her place in the contemporary world.

The works are also linked to the changes within the value systems in force in Gulf society. The loss of indigenous values and the increasing process of Westernisation present the conflict between traditional customs and forms of behaviour and the realities of contemporary life. All these changes are the result of rapid economic growth, the strong processes of globalisation and the expansion of the West bringing with it another culture and set of customs. The results of the economic changes within society are unhealthy relations between people, and the appearance of falseness, deceit and hypocrisy.

The problem of prisoners appears in both of the two short stories. Prisoners, after a long period of confinement, are unable to return to life in a society which has undergone radical changes in its behavioural patterns. The 'new' reality is so beyond them that they do not even attempt to make the effort to adapt to life in their new surroundings, for this turns out to be something beyond their power. Existence in the present world appears to them to be as absurd and as much a misconception as the search for safety and freedom in prison would be for

13 Muḥammad ibn Sayf al-Raḥbī, 'Dhākira...' (1993), 12–14.

others. As can be seen, the significance of the word 'freedom' can be as radically different as the reality one is to face.

The similarity in content and form in the two stories can be striking for the reader. Laylā al-ᶜUthmān and her work are known not only in Arab countries, but also in Europe, thanks to numerous translations. This problem also appeared for al-Raḥbī to be sufficiently important for him to opt to present it. Yet in the countries of the Gulf all of the matters mentioned above are discussed on a day-to-day basis. People write about them in newspapers, television and radio broadcasts, and other men of letters deal with these subjects. Through the help of 'other's speech' they have created a means of a literary illusion of reality. They have utilised a communicative style which results from the cognitive norms of contemporary man. The maxims and aphorisms created by the authors give the impression of universal knowledge — natural knowledge that is close to the recipient who receives their stylistic shape as a substitute for reality. The quotes the text contains are anonymous, non-locatable, irreversibly deformed, and yet they function as 'already read', 'already met'.

Let us note that the very titles of the short stories, 'al-Ru'ūs ilā asfal' [With Heads Downwards] and 'Dhākira lahā ṭaᶜm al-mawt' [Recollections of the Taste of Death] cite widely used sayings and metaphors. The words *al-Ru'ūs ilā asfal,* 'with heads downwards' which could also be translated as 'upside down', suggest something unnatural, something strange, at odds with ruling principles; the words *ṭaᶜm al-mawt*, 'the taste of death' conjure up an image of crime, revenge, fear, suffering.

The category of depression dominates the aesthetic tone of the works. There are amassed within them words and phrases associated with pain, suffering, loneliness, loss, disenchantment and incomprehension, for example:

> Despite the years I have not forgiven her...
> Let her be damned
> the world becomes cramped
> I do not know anyone here
> The world is cruel
> people with dour faces

where do I go now [14]
derisive words. ... sneering laughter
she was unfaithful
I hate you
Life as terrible as a nightmare
The spectre of the future,[15]

The world imagined has been presented in the works mentioned in a very similar way. The presentation of the narrative is equally similar, despite the fact that in Laylā al-ᶜUthmān's story the narrative is in the first person, while in al-Raḥbī's work it is in the third person. Retrospection appears in both stories, as does a break in the chronological flow of the narrative. The events which depict the first hours of freedom for the prisoners are intertwined with the distant past, betraying to the reader the motifs of crime and the mysteries of prison life. The present is intertwined with the past, the past with the present. In Laylā al-ᶜUthmān's text direct speech is dominant, while in al-Raḥbī's work seemingly indirect speech intertwines with direct. Direct speech characterises the speaker, conveying not only his thoughts, but also his temperament and involvement, as well as his individual linguistic features. Thanks to the seeming indirect speech, that narrator is able to perceive elements which could not have derived from him: colloquial sayings and perspectives. Besides, the open objectivism of direct speech and the partial objectivism of seemingly indirect speech illustrate the writer's relation to the quoted, or copied, 'other's speech', and reproduces the actual social contact.[16]

Laylā al-ᶜUthmān and al-Raḥbī belong to that group of writers which can boast the highest literary techniques. Every artistic means used, along with every technique employed, by them to visualise the world fulfils within the short story a definite function (informative, aesthetic). They have as their task the most successful imitation of reality. The unusual faithfulness of the literary representation conveyed by both works furthers the direction of attention towards the means of poetic transposition of a definite artistic technique and literary strategies which jointly create an image of almost tangible reality.

14 Laylā al-ᶜUthmān, 'al-Ru'ūs ...' (1983), 52–63.
15 Muḥammad ibn Sayf al-Raḥbī, 'Dhākira...' (1993), 8–14.
16 B. Chrząstowska and S. Wysłouch, *Poetyka stosowana* (Warszawa, 2000), 371–6.

In talking of the intertexuality that appears in the given works, one should pay attention to one more very important point. The very genre of the short story together with the techniques by which it is produced were, after all, taken from the body of Western literature, which is fairly well known to contemporary Arab men of letters. The analysis of the two realistic texts carried out above shows how intertextuality flows within one 'general text' which is comprised of the reality, national history, tradition, culture, literary ideology and stylistic manners discovered as pre-existing by the writers. In other words the reality is 'personified' in the sum of the texts. The writer, as an ordinary subject of speech, is unable to express himself in a way different from the people that surround him. He therefore imitates their style and ways of speaking. In the all-embracing world he does not think up texts, but reads, repeats, quotes — even when this is done subconsciously. Such citing of social styles of speech, stereotypes, clichés, undoubtedly exceeds the frameworks of individual texts, exceeds the framework of the literary body. Someone may, therefore, ask rightly: 'What is intertextuality?' The answer lies squarely with the researcher. It depends on how widely he understands the term. It is worth here emphasising that insofar as in the case of clear reference, citation, allusion, or reminiscences the value of intertextuality does not raise any doubts, in the case of realistic prose the interpretation is independent of the text. What is more, it often concerns not only intertextuality but also reality.[17]

A text is a mosaic of quotes, references and echoes of languages of culture both past and contemporary, which penetrate right through, creating an extensive sound recording. Intertextuality is a network in which every text is caught within the framework of another text. Intertexuality provokes one to reach for subsequent volumes, enriches interpretation, and guarantees the joy of playing with association, the construction of new meanings and paradoxes. It is a game between the author, the work and the reader, a game often played equally by researchers and translators.

Intertextual relations within Arabic literature constitute a great challenge both for the researcher and translator as well as the reader. The correct reading of a work's contents is undoubtedly connected not only with a knowledge of the body of literature but also with the knowledge of

17 Z. Mitosek (1998), 331–2.

the realities of a given area of the world, its traditions and cultures, the principles and rules it is governed by, the problems fought with, the way of thinking and opinions of people, the social and historical context. However, in order to understand a given work, it is not necessary to extract on the part of the reader all the intertextual relations it contains. We must remember that although the very process of translation wears down the range of intertextual links, while impoverishing its intertextuality, and although it limits interpretative possibilities, it does not rule out comprehensibility of the work as such. These mosaics of quotes, upon which every text is constructed, are the source of our journey through the endless labyrinth of interpretation which grows and develops along with our knowledge.

Select Bibliography

N.B. Individual entries from *The Encyclopaedia of Islam*, new ed. (Leiden: E.J. Brill, 1960–2004), and the *Encyclopedia of Arabic Literature*, edited by Julie Scott Meisami and Paul Starkey (London / New York: Routledge, 1998) are not listed separately in the bibliography.

ASQ = *Arab Studies Quarterly*
MEL = *Middle Eastern Literatures*
MES = *Middle Eastern Studies*
Ann. Islamol. = *Annales islamologiques*

^{c}Abd Allāh, ^{c}Abd al-Ḥalīm *Ba^{c}d al-ghurūb* (Cairo: Lajnat al-Nashr lil-Jāmi^{c}iyyīn, 1949).

^{c}Abd Allāh, Rāshid, *Shāhanda* (3rd ed.; Sharjah: Emirates Writers' and Literates' Union, 1998), 'Ihdā'' [Dedication].

^{c}Abd Allāh, Yaḥyā al-Ṭāhir, *Thalāth shajarāt kabīra tuthmir burtuqālan* (Cairo: al-Hay'a al-Miṣriyya al-^{c}Āmma lil-Ta'līf wa-al-Nashr, 1970).

Abisaab, Rula Jurdi, 'The Pessoptimist: breaching the state's *da^{c}wa* in a fated narrative of secrets', *Edebiyat* 13 (1) (May 2002), 1–10.

Aboulela, Leila, *Days Rotate. Glass Enclave, The Ostrich, The Way Home*, on-line <http://www.intangible.org>.

——, *Coloured Lights* (Edinburgh: Polygon, 2001).

——, *The Translator* (Edinburgh: Polygon, 1999; Columbia University Press, 2001); Dutch tr. Wim Scherpenisse, *De vertaalster* (Breda: De Geus, 2001; Brussels: 11.11.11, 2001; Den Haag: NOVIB, 2001). German tr. Jun Himmelreich, *Die Uberseterin*, Black Women series, Lamuv TB 314(Göttingen: Lamui, 2002). Spanish tr. Flora Casas, *La Traductora* (Madrid: Lengua de trapo Ocèano, 2002). French tr. Christian Surber Carouge, *La Traductrice* (Genve: Éditions Zoë, 2003).

Abū Hayf, ^{c}Abd Allāh, *al-Ta'sīs: maqālāt fī al-masraḥ al-sūrī* (Beirut, 1977; Damascus: Ittiḥād al-Kuttāb al-^{c}Arab, 1979).

Abū Jadra, Rashīd [Boudjedra], *La Répudiation* (Paris: Éditions Denoël, 1969).

——, *Ma*ᶜ*rakat al-zuqāq* (1986), French tr. *La Prise de Gibraltar* (Paris: Éditions Denoël, *c.* 1987).

African Writers Index http://www.geocities.com/africanwriters/ Authors-S.html#salih (n.d., viewed 3 September 2003).

Aḥmad, ᶜAbd al-Ḥamīd, 'Tawṣīfāt ᶜāmma ḥawla al-qiṣṣa wa-al-riwāya fī dawlat al-Imārāt', *al-Multaqā al-awwal lil-kitābāt al-qaṣaṣiyya wa-al-riwā'iyya fī dawlat al-Imārāt al-*ᶜ*arabiyya al-muttaḥida*, 27 February–1 March 1985 (Sharjah: Dā'irat al-thaqāfa wa-al-iᶜlām in cooperation with Emirates Writers' and Literates' Union, 1989), 9–22.

Aktaş, Cihan, 'Die "Geschichte" der islamistischen Frau', in *Die neue muslimische Frau*, ed. Barbara Pusch, Beiruter Texte und Studien, 85 (Istanbul: Orient-Institut and Goethe-Institut / Würzburg: Ergon Verlag, 2001), 123–36.

Alf layla wa-layla (Beirut: al-Maṭbaᶜa al-Kāthūlikiyya, 1889). Calcutta edition (1839–1842), Cairo edition (Bulaq, 1835); *Alf layla wa-layla* (Alf Layla wa Layla, A Thousand and One Nights, Mille et Une Nuits), Introduction by Dr Afif Nayef Hatoum (Beirut: Dar Sader, 1999), I–VI.

Āl Khalīfa, Suᶜād, 'al-ᶜAnkabūt', *al-Ghurfa al-mughlaqa* (Beirut: al-Mu'assasa al-ᶜArabiyya lil-dirāsāt wa-al-nashr, 2001), 25–38.

Allen, Graham, *Intertextuality*, The New Critical Idiom Series (London / New York: Routledge, 2000).

Allen, Roger, *The Arabic Novel: an historical and critical introduction* (2nd edition, New York: Syracuse University Press, 1995).

——, 'Translation translated: Rashīd Abū Jadrah's *Ma*ᶜ*rakat al-zuqāq*', *Oriente moderno* 16 (77), n.s. 2–3 (1997), 165–76.

——, 'Literary history and generic change: the example of the *maqāmah*', in *Studies in Honor of Clifford Edmund Bosworth*, I. *Hunter of the East* (Leiden: E.J. Brill, 2000), 3–14.

Anderson, Benedict, *Imagined Communities* (1983; rev. ed., London and New York: Verso, 1991).

Appadurai, Arjun, *Modernity at Large: cultural dimensions of globalization*, (Minneapolis and London: University of Minnesota Press, 1998), Vol. I, *Public Worlds*.

al-^{c}Arwi (Laroui), ^{c}Abdallāh, *al-^{c}Arab wa-al-Fikr al-Tārīkhī* (Beirut: Dār al-Ḥaqīqa, 1973).

al-^{c}Azzām, Muḥammad, *Masraḥ Sa^{c}d Allāh Wannūs* (Damascus: Dār al-^{c}Alā al-Dīn, 2003).

Badawi, M.M., *Early Arabic Drama* (Cambridge: Cambridge University Press, 1988).

Bakhtin, Mikhaïl, *The Dialogic Imagination: four essays*, tr. Caryl Emerson and Michael Holquist (Austin: University of Texas Press, 1981).

Barakāt, Ḥalīm, *^{c}Awdat al-ṭā'ir ila al-baḥr* (Beirut: Dār al-Nahār, 1969), English tr. Trevor Le Gassick, *Days of Dust* (Wilmette, Ill.: Medina Press International, 1974).

Barthes, Roland, *Roland Barthes par Roland Barthes* (Paris: Éditions du Seuil, 1975).

Bencheneb, Rachid, 'Les Mille et une nuits et les origines du théâtre arabe', *Studia Islamica* 40 (1974), 133–60.

Berking, Sabine, 'Liebe geht auf die Knie' (review of *The Translator*), *Frankfurter Allgemeine Zeitung*, WWW edition (6 November 2001), <http://www.literaturpreis.org/aktuell/uebersetzerin.html>.

Bhabha, Homi K., *The Location of Culture* (London: Routledge, 1994).

Borges, Jorge Luis, *Labyrinths: selected stories and other writings*, eds Donald A. Yates and James E. Irby (New York: New Directions Books, 1964).

Boullata, Issa J., *Trends and Issues in Contemporary Arab Thought* (Albany, New York: State University of New York Press, 1990; 2nd ed., Syracuse University Press, 1995).

Brontë, Emily, *Wuthering Heights*, World Classics (Oxford: Oxford University Press, 1983).

Camus, Albert, *Le Mythe de Sisyphe* (Paris: Gallimard, 1942).

Canard, Marius, 'Les principaux personnages du roman chevaleries Arabe Dhāt al-Himma wa-l-baṭṭāl', *Arabica* 8 (1961), 158–73.

Carroll, Lewis, *Alice aux pays des merveilles et De l'autre côté du miroir*, traduit de l'anglais par André Bay. Préface de André Maurois (119ème éd. ; Paris: Livre club du libraire, 1961).

——, *Tout Alice*, tr. Henri Parisot, chronologie, préface et bibliographie par Jean-Jacques Mayoux (Paris: Flammarion, 1979).

Childs, Peter, and R.J. Patrick Williams, *An Introduction to Post-Colonial Theory* (Hemel Hempstead: Prentice Hall, 1997).

Chraibi, Aboubakr, 'Texts of the *Arabian Nights* and Ideological Variations', *Middle Eastern Literatures* 7 (2) (July 2004), 149–57.

——, *Dreihundert Jahre '1001 Nacht' in Europa. Ein Begleitheft zur Ausstellung in Münster, Tübingen und Gotha*, eds Anke Osigus in cooperation with Heinz Grotzfeld (Münster: LIT Verlag, 2005).

——, (ed.), *Les Mille et Une Nuits en partage*, Actes du colloque « Milles et une nuits en partage », Paris, 25–29 mai 2004.

Chrząstowska, B., and S. Wysłouch, *Poetyka stosowana* (Warszawa, 2000).

Cooke, Miriam, 'Zaynab al-Ghazâlî: saint or subversive?', *Die Welt des Islams* 34 (1994), 1–20.

Culler, Jonathan, *The Pursuit of Signs: semiotics, literature, deconstruction* (Ithaca, New York: Cornell University Press and London: Routledge and Kegan Paul, 1981).

——, *Deconstruction: critical concepts in literary and cultural studies* (London: Routledge, 2003).

Darwīsh, Aḥmad, *Taqniyyāt al-fann al-qaṣaṣī ᶜabra al-rāwī wa-al-ḥākī* (Cairo: Longman, 1998).

Darwīsh, Maḥmūd, *ᶜĀshiq min Filasṭīn* (Beirut: Dār al-ᶜAwda, 1970 [1966?]).

——, *Arā mā urīdu* (1990; Beirut: Dār al-Jadīd, 1993).

——, *Aḥada ᶜashara kawkaban* (Beirut: Dār al-Jadīd, 1992).

Davidson, J.F., 'In Search of a Middle Point: the origins of oppression in Tayeb Salih's *Season of Migration to the North*', *Research in African Literature* 20 (1989), 385–400.

Deheuvels, Luc-Willy, 'Le Caire comme contre-utopie', Dossier spécial sur Le Caire de Mahfouz, *Qantara*, Institut du Monde Arabe, n° 50–51 (hiver 2003–printemps 2004), 56–58.

Dorigo, Rosella, 'Il teatro contemporaneo in Siria. L'impegno di Saᶜd Allāh Wannūs', *Quaderni di Studi Arabi* 1 (1983), 53–66.

Dorset County Council: Open Books, Summary of The *Translator*, Extract, Interview Q&A with Leila Aboulela. http://www.dorset-cc.gov.uk, (c.2000).

Dové, Peter, 'Probleme der Intertextualität im Werk von Zakarīyā Tāmir', *Asiatische Studien/Etudes Asiatiques* 55 (2001), 961–9.

——, *Erzählte Tradition. Historische und literarische Figuren im Werk Zakarīyā Tāmirs. Eine narratologische Analyse* (Wiesbaden: Reichert, forthcoming 2006).

El-Enany, Rasheed, *Naguib Mahfouz. The Pursuit of Meaning* (London / New York: Routledge, 1993).

Fähndrich, Hartmut, 'Viewing "the Orient" and Translating its Literature in the Shadow of *The Arabian Nights*', in *Yearbook of Comparative and General Literature* 48 (2000), 95–106.

——, 'Quelques réflexions sur le roman-conte de fées *J'étais une fois un prince* de R. Jābir', in *Romanciers Arabes du Liban* (Toulouse: CEMAA, 2002), 131–41.

——, *Die Hinrichtung des Todes. Unbekannte Geschichten von bekannten Figuren*, tr. from Arabic by Hartmut Fähndrich and Ulrike Stehli-Werbeck (Basel: Lenos Verlag, 2004).

Faure, Adolphe, 'Un réformateur marocain: Muḥammad b. Muḥammad b ᶜAbd Allāh al-Muwaqqit al-Marrākusī', *Hespéris* 39 (1952).

Fayyāḍ, Tawfīq, *al-Shāriᶜ al-aṣfar* (1968; Beirut: Dār al-ᶜAwda, 1970).

Friedman, A.W., *William Faulkner* (New York: Frederick Ungar, 1984).

Furrer, Priska, 'Propaganda in Geschichtentform — Erzählstrategien und Handlungsanweisungen in islamischen Frauenromanen aus der Türkei', *Die Welt Islams* 37 (1997), 88–111.

——, 'Zwischen Didaktik und Ästhetik — islamische Frauenromane in der Türkei', in *Die neue muslimische Frau*, ed. Barbara Pusch, Beiruter Texte und Studien, 85 (Istanbul: Orient-Institut and Goethe-Institut / Würzburg: Ergon Verlag, 2001), 111–21.

Genette, Gérard, *Figures III* (Paris: Seuil, 1972) ; English tr. Jane E. Lewin, *Narrative Discourse* (Ithaca, NY: Cornell University Press, 1980).

——, *Palimpsestes: la littérature au second degré* (Paris: Seuil, 1982); English tr. Channa Newman and Claude Doubinsky, *Palimpsests: literature in the second degree* (Paris: Seuil, 1982; University of Nebraska Press, 1997).

——, *Nouveau discours du récit* (Paris: Seuil, 1983) ; English tr. Jane E. Lewin, *Narrative Discourse Revisited* (Ithaca, NY: Cornell University Press, 1988).

——, *Paratexts: thresholds of interpretation*, tr. Jane E. Lewin (Cambridge: Cambridge University Press, 1997).

Ghazoul, Ferial J., *Nocturnal Poetics.* The Arabian Nights *in Comparative Context* (Cairo: American University in Cairo Press, 1996).

——, 'Halal Fiction' (review of Leila Aboulela, *Coloured Lights* and *The Translator*), *al-Ahrām Weekly Online* 542 (12–18 July 2001). <http://-weekly.ahram.org.eg/2001/542/bo4.htm> (2001).

al-Ghiṭānī, Jamāl [Ghitani, Gamal; El Guitani, Gamal; Ghitany, Gamal], *al-Zaynī Barakāt* (Cairo: Dār al-Ma'mūn lil-ṭibā^{c}a, 1975), English tr. Farouk Mustafa Abdel Wahab (1988, 1990) *Zayni Barakat* (London: Penguin, and New York: Viking; (2004) Cairo: American University in Cairo Press).

Ghulūm, ^{c}Abd Allāh Ibrāhīm, *al-Qiṣṣa al-qaṣīra fī al-Khalīj al-^{c}Arabī: al-Kuwayt wa-al-Baḥrayn* (Beirut: al-Mu'assasa al-^{c}arabiyya lil-dirāsāt wa-al-nashr, 2000).

Gołębiowski, B., 'Przedmowa' [Foreword], in Vladimir Propp, *Morfologia bajki* (Warszawa, 1976).

Greenberg, Clement, *The Collected Essays and Criticism* (Chicago and London: University of Chicago Press, 1986), Jonathan O'Brien (ed.), Vol. I, *Perceptions and Judgments, 1939–1944.*

Ḥabībī, Imīl, *Al-Waqā'i^{c} al-gharība fī ikhtifā' Sa^{c}īd Abī al-Naḥs al-mutashā'il* (Haifa: arabesk, 1974; repr. Jerusalem: Manshūrāt Ṣalāḥ al-Dīn, 1977).

Hafez, Sabry [Ḥāfiẓ, Sabrī], 'The modern Arabic short story', *Modern Arabic Literature* (The Cambridge History of Arabic Literature), ed. M.M. Badawi (Cambridge: Cambridge University Press, 1992), 270–328.

al-Ḥakīm, Tawfīq, *Yā ṭāli^{c} al-shajara* (Cairo: Maktabat al-ādāb wa-maṭba^{c}atuhā, 1962).

Hallaq, B., 'Autobiography and Polyphony' in Robin C. Ostle, Ed de Moor and Stefan Wild (eds), *Writing the Self: autobiographical writing in modern Arabic literature* (London: Saqi Books, 1998), 192–206.

Ḥanafī, Ḥasan, *Qāḍāyā mu^{c}āṣira*, 2 vols (Cairo: Dār al-Fikr al-^{c}Arabi, 1977; Beirut: Dār al-Tanwīr, 1981, 1983).

Hariharan, Githa, *The Thousand Faces of Night* (London: Women's Press, 1996; first published India: Penguin, 1992).

Haykal, Muḥammad Ḥusayn, *Zaynab* (1913: Cairo: Maktabat al-Nahḍa al-Miṣriyya, 1963); English tr. John Mohammed Grinsted (1989) *Zainab* (London: Darf).

Heath, Peter, 'Creativity in the novels of Émil Habiby, with special reference to Saᶜid the Pessoptimist', in *Tradition, Modernity, and Post-Modernity in Arabic Literature: essays in honor of Professor Issa J. Boullata* (Leiden: E.J. Brill, 2000), 158–72.

Helbig, Jörg, *Intertextualität and Markierung: Untersuchungen zur Systematik und Funktion der Signalisierung von Intertextualität*, Beiträge zur neueren Literaturgeschichte, Folge 3; 141 (Heidelberg: C. Winter, 1996).

Ḥimmīsh, BenSālim [Himmish, Ben Salim] *Majnūn al-Ḥukm* (1990; Rabat: Maṭbaᶜat al-maᶜārif al-jadīda, 1998).

———, *al-ᶜAllāma* (Beirut: Dār al-Ādāb, 1997, 2000).

Hobsbawm, Eric, and Terence Ranger, *The Invention of Tradition* (Cambridge: Cambridge University Press, 1983).

Hourani, Albert, *A History of the Arab Peoples* (New York: Warner Books, 1991).

Hourani, G.F., *Arab Seafaring in the Indian Ocean in ancient and early medieval times* (Princeton, NJ; Chichester: Princeton University Press, 1995).

Ibn ᶜArabī, Muḥyī al-Dīn, *Fuṣūṣ al-ḥikam* (Qum: Initishārāt Baydar, 1420 AH [1999 or 2000]).

———, *al-Futūḥāt al-makkiyya* (Cairo: al-Hay'a al-Miṣriyya al-'Āmma lil-Kitāb, 1972–1983).

Ibn Ḥazm, *Ṭawq al-ḥamāma* (Warszawa: PIW, 1976).

Idrīs, Yūsuf, *al-Jins al-thālith* (Cairo: ᶜĀlam al-Kutub, 1971).

Irby, James E., 'Introduction' to Jorge Luis Borges, *Labyrinths: selected stories and other writings*, eds Donald A. Yates and Jame E. Irby (New York: New Directions Books, 1964), xv–xxiii.

Irwin, Robert, *The Arabian Nights: a companion* (London: Allen Lane, Penguin, 1994).

———, *Night and Horses and the Desert*, The Penguin Anthology of Classical Arabic Literature (1999; London: Penguin Books, 2002).

Ismail, Ellen, 'Von Exil und Heimat, von Liebe und Glauben' (review of *The Translator*), *epd-entwicklungspolitik* 18 (2001) <http://www.literaturpreis.org/aktuell/uebersetzerin.html>.

Ismā^{c}īl, Ismā^{c}īl Fahd, *al-Kalima; al-Fi^{c}l* (Beirut: Dār al-Ādāb, 1981).

Jābir, Rabī^{c}, *Sayyid al-^{c}atma* (London: Riyāḍ al-Rayyis, 1992).

——, *Shāy aswad* (Beirut: Dār al-Ādāb, 1995).

——, *al-Bayt al-akhīr* (Beirut: Dār al-Ādāb, 1996).

——, *al-Farāsha al-zarqā'* (Beirut: al-Markaz al-thaqāfī al-^{c}arabī, 1996).

——, *Kuntu amīran* (Beirut: al-Markaz al-thaqāfī al-^{c}arabī, 1997).

——, *Ralph Rizqallah fī 'l-mir'āt* (Beirut: Dār al-Ādāb, 1997).

——, *Naẓra akhīra 'alā Kīn Sāi* (Beirut: al-Markaz al-thaqāfī al-^{c}arabī, 1998).

——, *Yūsuf al-inklīzī* (Beirut: al-Markaz al-thaqāfī al-arabī, 1999).

——, *Riḥlat al-Ghurnāṭī* (Beirut: al-Markaz al-thaqāfī al-^{c}arabī, 2002).

——, *Bayrūt madīnat al-^{c}ālam* (Beirut: al-Markaz al-thaqāfī al-^{c}arabī — Dār al-Ādāb, 2003).

al-Jābiri, Muḥammad ^{c}Abid, *Naḥnu wa-al-Turath* (Beirut: Dār al-Ṭalī^{c}a, 1980).

Jabr, Kaltham, *Waja^{c} imra^{c}a ^{c}arabiyya* (Qatar: Wizārat al-i^{c}lām bi-al-minṭaqa al-sharqiyya, 1993).

Jabrā, Jabrā Ibrāhīm, *al-Safīna* (Beirut: Dār al-Adāb, 1970); English tr. Adnan Haydar and Roger Allen, *The Ship* (1985; Colorado Springs: Three Continents Press, 1995).

Jarrar, Maher, 'A Narration of "deterritorialization": Imil Habibi's *The Pessoptimist*', *Middle Eastern Literatures* 5 (1) (January 2002), 15–28.

Jibrīl, Muḥammad, *Zahrat al-Ṣabāḥ* (Cairo: al-Hay'a al-miṣriyya al-^{c}āmma lil-kitāb, 1995).

al-Jīlī, ^{c}Abd al-Karīm, *al-Insān al-kāmil fī ma^{c}rifat al-awākhir wa-al-awā'il* (Cairo: Makabat Muḥammad ^{c}Alī Ṣabīḥ, 1945).

Johnson-Davies, Denys (selected and tr.), *Modern Arabic Short Stories*, Arab Authors 3 (Oxford: Oxford University Press, 1967; London: Heinemann, 1978; Washington, DC: Three Continents Press, 1984).

Kāmil, Salīm Maṭar, *Imra'at al-qārūra* (London: Riad El-Rayyes, 1990); English tr. Peter Clark, *The Woman of the Flask* (Cairo: AUC Press, 2005).

Kanafānī, Ghassān, *Adab al-muqāwama fī Filasṭīn al-muḥtalla* (Beirut: Mu'assasat al-Dirāsāt al-Filasṭīniyya, 1968).

Kazan, Fayad E., *Mass Media, Modernity and Development: Arab States of the Gulf* (Westport, Conn.; London: Praeger, 1993).

Kendall, Elisabeth, 'Literature, Journalism and the *avant-garde* in Egypt: from *al-Hilāl* to *Gallery 68*', unpublished D. Phil Thesis, University of Oxford (1997).

Khalīl, Yūsuf, 'al-Shakl wa-al-maḍmūn fī al-qiṣṣa al-qaṣīra wa-al-riwāya fī dawlat al-Imārāt al-^{c}arabiyya al-muttaḥida', *al-Multaqā al-awwal lil-kitābāt al-qaṣaṣiyya wa-al-riwā'iyya fī dawlat al-Imārāt al-^{c}arabiyya al-muttaḥida*, 27 February–1 March 1985 (Sharjah: Dā'irat al-thaqāfa wa-al-i^{c}lām in cooperation with Emirates Writers' and Literates' Union, 1989), 49–82.

al-Kharrāṭ, Idwār [al-Kharrāṭ, Edwār], *Rāma wa-al-tinnīn* (1979; 2nd ed., Beirut: Dār al-Ādāb, 1992).

——, *al-Zaman al-ākhar* (1985; 2nd ed., Beirut: Dār al-Ādab, 1992).

——, *Turābuhā za^{c}farān* (1986; 2nd ed., Beirut: Dār al-Ādāb, 1991); English tr. Frances Liardet, *City of Saffron* (London: Quartet Books, 1989).

——, *Ma'iyyāt 86*, catalogue with study on ^{c}Adlī Rizqallāh (Cairo, 1986a).

——, *Ta'wīl*. Prose poem on the painting by ^{c}Adlī Rizqallāh, 'Testimony of Anger'. Printed pamphlet (Cairo, 1986b).

——, *Yā banāt Iskandariyya* (Beirut: Dār al-Ādāb, 1990); English tr. Francis Liardet, *Girls of Alexandria* (London: Quartet Books, 1993).

——, *Ḥijārat Bobello* (Beirut: Dār al-Ādāb, 1992); English tr. Paul Starkey, *Stones of Bobello* (London: Saqi, 2005; Cairo: AUC Press, 2005).

——, *Makhlūqāt al-ashwāq al-ṭā'ira* (Cairo: al-Hay'a al-miṣriyya al-^{c}āmma lil-kitāb, 1992).

——, *al-Kitāba ^{c}abr al-naw^{c}iyya* (Cairo: Dār al-sharqiyyāt, 1994a).

——, *Iskandariyyatī* (Cairo and Alexandria: Dār wa-maṭābi^{c} al-mustaqbal, 1994b).

——, *Yaqīn al-^{c}aṭash* (Cairo: Dār Sharqiyyāt, 1996).

——, *al-Fannān Aḥmad Mursī, shāᶜir tashkīlī* (Cairo: al-Hay'a al-ᶜāmma li-quṣūr al-thaqāfa, 1997).

——, *Akhbār al-Adab* (Cairo: 28th November 2004).

Kristeva, Julia, *Sèméiôtikè: recherches pour une sémanalyse* (Paris: Seuil, 1969).

——, 'The ruins of poetics', in *Russian Formalism: a collection of articles and texts in translation*, eds Stephen Ban and John E. Bowlt (Edinburgh: Scottish Academic Press, 1973), 102–19.

——, *La Révolution du langage poetique* (Paris: Seuil, 1974) ; English tr. Margaret Waller, *Revolution in Poetic Language*, intro. Leon S. Roudiez (London: Columbia University Press, 1984).

——, *Desire in Language: a semiotic approach to literature and art*, tr. Thomas Gora, Alice Jardine and Léon S. Roudiez (New York: Columbia University Press, 1980).

——, 'Word, dialogue, and the novel', in T. Moi (ed.), *The Kristeva Reader* (New York: Columbia University Press, 1986).

Kruk, Remke, 'Warrior Women in Arabic Popular Romance: Qannāṣa bint Muzāḥim and other Valiant Ladies', *Journal of Arabic Literature* 1 and 2 (1993), 213–30 and *Journal of Arabic Literature* 25 (1994), 16–33.

Landau, Jacob M., *Studies in the Arab Theater and Cinema* (Philadelphia: University of Pennsylvania, 1958). French ed., *Études sur le théâtre et le cinéma arabe* (Paris: Maisonneuve et Larose, 1965).

Leeuwen, Richard van, 'The Art of Interruption: the *Thousand and One Nights* and Jan Potócki', *MEL* 7 (2004), 183–98.

Lessing, G.E., *Laocoön, or The Limits of Painting and Poetry*, tr. E.A. McCormick (Indianapolis and New York: Bobbs-Merrill, 1962).

Liyong, T.L., 'Tayeb Salih's concluded *Season of Migration to the North*: an exercise in a subjective, development-oriented approach to African (and Third World) literary discussion', in *Perspectives and Challenges in the Development of Sudanese Studies*. eds Ismail H. Abdalla with D. Sconyers (Lewiston, Queenston and Lampeter: Edwin Mellen Press, 1993), 265–85.

Loomba, Ania, *Colonialism / Postcolonialism* (London: Routledge, 1998).

Lowenthal, David, *The Past is a Foreign Country* (Cambridge: Cambridge University Press, 1985).

Maḥfūẓ, ᶜIṣām, *al-Zanzalakht* (1963; Beirut, Dār al-Nahār, 1969).

Maḥfūẓ, Najīb [Mahfouz, Naguib], *Tharthara fawq al-Nīl* (Cairo: Maktabat Miṣr, 1966).

——, *Taḥta al-mizalla* (Cairo: Maktabat Miṣr, 1968), English tr. Akef Abadir and Roger Allen of several stories in *God's World* (Minneapolis: Bibliotheca Islamica, 1973).

——, *al-Marāyā* (Beirut: Dār al-qalam, 1972); English tr. Roger Allen, *Mirrors* (Minneapolis, Mn: Bibliotheca Islamica, 1990; Cairo: American University Press, 1999).

——, *Ḥikāyāt ḥāratinā* (Beirut, 1974); English tr. Philip Stewart, *Children of Gebelawi* (Washington, DC: Three Continents Press, 1981; rev. ed., Pueblo, Colo. : Passeggiata Press, 1997).

——, *Layālī alf layla* (Cairo: Maktabat Miṣr, 1982). English tr. Denys Johnson-Davies, *Arabian Nights and Days* (New York: Doubleday, 1995).

——, *Riḥlat Ibn Faṭṭūma* (Cairo: Maktabat Miṣr, 1983); English tr. Denys Johnson-Davies, *The Journey of Ibn Fattuma* (New York: Doubleday, 1992).

——, *Adrift on the Nile*, English tr. Frances Liardet (New York: Doubleday, 1994; Cairo: American University in Cairo, 2001).

Malti-Douglas, Fedwa, 'A Literature of Islamic Revival? The autobiography of Shaykh Kishk', in *Cultural Transitions in the Middle East*, ed. Sherif Mardin (Leiden: E.J. Brill, 1994), 116–29.

McEwan, Joanne, Review of *The Translator* (6 December 2001), *Islam-Online.net*, 'The World in Crisis', <http://198.65.147.194/English/ Crisis/-BookReviews/article3.SHTML>.

McLean, Duncan (ed.), *Ahead of Its Time* (London: Jonathan Cape 1997: 2nd ed., London: Vintage, 1998).

Mehrez, Samia, *Egyptian Writers Between History and Fiction* (Cairo: American University in Cairo Press, 1994; 2005).

Milkāwī, Thābit, *al-Riwāya wa-al-qiṣṣa al-qaṣīra fī al-Imārāt, nash'a wa-taṭawwur* (Abu Dhabi: Cultural Foundation, n.d.).

Miller, Susan, 'A Conversation with Leila Aboulela' (2000). <http://literal-mind.com/leila.html>.

Mitosek, Z., *Teorie badan literackich* (Warszawa: PWN, 1998).

al-Mu'aqqit al-Murrākishī, Muḥammad ibn ^{c}Abd Allāh [al-Mu'aqqit al-Murrākushi, Mohammed Ibn Abdallah], *al-Riḥla al-Murrākushiyya*

(1932), French tr. *Les gens du navire, ou le XIVe siècle. Réforme et politique dans le Maroc des années 1930*, ed. and tr. Alain Roussillon and Abdallah Saaf (Casablanca: Afrique Orient, 1998).

Muḥammadiyya, Aḥmad Sa^{c}īd (ed.), *al-Ṭayyib Ṣāliḥ, ^{c}abqarī al-riwāya al-^{c}arabiyya* (Beirut: Dār al-^{c}Awda, 1976).

al-Muwayliḥī, Muḥammad *Ḥadīth ^{c}Īsā ibn Hishām* (Cairo: Dār al-Ma^{c}ārif, 1907).

al-Muẓaffar, Sa^{c}ūd, *Rimāl wa-jalīd* (Muscat: S. ibn S. al-Muẓaffar, 1988/9).

——, *Inna-hā tumṭiru fī Abrīl* (Muscat: S. ibn S. al-Muẓaffar, 1992).

Naga, Atia Abul, *Les Sources françaises du théâtre égyptien, 1870–1939* (Algers: Société Nationale et de Diffusion, 1972).

al-Na^{c}īmī, Hudā, 'Laylā wa-anā', *Abāṭīl* (Cairo: al-Dār al-Miṣrīyya al-Lubnāniyya, 2001), 43–50.

Najm, Muhammad Yūsuf, *al-Masraḥiyya fī al-adab al-^{c}arabī al-ḥadīth, 1847–1914* (Beirut: Dār Bayrūt, 1956).

——, 'Abū al-Ḥasan al-Mughaffal', in *al-Masraḥ al-^{c}arabī: dirāsāt wa-nuṣūṣ* (Beirut: Dār al-thaqāfa, 1961).

al-Naqqāsh, Mārūn, *Arzat Lubnān* (Beirut: al-Maṭba^{c}a al-^{c}Umūmiyya, 1869).

Nasrallah, Emily [Imilī Naṣr Allāh], *al-Layālī al-ghajariyya* (Beirut, 1998).

al-Nowaihi, M., 'Memory and Imagination in Edwār al- Kharrāṭ's *Turābuhā za^{c}farān*', *Journal of Arabic Literature* 25 (1994), 34–57.

al-Nuṣayr, Yāsīn, 'Jadaliyyat al-qirā'a al-thālitha', *al-Aqlām* 23 (3) (March 1988), 22–39 (24).

Nycz, R., 'Intertekstualność i jej zakresy: teksty, gatunki, światy', *Pamiętnik Literacki* 81 (2) (Wrocław, 1990), 106–14.

Olsson, Anders, 'Intertextualitet, komparation och reception', Staffan Bergsten (ed.), *Litteraturvetenskap: en inledning* (Lund: Lund studentlitterature, 1998), 51–69.

Ostle, Robin, Ed de Moor and Stefan Wild (eds), *Writing the Self: autobiographical writing in modern Arabic literature* (London: Saqi Books, 1998).

Ouyang, Wen-chin, 'The Dialectic of Past and Present in *Riḥlat Ibn Faṭṭūma* by Naguib Mahfouz', *Edebiyât* 14 (1) and 14 (2) (2003), 81–107.

——, 'Genres, Ideologies, Genre Ideologies and Narrative Transformation', *MEL* 7 (2004), 125–31.

Pagnini, Marcello, *Pragmatica della letteratura* (Palermo: Sellerio, 1988).

Parrilla, Gonzalo Fernández, 'La novela en Marruecos; un nuevo género literario en el proceso de formación de una literatura árabe nacional: el papel de la crítica', Tesis Doctoral, Universidad Autónoma de Madrid (Madrid, 2000).

Peled, Mattityahu, 'Portrait of an Intellectual', *MES* 13 (1997), 218–28.

Pessoa, Fernando, *The Book of Disquiet*, tr. by Richard Zenith (London: Allen Lane, 2001).

Piégay-Gros, Nathalie, *Introduction à l'intertextualité* (Paris: Nathan, 1996).

Planhol, Xavier de, *L'Islam et la mer: la mosquée et le matelot; VIIe–XXe siècle* (Paris: Perrin, 2000).

al-Raḥbī, Muḥammad ibn Sayf, 'Dhākira lahā ṭaʿm al-mawt', in *Bawwābāt al-madīna* (Muscat, 1993), 7–14.

——, 'al-Ḥikāya', in *Mā qālathu al-rīḥ* (Cairo, 1999), 11–14.

Ramsay, Gail, 'The Novels of an Egyptian Romanticist: Yūsuf al-Sibāʿī', doctoral dissertation, Stockholm University, University of Oriental Languages, Department of Arabic, Stockholm (1996).

——, 'Confining the Guest Labourers to the Realm of the Subaltern in Modern Literature from the Gulf', *Orientalia Suecana* 53 (2004), 133–42.

al-Rikābī, ʿAbd al-Khāliq, *Mawt bayn al-baḥr wa al-ṣaḥrā'* (Baghdad?, 1976).

——, *Nāfidha bi-saʿat al-ḥulm* (Baghdad: Dār al-Rashīd, 1977).

——, *Man yaftaḥ bāb al-ṭilasm* (Baghdad: Dār al-Rashīd, 1982).

——, *Mukābadāt ʿAbd Allāh al-ʿĀshiq* (Baghdad: Dār al-Rashīd, 1982).

——, *Ḥā'iṭ al-banādiq* (Baghdad: Dār al-Rashīd, 1982); English tr. *Wall of Rifles* (Baghdad?, 1983) including 'Ḥā'iṭ al-banādiq' (1982c), 'al-Khayāl' (1982a), 'al-Muḥārib' (1982b) short stories.

——, *al-Rāwūq* (Baghdad: Dār al-shu'ūn al-thaqāfīyya al-ʿāmma, 1986).

——, *Qabl an yuḥalliq al-bāshiq* (Baghdad: Wizarat al-thaqāfa wa-al-iʿlām, Dār al-shuʿūn al-thaqāfīyya al-ʿāmma 'Āfāq ʿArabiyya', 1990).

——, *Sābiʿ ayyām al-khalq* (Baghdad: Dār al-shuʿūn al-thaqāfīyya al-ʿāmma, 1994; Beirut: Baysān, 2000).

——, *al-Bayzār* (Baghdad: Dār al-shuʿūn al-thaqāfīyya al-ʿāmma, 1998).

——, *Nahārāt al-layālī al-alf* (Baghdad, 1998?).

Rimmon-Kenan, Shlomit, *Narrative Fiction: contemporary poetics* (London / New York: Methuen, 1983).

al-Rīsh, ᶜAlī Abū, *al-Iᶜtirāf* (Abu Dhabi: Mu'assasat al-ittiḥād lil-ṣiḥāfa wa-al-nashr wa-al-tawzīᶜ, 1982).

Rizqallah, ᶜAdly, *Ma'iyyāt naḥtiyya: sculptural water colours. Kullu hādhā al-shiᶜr* (Cairo, 1995).

al-Ṣaffār, Fawziyya, *Azmat al-ajyāl al-ᶜarabiyya al-muᶜāṣira: dirāsa fī* Mawsim al-hijra ilā al-shimāl *lil-Ṭayyib Ṣāliḥ* (Tunis: Mu'assasat ᶜAbd al-Karīm ibn ᶜAbd Allāh, 1980).

Ṣāliḥ, al-Ṭayyib [Salih, Tayeb], *Mawsim al-hijra ilā al-shimāl* (1966; 14th ed.; Beirut: Dār al-ᶜAwda, 1987). English tr. Denys Johnson-Davies, *Season of Migration to the North*, African Writers Series ([1969]; Oxford: Heinemann, 1991).

——, *ᶜAbqarī al-riwāya al-ᶜarabiyya*, ed. Aḥmad Saᶜīd Muḥammadiyya (Beirut: Dār al-ᶜAwda, 1976).

——, *Dūmat Wad Ḥāmid*, in Ṣāliḥ (1996), 501–17 (1st ed.; Beirut: Dār al-ᶜAwda, 1969). English tr., *The Doum Tree of Wad Hamid*, in Johnson-Davies, *Modern Arabic Short Stories* (1969; London: Heinemann, 1978), 83–94. (First edition included in Tayeb Salih, *The Wedding of Zein and Other Stories* (London: Heinemann, 1969).) .

——, *al-Aᶜmāl al-kāmila* (Beirut: Dār al-ᶜAwda, 1996).

Schweikle, Günther and Irmgard Schweikle (eds), *Metzler Literatur Lexikon. Begriffe und Definitionen* (Stuttgart: J.M. Metzler, 1990).

Sessona, Anna Zambelli, 'Intertextual Strategies and the Poetics of Identity in Imil Habibi's Literary Works', unpublished D. Phil. Thesis, University of Oxford (2001).

Sharabi, Hisham, *Neopatriarchy: a theory of distorted change in Arab society* (New York and Oxford: Oxford University Press, 1988).

al-Shārūnī, Yūsuf, *Fī al-adab al-ᶜUmānī* (Cairo: Markaz al-ḥaḍāra al-ᶜarabiyya, 2000).

al-Shidyāq, Aḥmad Fāris, *al-Sāq ᶜalā al-sāq fī-mā huwa al-Fāryāq* (Cairo: Maṭbaᶜat al-funūn al-waṭaniyya, 1855).

al-Sibāᶜī, Yūsuf, *Bayn al-aṭlāl* (1952; Cairo: al-Sharika al-ᶜarabiyya lil-ṭibāᶜa wa-al-nashr, 1960?).

―――, *Rudda qalbī* (1954; Cairo: Maktabat al-Khānjī, 1969).

―――, *Nādiya* (1960; Cairo: Maktabat al-Khānjī, 1966?).

―――, *Naḥnu lā nazraᶜ al-shawk* (1969: Cairo: Maktabat Madbūlī, 1979).

Siddiq, Muḥammad, 'The Process of Individuation in al-Ṭayyib Ṣāliḥ's Novel 'Season of Migration to the North', *Journal of Arabic Literature* 9 (1978), 67–104.

Spivak, Gayatri Chakravorty, 'Can the Subaltern Speak?', in *Marxism and the Interpretation of Culture*, eds Carl Nelson and Lawrence Grossberg (Urbana and Chicago: University of Illinois Press, 1988), 271–313.

―――, *A Critique of Postcolonial Reason* (Cambridge, Mass.; London: Harvard University Press, 1999).

Stehli-Werbeck, Ulrike, 'Der Poet der arabischen Kurzgeschichte: Zakarīyā Tāmir', *Arabische Literatur, postmodern*, eds Angelika Neuwirth et al. (Munich: Edition Text+Kritik, 2004), 179–90.

Szyska, Christian, 'On Utopian Writing in Nasserist Prison and Laicist Turkey', *Die Welt des Islams* 35 (1995), 95–125.

―――, 'Rewriting the European Canon: ᶜAlī Aḥmad Bākathīr's "New Faust"', in *Encounters of Words and Texts*, eds Lutz Edzard and Christian Szyska (Hildesheim: Olms, 1997). 131–45.

―――, 'Najīb al-Kīlānī on His Career, or: how to become the ideal Muslim author', in *Conscious Voices*, eds Stephan Guth, P. Furrer and J.C. Bürgel (Beirut: Orient-Institut / Stuttgart: Steiner, 1999), 221–35.

Takieddine-Amyuni, Mona, 'Tayeb Salih's *Season of Migration to the North:* an interpretation', *ASQ* 2 (1980), 1–18.

―――, (ed.), *al-Abḥāth* 32 (1984), special issue *Essays on Tayeb Salih's Season of Migration to the North* (contains also 'A Selected and Annotated Bibliography', 157–73).

Tāmir, Zakariyyā [Tamer, Sakarija], *al-Numūr fī al-Yawm al-ᶜĀshir* (1969; Beirut: Dār al-Ādāb, 1978); English tr. Denys Johnson-Davies, *Tigers on the Tenth Day and Other Stories* (London: Quartet Books, 1985).

―――, *Dimashq al-ḥarā'iq* (1973; Damascus: Maktabat al-Nūrī, 1978).

―――, *Nidā' Nūḥ* (London: Riad El-Rayyes 1994) [includes 'Shahriyār wa-Shahrazād'].

Ṭarābīshī, Jūrj, *Madhbaḥat al-turāth fī al-thaqāfa al-ᶜarabiyya al-muᶜāṣira* (London: Dār al-Sāqī, 1993).

——, *Sharq wa-gharb — rujūla wa-unūtha: dirāsa fī azmat al-jins wa-al-ḥaḍāra fī al-ᶜarabiyya* (Beirut: Dār al-Ṭalīᶜa, 1997), 142–85.

Tarawneh, Yosif, and Joseph John, 'Tayeb Salih and Freud: the impact of Freudian Ideas on *Season of Migration to the North*', *Arabica* 35 (1988), 328–49.

Ṭarshūd, Maḥmūd, 'Madrasat tawẓīf al-turāth fī al-riwāya al-ᶜarabiyya al-muᶜāṣira', *Fuṣūl* 17 (1) (Summer 1998), 27–39.

Tizzinī, Ṭayyib, *Mashrūᶜ Ru'ya jadīda lil-Fikr al-ᶜArabī min al-ᶜAṣr al-Jāhili ḥattā al-Marḥala al-Muᶜāṣira* (Beirut: Dār Ibn Khaldūn, 1978), I: '*Min al-turāth ilā al-thawra*'.

Tomiche, Nada, 'al-Ṭayyib Ṣāliḥ: le révélateur le plus sensible de l'acculturation: l'individu contre le groupe', *Ann. Islamol.* 17 (1981), 375–93.

Touraine, Alain, *Can We Live Together?* (Stanford, Ca.: Stanford University Press, 2000).

al-ᶜUthmān, Laylā, 'al-Ru'ūs ilā asfal', in *al-Ḥubb lahu ṣuwar* (2nd ed., Beirut, 1983), 52–63.

Walther, Wiebke, 'Modern Arabic Literature and the *Arabian Nights*', *The Arabian Nights Encyclopaedia.* 2 vols, eds U. Marzolph, R. van Leeuwen (Oxford: ABC–CLIO, 2004), I, 54–61.

Wannūs, Saᶜd Allāh, *Ḥaflat samar min ajl al-khāmis min Ḥazīrān* (Beirut: Dār al-Ādāb, 197-).

——, 'Bayānāt li-masraḥ ᶜarabī jadīd', *al-Maᶜrifa* 104 (1970), 5–32, special issue on theatre.

——, *Mughāmarat ra's al-mamlūk Jābir* (Damascus: Wizārat al-Thaqāfa, 1971).

——, *Sahra maᶜa Abī Khalīl al-Qabbānī* (Damascus: Ittiḥād al-Kuttāb al-ᶜArab, 1972).

——, *al-Malik huwa al-malik* (Damascus: Dār Ibn Rushd, 1978; repr. Beirut: Dār al-Ādāb, 2002).

——, 'Mulāḥaẓa ḥawla al-iqtibās aw al-iᶜdād al-masraḥī', *al-Ḥayā al-masraḥiyya* 6 (1978), 112.

Westney, Emma, 'Arabic Literary Modernism: the short-story cycles and episodic novels of Imīl Habībī and Idwār al-Kharrāṭ', unpublished D. Phil. Thesis, University of Oxford (2000).

Wielandt, Rotraud, *Das Bild der Europäer in der modernen arabischen Erzähl- und Theaterliteratur* (Beirut: Orient-Institut / Wiesbaden: Steiner, 1980) (=*BTS;* 23).

——, 'The Problem of Cultural Identity in the Writings of al-Ṭayyib Ṣāliḥ', in *Studia Arabica et Islamica: Festschrift für Iḥsān ᶜAbbās*, ed. Wadād al-Qāḍī (Beirut: Imp. Catholique. 1981), 487–515.

Wild, Stefan, 'Searching for Beginnings in Modern Arabic Literature', in Robin C. Ostle, Ed de Moor and Stefan Wild (eds), *Writing the Self: autobiographical writing in modern Arabic literature* (London: Saqi Books, 1998), 82–99.

Worton, Michael, and Judith Still (eds), *Intertextuality: theories and practices* (Manchester and New York: Manchester University Press, 1990).

Index

Abāṭīl (2001) 180, 185
^{c}Abd Allāh, ^{c}Abd al-Ḥalīm 167
^{c}Abd Allāh, Rāshid 164, 165, 182, 183
^{c}Abd Allāh, Yaḥyā al-Ṭāhir 37, 38
^{c}Abd al-Majīd, Ibrāhīm 36
Aberdeen 67, 68, 71
Aboulela, Leila 65–82
abstraction 106
Abū al-Ḥasan al-Mughaffal aw Hārūn al-Rashīd (1848) 117–30
Abu Dhabi 167
Abū Hayf, ^{c}Abd Allāh 118
Abū Jadra, Rashīd (Boudjedra) 9–11
Abū Nuwās (AD 757–814) 72, 73, 81
Abū al-Rīsh, ^{c}Alī 167, 168, 182, 183
adab (belles-lettres) 7
Adab al-muqāwama fī Filasṭīn al-muḥtalla 39
aesthetics 34, 37, 39, 40
Africa 13
Ahl al-safīna (1934) 14, 15, 18, 19, 28–30
al-Ahrām 153, 154
Ahwār region 45
Aḥada ^{c}ashara kawkaban (1992) 34, 35
Āl Khalīfa, Su^{c}ād 174, 184
Alexander the Great 137
Alexandria 134, 135, 137, 139, 140, 145, 149, 153, 159
Alexandrian Duet 135, 137, 140
Alf layla wa-layla 31, 46, 50, 55, 56, 59, 61, 103–15, 117–19, 154, 155, 162, 166, 189–91
Algeria 9, 10
Alice aux pays des merveilles see *Alices's Adventures in Wonderland*
Alice's Adventures in Wonderland 85, 88, 89, 93, 100
alienation 112
al-^{c}Allāma (1997) 8
allegory 15, 37, 43
allusion 88, 98, 158, 159, 188, 198
anachrony 149
analogy (*qiyās*) 90, 94
al-Andalus 9–10, 191
Anderson, Benedict 62, 63
Anṭūn, Faraḥ 165
al-Anwār 39
Apollo 151
Arā mā urīdu (1990) 34, 35
Arabian (Persian) Gulf 13, 162–86, 195, 196
Arabian Nights see *Alf layla wa-layla*
archetext 119
archetextuality 105, 108, 112
archetypes 161, 182
Ars Poetica (Aristotle) 141
al-^{c}Arwī, ^{c}Abdallāh 3
^{c}Āshiq min Filasṭīn (1966) 38
Asians in Gulf 163–4, 171–3, 184
Aṣdā' al-sīra al-dhātiyya (1994) 6
Aṣḥāb Jam^{c}iyyat al-Ṣawā^{c}iq al-Samāwiyya 15, 16
authenticity (*aṣāla*) 49–51, 60, 73
autobiography 135, 151, 152
'auto-intertextuality' 135, 136, 139, 140, 143
^{c}Awdat al-ṭā'ir ilā al-baḥr (1969) 2

Babylonian mythology 46, 54–55, 57
Ba^cd al-ghurūb (1949) 167
Ba^cthists 52
Baghdad 27, 31, 51, 119–24
Bahrain 161, 162, 174, 184
al-Bakhīl (1847) 118
Bakhtin, Mikhail 51, 61
Barakāt, Ḥalīm 2
Barthes, Roland 134
Basra 167
Bawwābāt al-madīna (1993) 193
Bayn al-aṭlāl (1952) 167–9, 183
Bedouin 163
Beirut 25, 39, 73, 84, 95, 117, 147
Bhaba, Homi 163–4, 173, 184
Biblical tradition 55, 57
Bloom, Harold 8
Bluebeard (*Barbe-bleue*) 174, 184
The Book of Disquiet 85, 86
Borges 50, 51, 55, 57, 59, 60
broadcasting 67, 196
Brontë, Emily 175, 177, 184
al-Bustānī, Salīm 165

Caine Prize for African Writing (2000) 67
Cairo 8, 42, 66, 110, 113, 148, 169; El-Hanager Art Centre 148
Camus, Albert 134
Carroll, Lewis (1832–1898) 85, 88–90, 94, 96, 97, 99
cartography 13
Catholics 117
Cavafi 146
censorship 107
China, ancient 83, 84
chivalry 182, 183
Christian tradition 81, 113, 155, 156
chronology 113, 123
City of Saffron (1989) 147, 149
'clash of civilisations' 79
Cleopatra 137
clichés 198
collage 147–8
collective imagery 131
colloquial poetry (*mawwāl*, *zajal*) 113
colonial discourse 164
colonisation, European 48
comic play (*riwāya muḍḥika*) 123
consumer society 180, 185
contextualisation, cultural 157, 158
Coptic traditions 150, 151, 159
Courbet (1819–1877) 142
creation myth 55, 57
Culler, Jonathan 1, 157, 161, 174, 182–4
cultural clubs 166

da^cwa 81
Damas aux incendies (1973) 42
Darwīsh, Maḥmūd 34, 35, 38, 39, 41
al-Datmā' 166, 167, 183
De l'autre côté du miroir see *Through the Looking Glass*
death 21, 138, 194
deconstruction 39
depersonalisation 137
desert 157, 179
dhahabiyya (boat) 20, 21
Dhāt al-Himma (Dalhama) 162, 166, 183
dhows 13
dialectics 34
dialogues 126
Dickens, Charles 174
discourse 107
displacement 29
dispossesion 41
The Doum Tree of Wad Hamid (1969) 72, 73
'doubling' (*al-muḍā^cafa*) 50, 51, 55–57

drama 42, 46, 117–32
dream 25, 50, 51, 55, 57, 59, 121, 122, 126, 131
Dubai 168
Dūmat Wad Ḥāmid (1969) 73
dysphoria 34

East–West dichotomy 76, 80
Egypt 6, 7, 21 22, 34, 35, 46, 63, 66, 68, 108, 117, 157, 159, 166, 168
Egyptian Delta 149, 151
EMTAR 7, 33, 135
English language 66, 67, 77, 81, 86
epilogue (*khātima*) 125–8
equivalence 91
Europe 3, 4, 13, 27, 48, 71, 77, 83, 101, 103, 118, 196
Europeans 3, 13, 17, 19, 173
exile 45
existentialism 41

fable (*ḥaddūta*) 109
fabula 39
fairy tales 191
fantasy (*al-wahm*) 23, 25, 49, 50, 51, 58, 114, 126
Farmān, Ghāᶜib Ṭuᶜma 51
fate 14, 20, 169
Faulkner, William 134, 135
Fayyāḍ, Tawfīq 39, 43
female writers: Arab 185; Lebanese 185; Qatari 185
Fī al-adab al-ᶜUmānī (2000) 163
film 107, 108
first-person narrative (voice) 52, 71, 131, 136, 152, 197
focalisation 90
folk beliefs 155
folktales 180, 182, 184, 185, 190
frame-story 107
frame-within-frame structure 56, 60
Fuṣūṣ al-ḥikam (1999) 55, 58
al-Futūḥāt al-makkiyya 55

Galland, Antoine (1648–1715) 103
Gautier, Théophile 142
gender 77
Genette, Gérard 51, 65, 70, 85, 87, 104, 106, 114, 149, 150, 161, 182, 188
genre 34, 55, 108, 118
Ghazoul, Ferial 76, 79
al-Ghīṭānī, Jamāl 5–7, 46–47, 51, 62
al-Ghurfa al-mughlaqa (2001) 174
Gibraltar 10
Girls of Alexandria (1993) 149
globalisation 106, 163, 173, 195
The Godfather (1969) 169–71, 184
Gothic traditions 174, 184
Great Expectations 174, 184
Greenberg, Clement 141–4
Grimm brothers 185
Gulf War (1991) 64

Ḥabībī, Imīl [Habibi, Émile] 5–7, 135
Ḥadīth ᶜĪsā ibn Hishām (1898, 1907) 4, 7, 46
Ḥaflat samar min ajl al-khāmis min Ḥazīrān (1968) 118
al-Ḥākim (Fatimid caliph) 9
al-Ḥakīm, Tawfīq 4, 42
al-Hamadhānī 7
Hariharan, Githa 189
Hārūn al-Rashīd, ᶜAbbasid caliph 119-120, 123, 124, 130–1, 192
al-Ḥasūd al-salīṭ (1853) 118
al-Ḥayāt, journal 83
Haykal, Muḥammad Ḥusayn 4, 34, 167
heritage (*turāth*) 20, 47–50, 58, 60–63, 80, 107, 119, 131, 162, 163, 180, 182–185, 195

heroes 53, 54, 84, 85, 89, 93, 95, 96, 97, 100, 109, 112, 157, 193
heroic epic 53, 54, 109, 112
heroines 166
hetereogeneity 85
Ḥijārat Bobello (1992) 149–60
hijra 18, 28, 29
Ḥikāyat al-Nā'im wa-al-yaqẓān (1889) 117
Ḥikāyāt ḥāratinā (1974) 5, 6
al-Hilālī, Abū Zayd 162
Ḥimmīsh, Ben Sālim 8, 9
Ḥiwār 73
historical romances 164, 165, 183
history 20, 25, 26, 46, 164, 165, 183, 199
Hobsbawm, Eric 62
Hood, Edward W. 135
Horace 141
Hourani, Albert 2, 8
al-Ḥubb lahu ṣuwar (1983) 193
hybridity 43, 115
hypercodage 35, 37
hyperonymy 34
hypertext 65, 87, 88, 105, 119, 161, 182, 184, 185
hypertextuality 105–7, 111, 112
hyponymes 34, 35
hypotext 65, 87, 88, 96, 105, 108, 114, 119, 152, 154, 161, 182–5

Ibn Baṭṭuṭa 9, 14
Ibn ᶜArabī 55, 58
Ibn Ḥazm 189, 191
Ibn Iyās 6, 7
Ibn Jubayr 14
Ibn Khaldūn 8–11
Ibn al-Rūmī 112
Ibrāhīm, Jamāl Muḥammad 79
al-Iᶜtirāf (1982) 167–9, 182, 183
identity 31, 39, 41, 47, 73, 74, 65–82, 163, 165, 175, 176
Idrīs, Yūsuf 36, 42

illusion 24, 29, 126
imagery 28, 141, 142, 161
imagination 114
'imagining community' 62, 63
imitation (pastiche) 105, 182
Imra'at al-qārūra (1990) 45, 60
Imru' al-Qays 158
India 189, 190
indirect (metatextual) commentary 107
Inna-hā tumṭiru fī Abrīl (1992) 169–73, 184
al-Insān al-kāmil fī maᶜrifat al-awākhir wa l-awā'il (1945) 55, 56
Introduction à l'intertextualité (1996) 87
iqtibās 129
Iram 19
Iran–Iraq War 45, 64
Iraq 27, 45, 46, 51, 52, 54, 63, 64
irony 120
irrationality 96
Iskandariyyatī (1994) 147
Islam 13, 15–17, 29–30, 65–82, 164–6
Islamic literature (*al-adab al-islāmī*) 69
Islamic traditions 155, 159
isnād 114
Israel 37
Italy 24, 83, 117, 118, 135, 170

Jābir, Rabīᶜ 83–101
al-Jābirī, Muḥammad ᶜAbid 3
Jabr, Dr Kaltham 175, 177, 184
Jabrā, Jabrā Ibrāhīm 5, 13–31
Jaffa 38
Jakarta, Indonesia 67
Jerusalem 138
Jibrīl, Muḥammad 103–15
al-Jīlī, ᶜAbd al-Karīm 55, 56, 58
al-Jins al-thālith (1971) 42

mirroring 29, 112
mixed media 133–48
Molière 118
Monet 135
Morandi, Giorgio 135
Morocco 14, 15
motifs 28, 33–43, 137, 138, 161, 184, 190, 197
muᶜāraḍa 79
Mughāmarat ra's al-mamlūk Jābir (1972) 118
Muḥammad al-Mu'aqqit, Muḥammad ibn ᶜAbd Allāh 13–31
Mukābadāt ᶜAbdallāh al-ᶜĀshiq (1982) 51
Mulḥaq al-Nahār 85
al-Muqaddima 9–10
Mursī, Aḥmad 146
Muslim(s) 15, 17, 29, 30, 65–82, 166
al-Muwayliḥī, Muḥammad 3, 4, 7, 46
al-Muẓaffar, Saᶜūd bin Saᶜd (Saᶜūd al-Muẓaffar / Saud Al Mudhaffar) 169, 172, 173, 184
myth 35, 190
Le Mythe de Sisyphe (1942) 134

al-Naᶜīmī, Hudā 180, 185
Nādiya (1960) 167
Naguib Mahfouz Prize (2002) 8
al-Nahār 84
nahḍa 12
Naḥnu lā nazraᶜ al-shawk (1969) 167, 168, 183
al-naksa 1–4, 21
Naples 27
al-Nāqid 45, 83
al-Naqqāsh, Mārūn (1817–1855) 117–30
narrative 13–31, 49, 133, 150
nasīb 159
Nasrallah, Emily (Imilī Naṣr Allāh) 185
nationalism 35, 62, 63, 165
nation-state 62–64
Nazra akhīra ᶜalā Kin Säi (1998) 84
neo-patriarchy 163, 168, 178–9, 183, 184
Neo-Platonism 139
nihilism 21–23, 30
Nile River 21, 36, 69, 74, 78
Nobel Prize 4
al-Nowaihi, Magda 133, 140
al-Numūr fī al-Yawm al-ᶜĀshir (1969) 37
al-Nuṣayr, Yāsīn 52

Occident 80, 103
Olsson, Anders 162, 183
Oman 161, 162, 169–73, 184, 188, 193
Omani literature 171, 173, 193
oral literature 55, 56, 61, 108, 113–15, 152
Orient 71, 80, 81, 94, 103
Orientalists 103, 187
originality (*aṣāla*) 49–51, 55, 58, 60, 61
Ottomans 7, 52

painting 140, 141
Palestine 24, 26, 35, 37–39, 41, 43
palimpsest 63, 85, 104, 185
Palimpsestes. La littérature au second degré (1982) 85, 104
paradise 36–38
paratext 105, 106, 109, 150, 151, 161
paratextuality 105, 109
Paris 103
Parnassians 142
parody 105, 107, 114
'Passeport', a poem (1970) 41

past 46, 47, 58, 60–63, 77, 137, 161–86, 187–99
pastiche 9, 87, 105, 182
pathos 167, 183
patriarchal society 106, 163
peritext 161
Perrault 174
Pessoa, Fernando (1888–1935) 85, 86
Pharsalie 11
Piégay-Gros, N. 87, 98
plagiarism 105, 110
platitudes 193
Poetics (Aristotle) 141
poetry 34, 35, 38, 40, 53, 113, 141, 142, 144, 146, 147, 151, 152
popular epic 55
Portuguese 85, 172
postcolonialism 47, 62, 80, 163
postmodernism 115
pre-Islamic poets 156, 159
premise 121, 122
press 66
La Prise de Gibraltar (1987) 11
prologue 125–8
prose poem 144
Proust, Marcel 158
Puzo, Mario 169, 184

Qabbānī, Nizār 40
Qabl an yuḥalliq al-bāshiq (1990) 51, 52
qaṣīda 112
Qaṭar 161, 162, 175, 177, 178, 180, 185
al-Qayyim, Dhākir 56
qiṣaṣ qaṣīra 6
quotations 188, 199
Qur'ān 11, 30; Qur'anic school (*kuttāb*) 11

Rābiṭat al-adab al-islāmī al-ᶜālamiyya 69
radio 67, 196
al-Raḥbī, Muḥammad ibn Sayf 188–91, 193, 196, 197
Ralph Rizqallah fī al-mir'āt (1997) 83–101
Rāma wa-al-tinnīn (1979) 133, 143, 147, 159
Ranger, Terence 62
al-Rāwūq (1986) 51–53, 60, 61
realism 34, 192
reality 24, 29, 114, 131, 142, 193, 196–8
Red Sea 13
reminiscence 188, 198
resistance literature 39, 40
retrospection 197
Riffaterre 188
Riḥlat Ibn Faṭṭūma (1983) 47
al-Riḥla al-Murrākushiyya (1932) 15, 30
al-Rikābī, ᶜAbd al-Khāliq 48–52, 61, 63
Rimāl wa-jalīd (1988) 172
riwāya 6, 151, 152
Rizq, al-Amīr 162
Rizqallāh, ᶜAdlī 146, 147
romanticism 164, 182, 183
Rouen 135
Rudda qalbī (1954) 167, 168, 183

Sābiᶜ ayyām al-khalq (1994) 48, 51, 52, 59–61, 63
al-Safīna (1969) 5, 14, 24, 28–31
Sahra maᶜa Abī Khalīl al-Qabbānī (1972) 118
Saᶜīd, Edward 69
Saint Simeon 138
Salih, Tayeb / Ṣāliḥ, al-Ṭayyib 65–82
Sallustus (d. 34 BC) 10
Santayana 7
al-Sāq ᶜalā al-Sāq (1855) 7, 46
Sayyid al-ᶜatma (1992) 83

Scotland 67, 69, 81
Scott, Sir Walter 165
sea 13, 14, 25, 28. 157, 158
Season of Migration to the North (1969) see *Mawsim al-hijra ilā al-shamāl*
second-person narrative 140
Sèméiôtikè (1969) 104
Serrano, Richard 11
Sessona, Anna Zambelli 133, 135
Shaddād ibn ᶜĀd 19
Shāhanda (1974) 164, 165, 182, 183
'Shahriyār wa-Shahrazād' (1994) 103–15
Sharabi, Hisham 163
sharīᶜa 17
Sharkān, prince 166
al-Shāriᶜ al-aṣfar (1968) 43
al-Shārūnī, Yūsuf 163, 171–3
Shāy aswad (1995) 98
al-Shidyāq, Aḥmad Fāris 7, 46
ships 13–31, 165
short story 46, 135, 162, 174, 175, 184, 185, 191–5, 198
al-Sibāᶜī, Yūsuf 167, 183
Sicilians 170, 171
similarity (*tashābuh*) 49
similes 25
Simon, Claude 11
Simonides (*ca.* 467 BC) 141
Sindbād the Sailor 13, 31
sīra dhātiyya 151
Sixties, generation of the (*jīl al-sittīnāt*) 51
Sixties, the 33, 43, 38, 40, 42, 51
social structure 19–20, 22, 25, 28, 29, 161, 168, 193, 195, 199
solipsism 34, 39
Sostrates, engineer 137
South-East Asia 13
space 13, 19, 20, 24, 26, 31, 35, 57, 92–94
stereotypes 173, 184, 193, 198
Stones of Bobello (2005) 149–60
story 47, 57–58, 109, 114
storyteller (*ḥakawātī*) 57–58
stream of consciousness 111
subconscious 140
subjectivisation 163, 172
subjects of reference 188
Sudan 65, 66, 71, 75–77, 79, 81
Sudanese literature 75, 77
Sufism (*taṣawwuf*) 6, 17, 56–60
Sumerians 45, 46
sunna 17
Superman 107
surrealism 41, 42
Switzerland 45
symbolism 20, 21, 24, 25, 27, 28, 34, 37, 38, 41, 42, 46, 47, 90, 132, 139, 141
Syria 37, 40, 106
Ṣarrūf, Yaᶜqūb 165

al-Takarlī, Fu'ād 51
tale (*ḥikāya*) 109
Tāmir, Zakariyyā (b. 1931) 37–39, 42, 103–15
taqiyya 80
Ṭarābīshī, Jūrj 63
Ṭarrāna 151
Ṭawq al-ḥamāma (1976) 189, 191, 192
technology 19
television 108, 196
textualisation 60, 61
Thalāth shajarāt tuthmir burtuqālan (1970) 37
Tharthara fawq al-Nīl (1966) 14, 20, 21, 28, 30
theatre 34, 39, 117–32
'theatre of the absurd' 34
theatre, European 118
thematic clustering 137
theme (*gharaḍ*) 161, 184

third-person narrative 19, 136, 140
Thousand and One Nights see *Alf layla wa-layla*
The Thousand Faces of Night (1993) 189
Through the Looking Glass 85, 86, 88, 91, 97, 99, 100
time 23, 28, 77, 136, 138, 139, 156
Tizzinī, al-Ṭayyib 3
toponymy 39
topos 33–35, 36–38, 40, 41
Touraine, Alain 163, 172, 184
transformation 182
translation 149, 150, 158
The Translator (1999) 65–82
transmission 53, 115
transtextuality 103, 104, 106, 108
travel 14, 18, 19, 25, 27, 28, 47, 50, 51, 55, 57, 60, 90, 91, 166
Tuḥfat al-nuẓẓār fī gharā'ib al-amṣār wa-ᶜajā'ib al-asfār 9
Turābuhā zaᶜfarān (1986) 133, 135, 147, 149, 159

ᶜulamā' 17
Umm Durmān 69, 78
umma 16, 19
United Arab Emirates (UAE) 161, 162, 164, 183
United Kingdom 52, 67, 77, 78
United States of America 170
urban society 168
al-ᶜUthmān, Laylā 193, 196, 197

Verhaeren 142

Wajaᶜ imra'a ᶜarabiyya (1993) 175, 178, 184
Wannūs, Saᶜd Allāh 117–32
Wāq islands 167
al-Waqā'iᶜ al-gharība fī ikhtifā' Saᶜīd Abī al-Naḥs al-Mutashā'il (1972) 1, 5
al-Wāsiṭī 10–11
The Wedding of Zein and Other Stories (1969) 72
West, the 19, 47, 48, 81, 161, 163, 175, 179, 183, 192
West Africa 190
Western literature 8, 19, 80, 81, 118, 119, 161, 163–5, 170, 182–3, 198
Westernisation 195
Westney, Emma 133, 137, 140
Wuthering Heights (1847) 175–9, 184

Yā banāt Iskandariyya (1990) 133, 135, 140, 147, 149, 159
Yā ṭāliᶜ al-shajara (1962) 42
Yaqīn al-ᶜaṭash (1996) 133, 143, 144
Yāqūt al-Ḥamawī 36
Yemen 67

Zahrat al-Ṣabāḥ (1995) 103–15
al-Zaman al-ākhar (1985) 133, 143, 147
al-Zanzalakht (1963) 42
Zaydān, Jurjī 165
Zaynab (1913) 34, 167
al-Zaynī Barakāt (1975) 5–7

EU authorised representative for GPSR:
Easy Access System Europe, Mustamäe tee 50,
10621 Tallinn, Estonia
gpsr.requests@easproject.com

www.ingramcontent.com/pod-product-compliance
Ingram Content Group UK Ltd.
Pitfield, Milton Keynes, MK11 3LW, UK
UKHW041914140426
5217IPUK00013B/153

9780719081897